The Menuhins

The Menuhins

A FAMILY ODYSSEY

Lionel Menuhin Rolfe

WITH ILLUSTRATIONS BY MICHAEL CORMIER

PANJANDRUM/ARIS BOOKS / SAN FRANCISCO / 1978

First Printing

Panjandrum/Aris Books
99 Sanchez Street
San Francisco, CA 94114

Library of Congress Cataloging in Publication Data:

Rolfe, Lionel Menuhin, 1942—
The Menuhins: A family odyssey.
Includes index.
1. Menuhin family.   2. Menuhin, Yehudi, 1916—
3. Musicians—Biography.   I. Title.
ML418.M27R6   780'.92'2 [B]   78-13051
ISBN 0-915572-22-2

Manufactured in the United States of America

This book is dedicated to
my wife Nigey Lennon Rolfe
and my children Heather and Haila Rolfe

ACKNOWLEDGEMENTS

Any book this large in scope inevitably is beholden to many people. Without them this book would not have been written. While I cannot mention everyone, there are those who must be included.

First, for a variety of reasons, not the least of which included typing and editing, my deep appreciation goes to Nigey Lennon Rolfe, my wife. Hal Silverman of the San Francisco *Examiner* as well as Stan Arnold of the San Francisco *Chronicle* helped me with the original research. Umberto (Nino) Tosi, a fine editor and writer, was the person who long ago suggested to me this was my inevitable first book. Bob Sherrill, who as an editor of the ill-fated Los Angeles weekly, *L.A.* actually got me started writing about my family. Gene Vier was always encouraging and helpful. Studs Terkel and Don Gold were important in getting this book launched. Leita Hagemann understood what I was doing sooner than I, and Dianna Rolfe did an heroic job editing and typing in the early stages. Carol Zedeck made valuable contributions in the early stages of the book.

Yehudi, Hephzibah and Yaltah, whatever their doubts, all gave generously of their time and advice. Yehudi was especially encouraging when it must have been difficult for him. And without Dave McQueen's hospitality as well as wisdom, this book certainly would have never been written. Thanks also to Howard Schrager and Renate Holdreith who became involved through my publishers in the editing process.

My thanks also to the following magazines and newspapers where portions of this book appeared in earlier forms: the Los Angeles *Times, Coast* Magazine, *L.A., Let's Live* and *City* Magazine (of San Francisco).

And it was through the considerable efforts of my publishers, Dennis Koran and L. John Harris, that this manuscript became whole.

CONTENTS

ILLUSTRATIONS

INTRODUCTION

A Menuhin Synopsis

The Menuhins is the story of the great violinist, Yehudi Menuhin, his talented sisters, their parents and all the remarkable Menuhin ancestors. *The Menuhins* is also my story, for I am the son of Yehudi's sister Yaltah. In coming to terms with this extraordinary family, and my relationship to it, it was necessary to trace the family's roots, for all the contemporary Menuhins have been greatly influenced by the tradition that has nurtured us.

Tracing one's family roots has become, it seems, a national pasttime, and for those who feel the pull of the past, the search often requires much effort and, yes, money. I had an easier time of it because my Menuhin ancestors, the Schneersohns, are a famous and well-documented family of orthodox Jews who created *Chabad* Hassidism and made their court in the Russian town of Lubavitch.

The Hassids, as you may well know, were a very spiritual group of Russian and Eastern European Jews who broke away from the established Judaism of their day—the eighteenth century. *Chabad* Hassidism was one of the most important forms of Hassidism. The exact definition of "Chabad" is rather complicated, but it designates the kind of extreme devotion and discipline practiced by this group of Hassids. *Chabad* Hassids aimed at achieving an ecstatic union with God, often by means of song. And the *Chabad* or Lubavitcher movement is still flourishing today, especially in America where *Chabad* "houses" or centers attract the young.

Soon after my mother told me of my relation to the Hassids, I began a study of my ancestors. A Lubavitcher rabbi in Los Angeles suggested I visit Rabbi Jacobson at the Lubavitcher headquarters in Brooklyn. Jacobson told me some of the names in my grandfather Moshe's line, but because of certain impurities within the Menuhin tribe today, as I shall describe later, he refused to go any further. Luckily, a trip to the great New York Public Library yielded a family tree of the Schneersohns. More pieces fell into place. The most important source of information on my family lineage was my mother's cousin in Israel, Hochy Zuriel. He completed for me the family line back to the first Schneersohn, Schneur Zalman. Hochy showed me a

rare book, a complete Schneersohn family tree, published in Tel
Aviv in 1940. To my surprise, my mother's name was included. Since
the book was written in Hebrew, I had to scribble down names and
facts as Hochy read all the generations from my mother back to Zalman.
In putting together my family odyssey, I have focused on the major
characters in the Menuhin past. The family's branches are twisted
and complex, and I have tried to stay close to the trunk and roots.
But, the reader may still feel at times at sea among the generations of
Yehudi's ancestry, and I hope the following synopsis helps to clarify
the Menuhin line, and proves a useful reference tool.

   Those characters dealt with in detail in my book are listed to the
left of the synopsis in bold print. The dates and names I am not
certain of are followed by question marks.

	On the gravestone of Rabbi *Judah Liva,* who died in 1440, it is said that he was a blood relation of the Bible's King David. Whether this is true or not, Rabbi Liva was the ancestor of *Gaon Betzalel,* a poor man with many sons.
The MaHaRal (1512-1609)	One of Gaon Betzalel's sons was the famed Rabbi *Judah Loewe,* also known as *The MaHaRal,* chief rabbi of Prague and the creator of the legendary Golem. He married *Pearl Reich,* the daughter of a rich and influential family of "court Jews."
	The MaHaRal had a grandson named *Judah Lieb,* who married a woman named *Sara.* Judah Lieb and Sara had a son named *Moshe,* who had a son named *Schneur Zalman.* This first Schneur Zalman married a woman named *Rachel* and they had a son named *Baruch.* Baruch married *Rebeka,* a descendant of *The MaHarShal.*
The MaHarShal (1510-1573)	The MaHarShal was a great Kabbalist from a Sephardic background and a close boyhood friend of The MaHaRal.
Schneur Zalman (1745-1813)	Baruch, who died in 1790, was the father of the legendary *Schneur Zalman* who founded not only *Chabad* Hassidism but

**Menachem-Mendel
Schneersohn
(1789-1866)**

Sara Liba _____ (?)
(? — 1939)

**Isaac (Yitzhak)
Mnuchin
(? — 1897)**

**Moshe Menuhin
(1893 —   )**

**Marutha Sher
(1891? —   )**

**Yehudi Menuhin
(1916 —   )**

**Hephzibah Menuhin
(1920 —   )**

**Yaltah Menuhin
(1921 —   )**

the Lubavitcher dynasty. This Schneur Zalman married a woman named *Sterna* and
had a daughter named *Deborah Leah*
(?-1792). Deborah Leah married *Shalom
Shankhna* and they had a son named
Menachem-Mendel, who took the surname
Schneersohn.

Schneersohn was the third Lubavitcher
Rebbe. (The Hassidim call their spiritual
leaders *Rebbe.*) His wife was *Hayyah
Mushka* and one of their six sons was
Israel Noah, who lived from 1816 to 1833.

Noah had a daughter named *Perla Deborah*
who married a Schneersohn relation whose
name may have been Zalmanson. They had
a daughter named *Sara Liba*, Yehudi
Menuhin's grandmother.

Sara Liba married *Isaac Mnuchin* (Mnuchin
became Menuhin in America), the great-
grandson of the famed *Levi-Yitzhak of
Berditchev* (1740-1809), the wise Hassidic
teacher who was a contemporary of the
great Schneur Zalman.

Old Levi-Yitzhak's immediate offspring
had married into the Schneersohn family,
and so the Mnuchins are also Schneersohn relations. The marriage of Isaac
Mnuchin to Sara Liba gave to their son,
Moshe, Schneersohn blood from both
maternal and paternal sides.

When Mnuchin died his son Moshe was
four years old. Moshe grew up in Russia
and Palestine and emigrated to America
a young man. He married *Marutha Sher*,
also believed to be a Schneersohn relation,
and they had three children: *Yehudi,
Hephzibah* and *Yaltah.*

Yehudi has four children: *Zamira, Krov,
Gerard* and *Jeremy.*

Hephzibah has three children: *Kronrod,
Marstan* and *Clara.*

Yaltah has two children: *Robert* and
Lionel.

I
A JOURNEY
INTO THE PAST

Yehudi the prodigy in 1927

ONE

My Link to the Menuhin Odyssey

B Y A TWIST OF FATE that to this day I am not entirely comfortable with, I was born into one of the great families in the history of world music —the Menuhins. My mother, Yaltah Menuhin, is the youngest sister of the great violinist, Yehudi Menuhin. Were it not for the fame of Yehudi, the Menuhin name might not have attracted your attention. My mother and her sister Hephzibah were both prodigy pianists. But Yehudi's fame towers over that of his sisters, and indeed, over nearly every violinist there is or has been. There is controversy, to be sure, about whether his playing has matured as he has grown older; but still, Yehudi is a star among stars.

With such a luminary in my immediate family, you can see why this book would have to be, in part, an examination of my own feelings while growing up within the Menuhin tribe. But the following pages have more to do with my mother, Yaltah, and my uncle Yehudi and aunt Hephzibah, and my grandparents Moshe and Marutha Menuhin—with their feelings, thoughts and ideas as I have heard and remembered them through the years, and particularly in conversations and "interviews" held primarily to compile material for this book. As a writer I have turned the stage over to them, which is as such a book should be—more a family memoir or odyssey than a biography per se. But I have reserved the right to comment where it seems to be needed. Whatever foibles or peculiarities of theirs I have recorded, I nevertheless respect the issues around which their lives are lived with deep commitment. World peace and music are equally important to my family, and a deep concern with the meaning of life moves in each one of them.

As I am writing this, Yehudi is in his sixtieth year, and by the time this book is in print he will have ended his second sabbatical. The last time he took a sabbatical was forty years ago, when he was making his widely publicized transition from child prodigy to adult violinist. Just before his most recent sabbatical, I walked with him into the Artist's Room at EMI Recording Studios in London. I was surprised at how humbly Yehudi mentioned that this had originally been the great Caruso's room. Yehudi himself had called this room home practically since his playpen days. He started recording at EMI in 1928, and his recordings now number in the hundreds.

By the time of his first sabbatical, Yehudi's very name, which means "the Jew," had become a fad. "Who's Yahoodi?" was a national joke during the Great Depression. Yet like the ineffable name of God, its power came from the fact that it sounded so exotic and mysterious. The joke had two appealing elements: the name had a lilt to it, and the joke implied a faint sneer.

The name's owner, however, had a magnificent and noble face as a child, and it became even more so as Yehudi grew older. The way he played the violin proved that the face was no mere mask. People loved the child and that love embraced his talented sisters as well.

Growing up so close to these illustrious people has left me with many questions and many anxieties. In reading about my Menuhin ancestors, and in talking with my relatives today, many old questions and anxieties were resolved, only to be replaced by others born out of my new awareness and out of the waves that the writing of my book sent through the Menuhin clan.

There are questions to which I have never really found adequate answers. What is the source of great genius like that displayed in the Menuhin family line? What psychological factors foster an entire brood of genius children? Or is genius purely genetic, or prearranged by fate, or a miracle? There are no easy answers. I do know that my mother has struggled mightily—and I believe Yehudi and Hephzibah have as well—to square herself with that tradition, as I also must. It is a tradition I felt compelled to study partly because of my own emotional and blood relation to it, but also because of the gaps between the public image of the Menuhins and the realities I saw. My story, then, is in part about the strong and sometimes troubled relationships between the Menuhins, past and present. It also describes how the Menuhin ancestors lived, and what they created within the tradition-bound community of extremely religious Jews in Russia who came to be known as the Hassidim. The inevitable problems of organization dictated that Yehudi be the focus of my book, as rightly he should be. His life, in a sense, forms the scaffolding from which I have tried to work the complex psychological and genealogical material of my family's story. And it is probably fair to say that Yehudi has been the focus of my life, as well. He was the almost mythic figure my mother, Yaltah, talked of constantly, and worshipped totally.

The facts of Yehudi's life are well known; a previous biography, countless news stories, and Yehudi's own recent autobiography have described much of it—the dates, the stories of his legendary youth, his honors, his political/social philosophy, the influence of his immigrant parents, etc. My own research confirms what I grew up knowing intimately—the details of Yehudi's life. Yet they had never explained to me the mystery of his gift, and the gifts of his two sisters. Nor did they explain how the Menuhins related to each other, or to the world. In the limelight of international news coverage, the Menuhin family projected genius, charm and confidence. But there has also been a secretiveness behind which they have lived, though cracks in the facade have appeared from time to time, particularly concerning Moshe, the family patriarch. His anti-Zionism was reported over the years, but his long and angry anti-Zionist, anti-Israeli tract, *The Decadence of Judaism in Our Time*, found its way into print only through the vanity press in America. Unreported storms raged within the Menuhin clan as they do in any other family, but somehow ours took on epic proportions because of the characters involved.

Yehudi first set bow to strings in a room in the Jewish section of San Francisco in the early twenties. Since then the greatest part of his life has been lived on concert stages, in recording studios, great hotels and estates and with the adulation of fawning aristocrats, seemingly far from his origins in the ghetto. Born shortly before the Russian

Revolution, Yehudi was a part of the great upsurge arising out of a crumbling order. Millions of his people had been expelled from Russia as the victims of this falling old order. His violin sang their song—and that is why they loved it so.

My uncle's early music was distinguished from that created by other child prodigies from the same ghetto by its profound and mature interpretation; he had something more than just astounding technique. The same could be said of several of Yehudi's ancestors who were called *illuy*, child prodigies. They displayed precocity not only in music but in science and writing, oratory and especially religion; religion, of course, combined all the others. As the nineteenth century came to an end, so did the tradition of all-encompassing religious scholastics. It's a good guess that the world lost some great religious leaders when the violin became a passion in the Russian Jewish world. The instrument was adopted from the gypsies who were associated with licentiousness, with sensuality; whereas Torah study was work for the mind, spirit and intellect. The violin became the bridge between body and mind. And when one masters the violin, one enters the realms of love, creativity, joy. That the child Yehudi could create a bridge to other worlds for his adult audiences seemed, indeed, a miracle. Only his parents knew, however, that Yehudi was not the first in his family's tradition of miraculous children. Child prodigies were the hallmark of Yehudi's Hassidic ancestors, the Schneersohns.

I didn't understand why my uncle possessed so much power until I began to see behind Yehudi our common family tradition of which I was not even aware until after my thirtieth birthday. Only then did I discover that our family, unique among Russian Jews, has a family tree that can be traced back generation by generation for five centuries. My discovery has left me awed and troubled.

I am awed because the family traces its power directly to the Kabbalah, the font of Jewish mysticism. Schneur Zalman, the founder of the Lubavitcher dynasty, and the first Schneersohn, was as important a musician as he was a religious leader. But I am also troubled because studying ancestors seems too pat a way to find one's identity. Yet ultimately I am a Menuhin, and the reader will see that to be a Menuhin is no simple matter.

I had always thought that I simply was not the type to go in for ancestor worship and family tree investigations. Yet late in 1972, on a trip to London and Zurich to see my mother, whom I had not seen for a number of years, a chain of events began that led me to a fascination with my own genealogy. Many of my mother's friends in Zurich were deeply involved with the psychology of Carl Jung. I became drawn to the notion of a collective unconscious, which Jung explains in part as a "certain psychic disposition shaped by the forces of heredity." My mother's description of our ancestors and my newfound fascination with Jung started the wheels turning that led, inevitably, to this book.

The year after the Zurich trip, I went to Israel, since my grandparents had lived there for many years. There I met a cousin of Yehudi's named Leah who surprised me by using the rather strong term "emotional cripple" to describe not only Yehudi but all the Menuhins. Leah said that they were out of touch with very important parts of themselves, but I rejected what she said because I knew of her bitterness about that side of her family. Now, however, I sometimes see that many of us in Yehudi's orbit could be described as lost souls, and perhaps that includes the great man himself. Leah's remarks came back to me when I later read a similar notion in Jung. He said that when a person becomes the instrument of a great art, that person, as well as many around him, must suffer for it in his personal life. Leah's bitterness was directed mostly at my grandparents, Moshe and Marutha, who had lived their lives solely for their children, and especially for Yehudi. Nothing and nobody would be allowed to interfere with that, including relatives.

One can see in Yehudi, Hephzibah and Yaltah, as Leah in Israel might explain, much that smacks of those who have suffered from psychological repression, suggesting perhaps more their connection with the priestly than with the prophetic tradition from which they grew. They worship the light and shun the dark in their tastes in both literature and music. Yehudi and Yaltah equally express distaste for writers who reveal the sleazy and violent aspects of life. It's as if they fear their own negative, dark sides. Still, quite recently, my mother wrote to me expressing her own resentment of her parents and especially the way they have treated her own sons, my brother Robert and me. "I feel you have lightened the burden for me," she said to me in her letter. "I've just carried it silently, whereas you have transformed it into something creative and concrete. You, in great pain, searched for the answer and wrote your book...you have

My mother and I in front of Yehudi's
health food restaurant on Baker Street in
London. My wife Nigey snapped this
picture in 1973

worked out mysteriously what I could not face." Now she is appalled at "the whole mechanics of hellish intrigues and climbing," which she feels came out of her parents' fear of poverty and particularly her mother's desire to escape her Jewishness.

All three of the Menuhin children today live as expatriate Americans in London. Their lives have been molded by the legend of their precocity, and they seem to resent it sometimes. Yehudi uses quotation marks around the word prodigy, as if he doesn't believe there really are any. If there was any "miracle" that occurred in the 1920's in the San Francisco of his youth, he attributes it to the clean air and water and the nutritious food of that period. There were a number of prodigies from that area, he points out—he was merely the first and the most famous.

One could dismiss the simplicity of Yehudi's explanation because he is, as a great many people know, a crackpot on the subject of nutrition. Yet there was, indeed, Ruggiero Ricci, a child prodigy of Italian immigrant parents. He was born two years later than Yehudi and was taught by the same teacher, Louis Persinger.

Poor Ricci idolized Yehudi. Ricci's father was convinced that of his eight musical children, one would surely equal the Jewish boy's precocity on the violin. Ricci used to go to Yehudi's San Francisco concerts with his fists clenched. He became a great violinist in his own right, but his career never took on the legendary aspects of Yehudi's. Perhaps his childhood lacked the wholesomeness, along with the inspiration and encouragement, that Yehudi lists as essential to the care and feeding of young musicians. Ricci's father's method of encouraging his son was to shout at him: "Be a fiddler or be a garbage man!" Ricci was obviously not as lucky in his choice of parents as was Yehudi.

There was also Isaac Stern, the last of the three great San Francisco violin prodigies. Stern was born two years after Ricci. One of the better-kept secrets of the Menuhin family is that Yaltah and Marutha personally delivered the promising Stern his first violin.

Today there are those critics who would compare Stern's violin playing quite favorably with Yehudi's, yet Yehudi's career and name have a certain magic, a charisma, that few violinists possess. People are forever calling Yehudi "the former wunderkind." Something about Yehudi sets him apart from the other violinists, and this may be the ultimate difficulty of his tale. It has been suggested that he was the greatest musical prodigy of this century. Yet, much as anyone else, Yehudi is at a loss to explain his amazing talent. "Make sure, Lionel," he has said to me, "that you don't compare me to Mozart. Mine was not that kind of gift."

The more I studied our common ancestry, the more it became apparent that somehow many of the forces in history and culture had been transmitted down the generational chain to Yehudi as surely as if they had been quantified as a chemical in his genes. (And some of them may well have been.) This, of course, might contradict the great science of genetics, but a more mystical explanation than the molecular structure of the genes appeals to me. I suspect that what is at work here is the ancient secret, understood by studying Kabbalah, not chemistry—and Yehudi's father, Moshe. The mysterious alchemy of great child prodigies often includes a driven and driving father.

The ancient Hebrews knew the magical power of music. David played the lyre for Saul to drive away the evil spirits of melancholy and depression that plagued the king. Yehudi, who gave his first public performance at six years of age, is said to be a direct descendant of the Old Testament's greatest child prodigy. This is because the Schneersohns are, according to the Lubavitcher tradition, directly descended from David.

In the eighteenth century, song was the wise man's—the *tzaddik's* —way into heaven. Schneur Zalman was not only the last of the *tzaddiks*, but also the last great composer of Jewish liturgical music. Myth and music were the two areas in which the Hassids excelled. Through myths, tales and parables, the *tzaddiks* explained the relationship between God and man, heaven and earth. Through music, they transcended opposites.

Schneur Zalman lived seven generations before Yehudi. Yet when Yehudi first emerged from the Jewish section of San Francisco in the 1920's, his father, Moshe, went out of his way to deny that there had been any unusual musical ability among his son's ancestors. Nor did he mention the influential role of the family in Jewish tradition.

Perhaps Moshe knew how strange the boy might appear to American eyes if the whole tale were told. The Messianic impulse is not a quality that Americans find endearing in immigrants, especially when it is expressed as aggressiveness. One dictionary defines Messianism as a "mystically idealistic and aggressive and crusading spirit," which—it is not unfair to say—Yehudi's ancestors had exhibited.

Often, the Menuhins seem more like seers than artists. Yehudi warns of terrible, gigantic natural catastrophes that he feels will inevitably overcome mankind. Hephzibah sees a new world coming into being out of social chaos, a new and far better world. Moshe prophesizes disaster for his people, the Jews, because they created a political state in Palestine.

Yaltah feels this world is not as real as other worlds, and thus, there is something unworldly about her. Yet in some ways she is closer to her feelings than either her brother or sister. You sense that when she says "My brother is a man who lives with a loneliness we will never know," she knows it quite well. For suffering, she says, is the paramount fact of life, and either you wallow in it or you use it in a creative, positive way. That, according to Yaltah, is what her brother is all about. She talks of how he withdraws into his universe of music, sliding in and out of our world. When he is playing well, she says, he is bringing messages from up there down here. And that is certainly the way my mother plays her music as well.

Being in touch with the ancient secret in our modern world must be a terrible burden. I think of what a friend of mine once said after attending with me one of Yehudi's concerts. She was impressed, of course, by his playing. But when she saw him up close after the concert, she commented, "He looks so tired. It must be hard being a legend in your own time." Yes, I thought, especially a legend that has been incubating not only during his own time, but for centuries.

While I was writing this book, Norman Mailer announced that his biggest opus since *The Naked and The Dead* was to be a novel about every generation of an archetypal Jewish family since Egyptian days. His story is fiction, whereas my family tree is real, to be sure. The story of the Lubavitchers is a migration through wars, revolutions and pogroms in search of salvation across the continents and

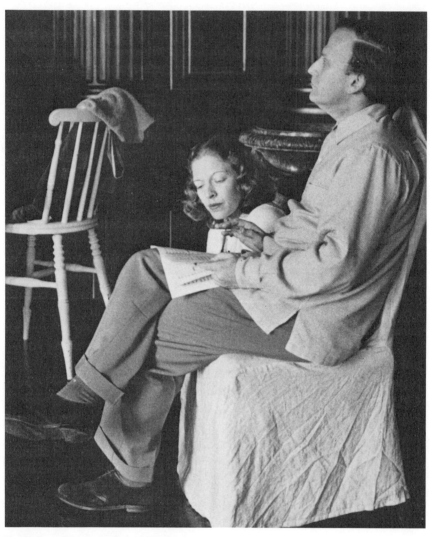

English photographer Erich Auerbach
captures characteristic expressions of both
Yehudi and Yaltah

oceans. The migration ended in San Francisco where the tale of Yehudi begins. Yehudi is a culmination of the whole historic flow of the great mystical and revolutionary movement known as Hassidism. To know what went into the making of Yehudi, the prodigy, you must learn history. You must also understand the mechanisms by which a family tradition is maintained at almost any price.

Being both a Menuhin and a Rolfe, I have been as ambivalent about my book as have been my relatives. I have agonized over my loyalties but have ultimately decided to tell the story of the Menuhins as completely as I know how—and it is, after all, a story that deserves to be told.

If there is some bitterness in my own story, my family odyssey was not motivated by it. For years I had resisted suggestions by friends and editors to write about my family. The discovery of my own link to the Hassids got me started, and as the ghosts of the Menuhin past became more real, Yehudi's image started changing. Too awe-struck by my connection to the Menuhins, I did not suspect that awe could turn to rage during my search for my family's roots. Part of the rage was a feeling that I was but another of the distressed souls who surround Yehudi. Yet side by side with rage, my awe of the Menuhin legend and the Menuhin music remains as strong as ever. If it was necessary to go beyond official Menuhin legends and facts, then it was equally necessary for me to go beyond my personal resentments in recording what is the Menuhin odyssey.

TWO

Moshe the Patriarch

IN SEPTEMBER OF 1971, I went to Villa Montalvo, a retreat for writers and artists in Saratoga, five miles from my grandparents' home in Los Gatos, California. I was then approaching my thirtieth year, and I knew, somehow, that big changes were coming in my life. At Villa Montalvo, I was installed as a writer-in-residence in that grand, old mansion built by a former San Francisco mayor named Phelan, who, in the twenties, used it as a stage for grand parties, poetry readings and—according to legend—orgies. These days it models itself on its more ethereal beginnings. It is run as a sanctuary for birds, trees and the arts by a group of patrons of the arts and by Santa Clara County.

It wasn't hard for me to become accepted as a writer-in-residence at Montalvo, since Yehudi was on the board, and besides, I had accumulated a fair collection of magazine and newspaper articles I had written about California. At Montalvo, I wanted to consolidate some things in my life, and I also wanted to write. In addition, I wanted to be close to Los Gatos, to look up and talk to my grandfather, who had been my most influential teacher while I was growing up.

My memories of the years I spent with Moshe when I was a young boy seem blissfully free of conflicts. Undoubtedly this is a selective memory, but it is what I remember. I often rode on the day train, the Daylight, between Los Angeles and Los Gatos. Those trips

My grandfather Moshe and I in the patio
at Rancho Yaltah in 1946

back and forth between my parents and grandparents became very important to me. They were my first taste of freedom. Even today I occasionally ride the Daylight, hoping to capture the memories: those long, dark tunnels across the Cuesta Grade between San Luis Obispo and Paso Robles, the haunting dark green of spring's first moments of glory on the rolling hills just north of Watsonville. Racing alongside Highway 101, vestibule open and the wind blowing my hair, I was forced to squint my eyes until everything was a blur, hoping all the time that the conductor wouldn't show up and make me go back inside the coach.

At my grandparent's home, I would go to sleep in the farthest bedroom in the wing closest to the chicken shed. It was a thick-walled, Spanish-style bedroom with windows that looked out onto gigantic trees and the lawn on which I'd be playing by afternoon. In the morning the lawn was shadowy and huge like a forest, particularly just before the sun came up. The steam engine of the Los Angeles-Santa Cruz train would come wailing and thundering across the nearby San Jose orchards, its revolving light searching the far corners of my bedroom. I could feel the steam hissing me back to sleep as the train sped on towards San Francisco.

I don't remember hearing Moshe sing the Hassidic songs he used to sing for Yehudi, songs Yehudi remembers his father singing as their car went down the sunny Sierra slopes from Yosemite, never faster than fifteen miles per hour because, says Yehudi, "that was Aba's [Moshe's] top speed."

Instead I remember my grandfather's eyes. They were the eyes of a Hassid, straining to give themselves up to God even as he was delighting in the mechanics of setting a gopher trap. My grandfather's bubbling energy was that of a Hassid, chanting from the soul of the God that burned constantly inside him. Yet, Moshe, who is now in his eighties, has not been inside a synagogue in years; he doesn't believe that the Jews are a chosen people, but he does believe in the universal prophecy that is Judaism.

Mostly I remember the intensity with which he did everything. I remember pulling Mark Twain and Robert Ingersoll off the dark, book-lined shelves in the Persian rug-covered hallways at the elder Menuhins' home, and becoming excited by their lack of religiosity. My budding atheism seemed to please Moshe, but when I acted on the other half of those authors' irreverence and poked fun at the flag,

Moshe became furious. He put up the American flag on every holiday, and once showed me how it was done. Then he carefully explained that you don't put up the flag every day. That would show disrespect.

My grandfather's patriotism excluded religion; the tradition at the Menuhins' home in Los Gatos, Rancho Yaltah, was not a Jewish tradition. We celebrated Christmas with the biggest Christmas tree around. The tree always reached to the top of the high ceiling, and it was always a beautiful specimen. We celebrated Christmas like Gentile families, proud of how big our tree was.

On one of those holidays at Los Gatos, Yehudi came to celebrate with his parents, and he brought me a toy. (As I recall, it was an erector set.) Even at that young age I knew my uncle was a famous man, because everyone in the family constantly discussed his doings. But it was all grownup talk; it hadn't much to do with the shadowy mornings when the world was so mysterious and life seemed such a grand and somehow frightening journey.

On the third day of my stay at Villa Montalvo, I received a letter from the mountaintop manor of Moshe Menuhin. It said that he had no time to see me, that he was old and ill. But then he had been saying that to me for years as an excuse for not wanting me to visit, yet he had Yehudi's sons staying with him frequently. This didn't seem fair, because I had really loved Moshe.

Moshe's letter was bitter, and the essence of it was that he never wanted to see me again. It was painful for him to have to write me again, refusing further to explain or discuss his reasons for not wishing to see me. He was sure that my mother and father were mature and wise enough to have thought everything over, and that they should be able to explain the "situation" to me.

I was angry at this letter, but not surprised. Because my mother was the least favored of the children, it was, I suppose, inevitable that her sons, to a lesser degree, would suffer. The same thing also happened to Hephzibah. Yehudi, however, even when he was in disfavor with Moshe, remained the eternal saint who could do no wrong. If he ever did anything wrong, it was because he had been surrounded by "evil people." Most people, one sensed, fell into that category if they happened to be around Yehudi much. All of this inspired Hephzibah to form an organization for rejected Menuhins called "Menuhins Anonymous." Being a Menuhin is a hard habit to break, however. I still felt the tremendous need to see my grandfather before he died, because for the past year I had forgotten all the nastiness and had been remembering only the good things about him. But this letter brought everything else back into focus.

I had heard throughout my youth that when my mother eloped with my father, Moshe had greeted the marriage announcement with a scornful, "he's worse than Hitler." My earliest years were spent in San Francisco, and Moshe and Marutha came to our house every weekend. I was often their house guest, and they treated me as a prized grandson. But I also had asthma, which I would get especially when the fog rolled in from the ocean. It wasn't the fog that caused it, however: it was the tension in our house, between my father and his in-laws, and between my father and Yehudi, who also did not take a liking to him. Finally my parents decided to move to Los Angeles, ostensibly to get away from the San Francisco fog that brought on my asthma. Actually, of course, it was to get away from the meddling in-laws. So intent on breaking up my parents' marriage were Moshe and Marutha, they sent a gigolo down to see my mother hopefully to seduce her away from my father!

My mother was never able to explain to me what the "situation" was, as Moshe had claimed she would be able to. Once she told Moshe, in what was a great show of strength for her, because none of the Menuhin children have learned how to talk back to the old people, that she would not see them again until they learned how to treat her children right. What did she care, Moshe replied, if he was not going to receive her children with open arms. "He [Lionel] is in the will along with the other grandchildren."

As far as I can tell, Moshe took a dislike to my father because my father was neither rich nor a Gentile. Moshe, rejecting the poverty and Jewishness of his past, expected both in whomever was to be Yaltah's mate. I can only assume that the offspring were also to be damned with the sins of their father. To this day I can offer no better explanation than this. I certainly never felt that I deserved such treatment.

No, my mother was not able to explain the situation. Rather, she wrote Moshe, asking him for an explanation after I had sent her a copy of the letter he had sent to me at Montalvo. He wrote back to her, saying that countries, clans, even blood relations do not concern him any longer. Even grandchildren, he said, no longer fit into his already preoccupied emotional life. He claimed that he was a universalist on the one hand, and an individualist on the other, and that both extremes merge into a harmony of merit, decency, honesty and morality.

Two years later, he again wrote in reply to a letter from my mother, who had asked him to "feel soft-hearted and compassionate and drop Lionel a line." Moshe replied to her that my life problems did not merit a letter from either him or Marutha. In another part of the letter, he claimed that my brother and I never loved or cared for our grandparents. When my brother was finishing high school, before he went on to get regent's scholarships as a star physics student from the University of California, and eventually a Ph.D., he received a letter from Moshe. Our grandfather suggested that decent work, a trade, would be the best thing for him. He also told my brother that his advice to me had fallen on deaf ears. Moshe wanted both of us to give up any notions about becoming intellectuals or scientists. Most insulting was Moshe's implication that our affluent lives made it possible for us to consider careers that we were not cut out for.

Even now, as I reread these letters, I feel anger, yet also a curious sense of irony, for I felt that I had loved my grandfather more than I had either of my parents, or anyone else in my family. At least in my early years this was true. My grandfather talked of philosophy and politics, and he told me about his own childhood, especially in Palestine. He was kind and patient. He introduced me to books and ideas. I guess he considered me a poor student, but he didn't say anything then.

Now I see something else. I keep recognizing the same awful patterns in effect between all the Menuhins and their offspring, a cruelty that goes from one generation to the next. A curious kind of distance and coldness seems to come between the various generations of Menuhins. I know that sometimes I feel I have done this with my own children. Between my mother and me, although in many ways we were always very close, there has been an unusual detachment for a mother and son. I don't think this is a Jewish or Hassidic trait; it has more to do with Moshe Menuhin.

One thing Moshe's letter did for me, however, was force me to begin a quest to fill the vacuum. My early years had been yanked out from under me. I started to search for my roots, because now I knew they had to be beyond Moshe. Moshe, I sensed, had just been a sort of conduit.

THREE

My Mother, Yaltah

YALTAH'S DEVOTION TO YEHUDI has greatly colored this book. If you met me on the street, I probably would not tell you about Yehudi, my famous uncle. But you would find out soon enough once you got to know me, because his effect on me has been great, especially through my mother. This is one way the past has put its hooks into me. For much of my life, my uncle Yehudi was a shadowy but ever-present figure. During my childhood, I perceived him through my mother's eyes since I was very close to my mother and she was always close to him, if not in person, then in thought. She tried to mold me in the child prodigy tradition. She failed because I was not the right kind of material and because I could not stand the constant comparison to Yehudi.

I grew up hearing my mother talk about her childhood days in Europe, and also about her famous brother Yehudi, and sister Hephzibah. I was thirty when, in 1972, rather down and out, I took the insurance money from a car accident and purchased a round-trip ticket to London and Zurich. My mother had divorced my father and left for Europe a decade before. I discovered that being a Menuhin meant something in Europe. In California, as a newspaperman, I had been moving from town to town, not knowing what I was looking for. I was at that time a Marxist, forever railing against the evils of

As a child I tried to fit into the Menuhin musical tradition

capitalism. But in England I quickly found myself becoming the worst kind of snob, a reactionary who not only wanted to keep the present order, but who also suspected that the previous one was even better.

One evening, my mother took me to the London premiere of a film called "The Way of Light," which was about Yehudi and the family. In the film, my mother was talking about *me*, and there I was, sitting next to her in the theatre. In the film, she said that she had not understood just how great a genius Yehudi was until she had her first son. I am her first son. Suddenly, all those frustrations about not being able to live up to her expectations came back to me.

The next morning we had it out. "You love your brother as if he were a god, the Messiah," I shouted at her. Now I knew why I had left home at nineteen and spent so many years escaping the influence of my family. My mother did not deny the charge, but added, "He is, after all, a genius." Then she showed me a book; on its cover was Schneur Zalman, an impressive-looking gentleman who, some two centuries ago, had been the Jewish equivalent of a great guru. He was my direct ancestor, my mother told me, and the founder of the Lubavitcher dynasty. My first thought was, "Oh no, another Yehudi." The thought was flip, but the moment was important.

As a musician, Yaltah is her brother's and sister's equal. Yehudi says she hasn't the strength to follow a grueling concert schedule, but that is only partly true. My mother very definitely suffers from, as she describes it, "third child syndrome." She has internalized the persecution she suffered during her youth, persecution that came from her mother, brother and sister. Her father was the only family member who did not persecute her, and perhaps they even became allies because Marutha was hard on both Moshe and Yaltah. Yaltah is aware of all this, but remains remarkably un-bitter. Her love for her brother, sister and parents is like that of a devoted puppy. Yet in a terrible moment of candor, she once told me that she thought of herself as a victim of all the things feminists talk about. As a young girl, she was made to wash dishes and sew while her brother and sister practiced music. Yehudi once apologized to me for the way he and Hephzibah had treated Yaltah over the years. Yet somehow I don't feel that the basic relationship has changed.

Just how powerful a syndrome being the third child of three prodigies is came home to me on that first European visit. Gabrielle, the wife of the banker in whose Zurich house we stayed, said that my mother's was a "Cinderella story," and added that the leading music critic in Zurich thinks Yaltah is the best musician of the Menuhins today.

Certainly my mother would not agree. There has always been one man foremost in her life, and that is her brother Yehudi. She does not consider herself a genius. Yehudi, on the other hand, is not only a genius but a god. Yet she also told me, almost proudly, that she read a book in which her particular case had been described. It was this book that claimed that her career had never matched her gifts simply because she was the victim of what the author considered a "third child syndrome."

Hephzibah believes my mother would have been happiest three hundred years ago, at a court, playing music and writing poetry to her several lovers. My mother's concerns are ethereal. She's more like Yehudi in this than she is like Hephzibah. My mother knows she is playing the traditional role assigned to her as a woman, and she is not particularly happy with it, but her pride is her strength.

To this day, Yaltah is the spunkiest of the three Menuhins. Hephzibah guides her brother's thoughts away from conservatism with the notion that the world has finally left the paternalistic age, and for this it should be thankful. Now we can make a renaissance or a nightmare of the event—it is up to us. But Yaltah plays the gadfly to both her brother's and sister's pet theories. She asks her impertinent questions that, for all their underlying charm, are nonetheless deeply cynical.

Whatever Yaltah is, and there are many impressions still in my head ranging from child to tyrant and many things in between and beyond, my ambivalent feelings disappear when she plays. God knows, as with any mother and son, there are vast differences between us, from politics to basic questions of lifestyle. But as Yaltah knows Yehudi's music, I feel that I know hers. It is a strange way for a mother and a son to relate, but music is, after all, communication—surely the highest and most mysterious form of it.

My mother ran away from her parents by eloping with my father

Yaltah in 1945 at NBC

Benjamin Lionel Rolfe. Her parents never approved of him or me. From the beginning, my life as a Menuhin included happy and even exalted moments, but also much pain and deep ambivalence.

On the cold Oregon morning of the day I was born, October 21, 1942, my entrance into this world was watched, amidst trauma, by my grandparents on both sides. Early in the day, they had all gone for a ride in the lush countryside around Medford, Oregon. They stopped at a small market to buy fresh salmon, the local specialty. Then everyone but my mother jumped back into the car.

Yaltah was slow. She is barely five feet tall, and I had added twenty pounds to her tiny frame. As she came out of the store, Moshe drove off without her. My mother ran crazily after the car, trembling and crying because she thought her father was leaving her behind. By the time he stopped and turned back to get her, her face was red and she looked violently ill. Yet all her mother, Marutha, could do as Yaltah crawled miserably back into the car was to insult her in Hebrew.

Later in the hospital room my mother was holding the hand of my father's mother, who had been there and was quite shocked by the scene. "You are a good person, Bea," Yaltah said to her mother-in-law. "My mother, Marutha, is so cold, so very cold."

My entrance into the world, as my mother described it, was not entirely pleasant nor auspicious.

In 1948 my parents left San Francisco, even though Moshe and Marutha purchased a house for them there, because the elder Menuhins were trying to split up their marriage. We moved to West Los Angeles, and I grew up near the University of California campus. Those years were hell for my mother. Although she had a circle of friends that included many of the city's most gifted musicians, Los Angeles was a backwater. For my mother, who speaks French better than English, culture began in Europe and only eventually permeated here. So miserable was she that one day, while driving home on the freeway, she pulled over and cried. She was crying because it seemed that the only music you could hear in this flat, smoggy place (outside your own home) was the jukebox variety.

I grew up sharing her prejudices. I hated plastic, freeways, suburbs, the glitter of Beverly Hills, the pretenses of the nouveau riche, and all the mediocrity. Yet, I am the product of Los Angeles as much as of the elder Menuhins. I grew up in an age of plastic and I am,

Yaltah Menuhin Sees Hubby

BENJAMIN ROLFE, 27, Fort Ord, Calif., selectee, and former Minneapolis lawyer, and his bride, the former Yaltah Menuhin, 20, younger sister of the famed violinist, Yehudi Menuhin, are shown at Fort Ord October 21, when the bride visited with her husband. They eloped to Reno, Nev., and were married October 18.   *(Associated Press Photo.)*

My parents eloped with much media
attention and family outrage in 1941

despite the hopes and lessons of my mother, a plastic man. I am as sleazy as my family is elegant. Where much is sacred to my uncle, little is sacred to me. When a four letter word is needed, I use it freely. I live an everyday life, unlike my cousins, because I wasn't born with a silver spoon in my mouth—I was born with a plastic one.

A plastic Los Angeloid must find meaning behind a steering wheel on a freeway. My mother faces the void with a Steinway, my uncle with a Stradivarius. From behind my typewriter, as I write, my view is of a flamingo-pink stucco apartment building, the type derided in every article written about Los Angeles.

Actually, my mother was not terribly enamored of all great culture. It bothered her that concertgoers rarely wanted to hear any contemporary music. Partly, concertgivers did not encourage contemporary works, simply for economic reasons; only live composers get royalties. My mother championed many modern works; she premiered chamber music by both George Antheil and Eric Zeisl, as well as works by Darius Milhaud, who is perhaps the best-known of these composers. She also premiered many works by Leon Levitch, her piano tuner. Levitch is a student of Roy Harris and Mario Castelnuovo Tedesco; he has recorded some of his compositions on Orion Records but makes his living as a piano technician. My mother believes composers should be appreciated while alive, and should not have to wait until they are dead to get performances of their work.

From time to time I find myself remembering the beautiful elements of my childhood, waking up to the sound of Beethoven's Kreutzer Sonata filtering into my room from downstairs. Often, fine musicians would come to our house in West Los Angeles, people like violinist Israel Baker and cellist Gabor Rejto; their performances make up my happiest childhood memories.

At other times my mother would take me along on visits to Gregor Piatigorsky's house, or to the home of the great violinist Joseph Szigeti in Palos Verdes. Szigeti's house had a huge tiled swimming pool. With the sun pouring down, the water became magical with colors. The days were blue and sunny there by the Pacific. I would go down and swim in the pool, and if I was lucky they would be playing the Kreutzer, and I would hear it most of the afternoon. If they played it enough times, I would come upstairs and turn pages for my mother; but I was afraid of making a mistake under the stern glare of Szigeti. Sometimes, in the most intricate passages, toward the end of the page, I would lose my place and turn at the wrong time.

I suppose my love of the Kreutzer speaks for my elegant side. But these days, the sleazy has more reality for me. I spend too many hours driving on Los Angeles' freeways, and at times it seems as if the only reality is breathing lead in the yellowish smog; and if you have been doing it long enough, you feel a kind of weariness. You end up drinking or smoking or going to rowdy parties because you need to be sleazy in Los Angeles.

Another influence in my childhood was Hollywood itself. To my mother's way of looking at it, Hollywood was evil, and to toil in its vineyards made one worse than a whore. And what about the movies? I had to sneak to see them. I grew up in a city that, perhaps more than any other, is the product of twentieth century media, yet my access to the world was limited for many years to the media of previous centuries—old books, music, etc. I was brainwashed, in a sense. I think I was attracted to journalism because my mother and all the Menuhins thought journalists low creatures.

One Saturday afternoon my mother caught me before I could go off to the Pickwick Theatre at Westwood and Pico to see the latest Victor Mature saga. Yaltah thought him particularly repulsive, and I remember that I had to stay home and receive a stern lecture on the evils of Tinseltown brainrot.

Although my mother created a European ambience in our home, Los Angeles was still outside. I did not go out of my way to read Dante's *Inferno*, which to my mother was one of the first things an educated person does. Although my father had read the *Inferno* in the original, early Italian, to my mother he still represented the sleazy, because he liked boxing and fishing. My mother detested sports, and to this day when I walk into a room where friends are watching a football or baseball game on TV, I instantly get depressed.

My early literary adventures included snickering over Henry Miller's *Tropic of Cancer* on the steps around the corner from the boys' room at Westwood Elementary School. I can hear my mother's voice now as I think back. "How can you be my son?" Indeed, how could I? Part of being sleazy is resisting the classical mode of thought. My mother, horrified at my incipient lowbrowism, sent me to boarding school, where I learned that there is such a thing as homosexuality, and that children can be terribly cruel. I never studied Dante's *Inferno*, but I felt as if I was going through one at those schools.

Yet I must have learned some of the Menuhin lessons, for now, listening to Yehudi talk of his "own little world" and the self-discipline he uses to get there, I find myself agreeing. I heard my mother give the same lecture a hundred times: "Discipline is not really something imposed against your will, which is the usual conception of it, but it is actually something embraced as an ally, something which one yearns for."

My mother hated Los Angeles, but her music and her pride kept her functioning. With music, her mood would recover. Instead of sternly lecturing me, she would tell me things about the music she was playing, about whatever interested her. Of course, during the day I was going to school and growing up in the world of the 1950's that had little to do with my Menuhin home. Yet I loved the music. My mother relied on my judgement of how she had played.

Whatever elegance I might possess has come from this orientation: the ability to create a world outside of daily life. If you can play a piece of music well, then maybe you can almost as easily form a perfect society. But music, of course, is more malleable than is reality. I can sit and write a great piece of poetry about man's future, his place in the universe, the entropy of that universe, or its harmony and mysterious functions, then walk out my front door and get run over by a garbage truck.

My mother has said that she married my father because he was "normal." Yet he was a would-be artist from the Depression who became a lawyer instead because his parents wanted him to. He was the black sheep in a family of businessmen, whose artists were successful hack screenwriters. He later became a judge and continued to enjoy writing poetry, painting, and reading ancient Hebrew and Italian texts.

My mother had little understanding of hard-living people. One evening my father came home a few hours late from work, his breath smelling of liquor. They had a terrible fight, even though it was a first-time occurrence. My mother thought my father was bourgeois because he came from a working background.

Yet, at times, my family was a very closely knit group. We took weekend trips to nearly everywere you can drive from Los Angeles.

This photograph of the Rolfe family appeared in the Long Beach *Independent-Press Telegram* in 1956, six months before my parents separated. The story told how a women—my mother Yaltah—combined a successful career and marriage. From left to right are my brother Robert, Yaltah, Benjamin and Lionel

Sometimes we went as far as the Southwest or deep into Baja California, before the new superhighway cut into it. Conversation was not a lost art in our house, in great part, it now appears, because we were the only family on the block without a television set.

Writing was also a favored activity during my childhood. My mother loves to write letters and poems. Her love of writing has earned her much valuable correspondence. One Sunday morning, Yaltah took out all her letters from Willa Cather, the author of several important American novels. Yaltah was very close to "Aunt Willa," who gave her the love she never received from her mother. Willa, in turn, liked Yaltah best of all the Menuhin children.

My mother had still been young when she married my father, who was then a young soldier in the Army gone AWOL to marry her. Amidst a storm of publicity, aided in part by Moshe's open hostility to the marriage, the couple eloped. My father hadn't much money, and my mother had never worried much about that particular commodity. As I was growing up, however, she lived in dreary, cockroach-infested Southern boardinghouses, which many young Army wives did in those days when their husbands were stationed in that part of the country. My crib was the top drawer of an old bureau. I shudder to think how miserable my mother must have been then, suddenly faced with the realization that her world now included the salt-of-the-earth she had only read about. She wrote long letters to Willa Cather, and Cather wrote long letters back. Cather was amazingly romantic. She said that from the pictures my mother had sent her, she thought I was the most beautiful baby she had ever seen. She also advised my mother, who must have been contemplating divorce, to stay with my father even in the face of so much scorn from the elder Menuhins.

The rest of Willa's letters were full of philosophy and practical advice in matters of romance. "Aunt Willa," of course, had a life-long relationship with another woman, Edith Lewis, which was scandalous in those days. As her writings bear out, Cather was extremely perceptive in human matters.

From these letters, I saw my mother as young and vulnerable, and felt sorry for what she must have suffered. I know that later when my father was stationed at Oakridge, Yaltah found intellectual companionship, at least musically. She played chamber music with Albert Einstein, who loved music intensely and played the violin not so terribly well.

My parents divorced when I was sixteen, and I began to frequent coffeehouses in Venice, California. I chummed with beatniks, roomed with heroin addicts and went to jail protesting segregation. These were almost prerequisites for my generation in the sleazy Los Angeles of the fifties and sixties. After the divorce my mother moved to New York and then to London. For about five years I didn't see her. The world she had created during my childhood was slipping away. She assumed I would keep in touch with her genteel friends, but I wasn't moving in those circles.

The night I arrived in Zurich, Yaltah met me at the airport and before we went back to the house where she was staying, we stopped at a nightclub and heard American disco music. The audience looked for all the world like the plastic swingers of San Francisco's Union Street or Sunset Boulevard in Los Angeles. She was not comfortable with the music, although she was listening to it, which is a change from what she once would have done. I'd like to be able to report that she is a secret lover of rock'n'roll, but this is not the case. Later on, we went up the hill to our quarters in the banker's house. It was a great mansion with three stories crammed full of the most amazing things, such as the first encyclopedia in French, some three centuries old. My mother "tucked" me into bed, which was a wide, very comfortable antique, with very soft blankets. I felt like a child. For a delicious moment I *was* a child, without a care in the world.

That first night in Zurich, my mother told me that I had the blood of the Hassids in me. She did not explain what that was, and I passed it off because I knew it had something to do with the Schneersohns, those "storefront rabbis" of Moshe's in Brooklyn, who were such a joke to him. The seed had been planted, although I did not seek out my Hassidic relatives in Brooklyn until the summer of 1973.

FOUR

Disillusionment at the Ancestral Court

I WENT TO NEW YORK with much excitement about the prospects of learning more about my Hassidic ancestors. The first morning after my arrival in New York, I emerged from the black pits of the subway to find that number 790, the address of the Hassidic headquarters, was quite a bit further down Brooklyn's Eastern Parkway. I found myself in front of the Brooklyn Museum. The hour was early enough that the sun's rays were still stark and slanted, and the streets of the surrounding black ghettoes were deserted, save for a few children still too young and full of energy to appreciate sleeping late on the Christian Sabbath.

As I began the trek down the broad, shabby but still dignified boulevard, I felt my balding head and cursed myself for not having followed the advice of people who had told me to get some cover for my shiny dome. It doesn't have to be a *yarmulke*; any type of hat would do, I had been told. "But wouldn't that be dishonest?" I had asked. "I mean, I'm not an orthodox Jew." "Just to show them respect," had been the answer. Ah, in that case, I knew what would have been ideal: one of those jaunty black berets that my grandfather Moshe always used to wear. Moshe used to have an endless supply of them, one in this room, another in that, maybe even one in the chicken shed. I came to share my grandfather's love of black berets, and my grandfather never seemed to be very angry at me when I would lose a beret and have to ask for another.

So a beret would be more honest than a *yarmulke*, and it would solve a couple of problems. A writer could certainly wear a beret without straining his credibility and still cover his head. Maybe, in fact, that was where Moshe had gotten the habit. A beret made you a dapper, worldly gentleman, and yet if you had come from the ghettoes of Eastern Europe, it eased your conscience about your naked head. At the same time, it showed the disdain he had for the orthodox in Judaism. A dapper, black, Parisian, Left Bank beret.

But there were no berets in the ghetto shops. One sad-looking place was right next door to a cleaning shop; in fact, the shop and the cleaners' adjoined in a two-shop arcade, barricaded this early in the morning by enormous jail-like bars. I peered through the bars and the dirty window. Definitely no berets there. I cast a wary eye at a group of Puerto Rican youths who were eyeing me, then hurried along.

My pace quickened, and as it did so, the whirring worrying in my head that I would have to brave the Lubavitcher Court hatless also increased. With alarm I saw that the numbers were climbing faster than I thought they would, and I cut my stride, not, as I was telling myself, because it was so early that no one would be there yet, but because of the reception I expected. Many a writer had been thrown bodily out of the Lubavitcher Court. On the other hand, the Schneersohns, the Lubavitchers, were my cousins. The Menuhins were but an offshoot of the famed Chabad father-to-son dynasty which presided over the Polish-Russian town of Lubavitch.

Once the Lubavitchers had been the major leaders of half of Russia's Jewish population, which numbered several millions. But the pogroms at the turn of the century, the mass exodus of the Jews before the Russian Revolution, and then Hitler, reduced the Lubavitchers to holding sway over 25,000 souls. They had done so for much of this century in unexotic, sleazy Brooklyn, ever since Rabbi Joseph Isaac Schneersohn, the sixth generation head of the Lubavitcher dynasty, had been released from a Soviet prison in the 1920's. He had made his way first to Paris, then to Brooklyn.

It turned out that number 790 was one of several buildings spread out over several blocks in the Crown Heights area. Hassidim in their long, flowing black gowns and hats strode and shuffled everywhere. Many were old, but not as many as I had expected. Busloads of Hassidic children pulled up in front of the entrance to 790.

Now I stood in the foyer behind the heavy entrance doors, uncomfortable because I could be naught but a stranger to the bearded Jews chanting in the next room with a passionate, melodic, electric hum that I recognized. Although in my youth my grandfather did not sing Hassidic melodies to me, there was an intense melody in the hum of his activity. Even if he was merely showing me the right way to pull up a weed or to dig a hole to trap a gopher gnawing at the roots of an orange tree, or tamping down the compost heap back of the chicken shed, that old Hassidic energy was there, an almost melodic energy.

Standing there inside number 790, I had feelings of déja-vu. Suddenly I understood where my grandfather's strange rhythm had come from. And now Hassidim emerged from the room where they had been chanting and *davaning*; they kissed the *mezuzah* on the door and went outside. I thought about how my grandfather had once been one of those worshipping, praying Jews; how I, too, in an earlier age, would have been one of them; how, even when one rebels, as had my grandfather, the effort is rarely · completely convincing. No, I hadn't sprung from the air. I understood that now, as I watched these Hassidim and remembered the childhood days I had spent with my grandfather.

My mind became involved in the kissing of the door's *mezuzah*, and I wondered if they expected me to do it. It was a whole celebration. In fact, that is the basis of Hassidism. Every second is meant for celebrating. God did not create once; he constantly creates. When a Hassid, a thin, pale-looking young man, had finished kissing the *mezuzah*, he looked straight at me, without giving me a sign of acknowledgement. He did not even ask me what I was doing there and left the building. Seconds later, another Hassid, with a more authoritative bearing, walked in the door and asked me what I wanted.

What did I want, I grinned inwardly, in 5,000 words or less? I heard my voice mumble something, and found I was being pointed at a door I assumed was an office. "Somebody should be there soon," a passing Hassid told me. Finally someone did come, an "American" rabbi. "Americans", as the Hassidim know them, are the younger generation who have stayed in the faith, but were not born in Russia. They talk like Americans and are hardly Jews in the eyes of the elders.

I began to explain my purpose to him, and he confirmed what I had been told by the Los Angeles Hassidic American rabbi, that Rabbi Israel Jacobson was the man I should talk to. Was that Rabbi Jacobson? I asked someone after the "American" rabbi had left, pointing to an extremely pale, delicately old man with a long, wispy, flowing beard. "No, no," said the *yeshiva* student who had suddenly appeared at my side. "That is the rabbi who deals only in questions of the Torah," he explained with unmistakable awe and reverence.

The "American" rabbi had returned. He kept glancing up at me. Something was making him nervous. Then I laughed. "Have you a *yarmulke*?" I asked him. He looked relieved. "Yes, yes," he said quickly, and rummaged through a cabinet, coming up with a red *yarmulke*. I put it on, and the rabbi looked as if God Himself was smiling in His Heaven.

Now the *yeshiva* student became very friendly. He wanted to talk. I asked him if he had ever heard of Yehudi Menuhin, the violinist. "No," said the student. "Well," I said, suddenly feeling silly, "he's my uncle, and one of the world's most famous violinists. I'm surprised you haven't heard of him, for he is also a Schneersohn." I talked for awhile about the Menuhins and the Schneersohns, and about the book I was writing. "I am related to the family, too," said the student proudly. I looked at him and saw that his broad, beaming countenance could be said to look like my own. I told him I had not been raised religiously; in truth, I hadn't even been *Bar Mitzvah'd*. It wasn't until six months ago that I had even started to look into my family background. I hadn't known how extraordinary and eccentric my family was. I had always known they were famous musicians, but not religious figures, too. "I've been reading a lot about my ancestors," I said.

"Follow me," the student replied. We went down a narrow, winding stairway to a basement synagogue, a gigantic room filled with noise and hubbub. Everyone was chanting and talking; it was chaotic, and no one person seemed in charge. Even the student didn't quite know what to do with me. I spotted the "Torah rabbi," and to my surprise, the student went up to where the rabbi was praying and interrupted him! The rabbi was surprised too, and angry. He glared at the student as if to say, "Deal with it as you will." So the *yeshiva* student returned to me and said I should put on *tfillin*, the Hebrew phylacteries. For the second time in my life, I did so. I repeated the

Hebrew words without knowing what they meant.

Knowledge in and of itself is not necessary, only faith. And while I couldn't claim to have much faith, I could feel it. If ever I were to have any kind of religious faith, this Hassidism might be it, if only because I regard reform Judaism as simply an attempt by Jews to be like Christians. If I were to be religious...I remembered that the Los Angeles rabbi, who had helped me considerably with my research, had once seen a picture of Yehudi standing at the Wailing Wall in Jerusalem. Well, Yehudi might have gone to the Wailing Wall, but he was no more a practicing Hassid than I was. Still, the fact that Yehudi had prayed there seemed to mean a lot to the Los Angeles rabbi.

After the prayer, which seemed to make the student happy, we talked, and the student seemed to understand what I had come for. He asked me to live with the Hassidim for awhile, "just to get a feel for what you are writing about," he said. The idea appealed to me.

We went upstairs, and the student said he would help me find Rabbi Jacobson. The student talked to several people and discovered which of the *yeshiva* buildings Jacobson was in at the moment. He pointed to the right one. I shook his hand and began walking, and came upon what looked like an abandoned building. From down at the end of one of its darkened halls, however, came the sound of voices, and finally from the shadows emerged the man who, I knew, had to be Jacobson.

"I want to talk," I said to the rabbi, and got the feeling that he had been expecting me. Jacobson merely nodded and pointed to the door at the far end of the building. I followed the little man.

It was a small, dark room with a rough bench and some chairs. At first Rabbi Jacobson couldn't understand, and my heart sank. "Moshe Menuhin, my grandfather," I said. Finally Jacobson took out a piece of paper and wrote the name down, and I began worrying. To whom could I go if this man didn't know? Jacobson had become my link with the past. "Meshe," the rabbi finally said slowly, and his face lit up. "You're related to him? How are you related to him?"

"He is my grandfather."

"And what do you do?"

"I am a writer. I am writing a book. I am told we are related to the Schneersohns."

Rabbi Jacobson nodded. "I have a letter," he began explaining, "written to me from Russia many years ago about Meshe, the father of Yehudi Menuhin. Your grandfather is the direct descendant via a marriage with a daughter of the great *tzaddik*, Menachem-Mendel Schneersohn, the famed grandson of Schneur Zalman. And on his father's side he was the great-grandson of Levi-Yitzhak of Berditchev."

He scrawled the name "Levi-Yitzhak" on the back of an envelope. I knew who Levi-Yitzhak was. I remembered having read about the saintly but eccentric teacher, and saying to myself, "That man reminds me somehow of myself." Now I was learning that there might be a reason for this.

"I want to see the letter," I said.

"It's in Hebrew," the rabbi told me. Suddenly his tone of voice became suspicious. He was no longer friendly. He began to scowl, and began asking me questions like a prosecuting attorney hot on the trail of a confession. I was taken aback, but, without thinking, I found myself answering everything truthfully, for I had the naive belief that that would be best. The rabbi questioned me about my family, my Jewishness, my upbringing. I had hoped that he would simply understand that I was coming from a different place, much as I felt I could understand these relatives of mine who had come from another culture and identify with them. For example, I said that my brother Robert was a physicist at Los Alamos, New Mexico. "What's a physicist?" asked the rabbi. "Is that like a doctor?" The thought struck me hard: the rabbi didn't even know what a physicist was. I tried to explain, but the more I said, the more it became apparent that the rabbi had no way of conceiving what a theoretical physicist does, and besides, I had the feeling I'd best not talk too much about the relentless pursuit of the mechanics of matter, for Hassidim are, after all, mystics, who treasure the universe's mystery as God's very own cloak.

Then I mentioned my daughters, and the rabbi asked the question, "Is the mother Jewish?" My first wife had not been Jewish, I had to admit.

The rabbi raised his hands in horror and announced that he had no intention of contributing to a book such as mine. "I will not besmirch the name of the Schneersohns, one of the greatest of Jewish intellectual family names, by linking it with that of the Menuhins," he said dramatically. "I will tell you no more."

My anger exploded. "The Schneersohns have nothing to be

ashamed of by being linked to the Menuhins," I replied. "And you
have no right to talk to me that way. I am every bit as much a Jew as
you are."

"Is your mother Jewish?"

"Of course. She's a Menuhin."

"And your father?"

I nodded. "Fully."

"But your children aren't."

"What do you expect me to do—disown my own children?"

"I'm not running a charity," said the rabbi. "I can't worry about
every lost soul. And Yehudi Menuhin, he's not married to a Jew
either, is he?"

"He's not."

Silence. I thought I would make an attempt to explain myself
again, to put my cards on the table. Certainly Jacobson would see he
had nothing to fear by helping me. There was no reason he should
refuse to help. But the more I talked, the worse things became. For
Jacobson had his idea of what should happen. He said that before he
would help, he would want the Menuhins to return to the fold. In
fact, he made it plain that the Hassidim would be very honored if the
Menuhins would return to the religion of their ancestors, as though I
could convince them to do so even if I wanted to.

Now Jacobson had another idea. "Listen," he said. "I will
maybe help you if you go back to the *yeshiva* and start by getting to
know some of the young men there." I shook my head. I said I had to
be in London soon, which was only partly true. But I knew I didn't
want to spend much more time in New York, let alone with the
Hassidim. "All right then," said Jacobson, "when you get to London,
look us up there. Associate with the right people. Stay away from the
shiksas." If I did all those things, maybe Jacobson would then
consider revealing all the details of my family tree.

I left the little room without talking to anyone there. Before I
walked out the front door, I passed a room where several *yeshiva*
students were gathered. They smiled at me as I walked out, but they
seemed to be too young to talk with. What would I say to any of
them? Perhaps, if my first friend had been there...I had felt some
closeness to him. Maybe I should simply go back to my Manhattan
hotel and catch the next plane out. I was still seething. But no, I owed
it another try. I would go to an afternoon of lectures by one of the

Lubavitcher rabbis.

The lecture was on *Tanya*, the great opus of Jewish psychology written in 1797 by the Alter Rebbe himself, Schneur Zalman. The *Tanya* lecture concerned Jewish souls and non-Jewish souls. According to *Tanya*, all human beings have souls, but only Jews have higher souls. I was again reminded of my inner turmoil at the way my own children had been so cavalierly dismissed. Yet the rabbi had said a few non-Jews might be Jewish souls in disguise and could thus be saved from the *goyiche*—that is, Gentile—culture.

One of those around the table listening to the rabbi's lecture was a loud, aggressive-sounding fellow who, as it finally came out, was a member of Rabbi Kahane's Jewish Defense League, the militant Zionist political organization centered in New York City.

Zalman's *Tanya* seemed to have struck a responsive chord in the fellow, who was now describing an incident in which he had silenced a "Jesus person" by quite pointedly ignoring him and addressing himself to the Jew the Jesus freak was trying to convert. When the Christian started to break into the conversation, the Kahane fellow turned to him and screamed, "Shut up, you uncircumcised dog! I'm not talking to you."

As the words "uncircumcised dog" came tumbling out, I knew I wasn't going to stay much longer in Brooklyn. I tried to imagine sleeping in the same room with Hassidim, but couldn't. I had never been *Bar Mitzvah'd* and worse, although I was supposedly circumcised at birth, my wife insists that it doesn't look that way. That's all I needed, to have a roomful of Hassidim telling me I should get an operation.

London seemed a much better fate than a retroactive circumcision.

My visit with the Hassids was of great interest to my family. I met with Yehudi, Hephzibah and Yaltah on various occasions and described my experience with Jacobson. Yehudi's first reaction to the story was to say that "the tightness is the heart of their survival, the key to their survival. You must respect it."

Hephzibah grinned a bit and said, "My God, they make Aba [the Hebrew word for "father", by which most of the Menuhins call Moshe] look like a tolerant man." Needless to say, tolerance is not one of Moshe's most notable traits.

Yaltah remarked, "You see, that's what Moshe was trying to escape from all of his life, that kind of attitude."

Later, Yehudi expanded on his point. "After all," he said, "you have to admire a people who can go around ignoring the conventionalities of the culture they live in. Devotion to principles is the hallmark of the Hassidim. It's the difference between the kinds of Jews who become philosophers and those who become merchants and bankers."

But he couldn't resist telling a story his father had often told. A little Hassidic boy, so Moshe's tale went, came home one day to tell his father about something he had discovered. He had seen the Red Sox and the White Sox in a baseball game on television and had found the whole thing enchantingly different from anything he had ever seen before. But when he tried to describe what he had seen, the father looked at his son quizzically and could make no sense of it at all. He couldn't grasp the concept of why two groups of men would stand around trying to hit balls at each other with sticks and then run around the battlefield playing a game of tag. The Hassid's son persisted with his explanations, until finally both realized it was an impossible situation. "Listen," said the Hassid, "just answer me one thing. This Red Sox and this White Sox, is it good for the Jews?"

Several days later, Yehudi suggested going for a walk. He had just come from a full day's recording at EMI's Abbey Road studios. He jogged up to the front door of his house, then walked up the stairs. "We'll have a walk. Would you like to walk? But not like the walk we had a long time ago." He looked meaningfully at me.

I searched my mind. "Where was that? At that big house on the Florida coast? I hardly remember it. I remember there was a pier."

"Yes, I remember that pier, too," said Yehudi.

"Why did we go for a walk?"

"You were very unhappy. And I thought if we talked, it would help. So we walked most of the day."

'I wish I remembered it better."

"Well, it doesn't matter that much," he said. It was during a month-long reunion of the three Menuhin children after World War II. "It was just before I married Diana."

Then Yehudi went upstairs and came back down wearing different clothes. He asked Diana if the red sweater he had just put on was all right. She adjusted it and said it was fine. We dashed just a little dangerously across the street in front of Yehudi's house in Highgate Village. Then we walked several blocks to the park nearby.

From Highgate, which is the highest point in London, you could see the whole city. "Ten years ago," said Yehudi, "you didn't have all those ugly skyscrapers." For awhile our talk was about the grotesqueness of land developers and the profit system. "It served a purpose once," said Yehudi.

We talked about squirrels, stopping to admire one scampering up a tree; and about the beauty of a particular, huge, almost purple tree. He spoke of the Hassidim. "It's a passion, a kind of lunacy," he was saying. "They are the kind of people who say, 'I'll be the best violinist in the world,' or 'The world has to be perfect,' even when it can never be. And they won't understand that it never can be, because between studying and praying they are not a part of the world. They are possessed." Maybe, I thought then, Yehudi's being one of the "best" violinists in the world is not unrelated to his Hassidic background either. If the Hassids are the possessed, I thought, then he is one of the possessed as well.

FIVE

Two Supreme Mysteries
—Myth and Music

T HE POSSESSION THAT Yehudi ascribes to the Hassids bothers him when it is applied to himself.
He is not fond of discussing his own precocity
and even seems to minimize it. Yet, after reading an earlier version of
this book, he complimented me and said that there was indeed something miraculous and mysterious about his precocity. It was a rare
personal admission for one who usually talks as if he were just
another boy, grown up into an ordinary man.

I think I first accepted the reality of Yehudi's incredible precocity
on a yellow, smoggy day in Los Angeles. I was eating a hot dog in
front of the UCLA research library, and I had just been looking
through some old news clippings of Yehudi's early life and exploits. I
had been reading the perhaps overly zealous words of some of the
awed reporters who had greeted the boy violinist at the beginning of
his career. I had begun to realize that there was something very
special about Yehudi. So special, in fact, that as I sat there eating that
silly hot dog, tears came to my eyes. I tried to describe to Nigey, my
wife, what it was about the phenomenon that had so affected me. I
don't know if I conveyed to her my sense of the miraculous which
Yehudi inspired in me, but I felt it. Suddenly I realized how seldom in
history a child is born who can so move people that they abandon all
pretense to anything but awe. Now I understood that while it might

have been cruel, my mother was right to realize after having me that her brother had been a miracle. He was a miracle, or had been, and the shadow under which I had been raised was not just a shadow; it was real.

My eyes were full of tears of discovery, for I had also been learning much more about my ancestors, gurus and wise men, many of whom as children had left their marks on history. If they are my ancestors as much as they are Yehudi's, I thought, then some of their spirit must move in me. I was not just a man sitting in front of a library in Los Angeles, I was a product of a centuries-old tradition that had molded me without my knowing it.

The first trip to London and Zurich (before I was even thinking of writing this book) had introduced me to the existence of the Schneersohns and the Lubavitchers. When I returned home to Los Angeles, I had gone to the local Lubavitchers and read much of the literature relating to my Schneersohn ancestors. The first thing that struck me was the pattern of child prodigies among them. Now, in the UCLA library, I was beginning a search of research facilities, looking all the while for an understanding of what child prodigies were. I read everything I could get my hands on, so fascinated had I become with the subject. It soon became apparent to me that what science cannot easily quantify or prove it soon denies as a valid phenomenon.

I became more convinced than ever that psychology is really nothing but a modern version of the old shaman's art, if that, for the one conclusion psychologists seem to be sure of in regard to prodigies is a cliche that is not true. They observe that music is the area where children can achieve exceptional success because music does not require experience as do writing and painting.

Yet, music requires the experience of all the ages. That kind of experience, in fact, which one has at birth and death, is greater than that known of by the psychologists, according to Yehudi. Yehudi was a six-year-old boy, but he seemed to have the wisdom of centuries. In the early 1920's, when his genius first became public, people recognized in his playing not only superb technique but sensed an intellect and a mind as profound as a sage's. Normally self-possessed men and women wrote about him as if he were a miracle.

The only school of psychology that might shed some light was one I had at one time strongly disagreed with. I was very bothered by my mother's friends in Zurich who were prominent in Jungian circles. I saw them as rich fascists, and I distrusted their idol. Hephzibah had also told me a story about an encounter she had had with Jung that convinced her he was just another money-hungry psychiatrist. Someone had suggested that Hephzibah's work in community organizing and Jung's work with the psyche would make for some interesting dialogue. Jung agreed but wanted to charge Hephzibah by the hour for the conversation, which to Hephzibah proved him a fraud.

My feelings about Jung were changed by my mother's husband, Joel Ryce. He was in the process of becoming a Jungian analyst, and he showed me a book on archetypes, psychic symbols that have endured universally throughout man's history. In it, Jung talks of myths which are the universals shared by all minds. "Myth is the natural and indispensable intermediate stage between unconscious and conscious cognition," Jung said. "True, the unconscious part of the mind knows more than the conscious does, but it is knowledge of a special sort, knowledge in eternity, usually without reference to the here and now, not couched in terms of the intellect."

Myths were not a simple thing to Jung. The more I read, the more it seemed to me that myth, in his eyes, represented everything and nothing. In some places he described each person's life as that person's myth. He said that it does not matter if myth is true or not, just that it *is*. He also insisted that myths are real, that they are manifestations of God. Myths tell us more about ourselves than do science or rationality. Each of us has our own unique myth, yet we also have broad categories which he calls the child-myth. A child-myth is larger than any one child and yet it is the myth that molds all children.

I was dubious about Jung's theories, but I also remember that when Joel showed me the book on archetypes, I had a sense that something larger than myself was being touched.

In the intervening months between my first experience with the Jungians in Zurich and my becoming involved in the writing of this book, I had largely forgotten this business of myths. But once back in London, I came across the work of the French anthropologist, Claude Levi-Strauss, and found in a passage a discussion of myth and music as the two supreme mysteries science had not yet unraveled. Levi-Strauss' words jumped out of the page at me, for suddenly I saw why I had found nothing satisfying about child prodigies even though I had searched in libraries halfway across the world. I was dealing with myths, the mind-boggling complexities of myth and of music.

Levi-Strauss suggested that the unraveling of the mystery behind music might be the key to a real scientific renaissance. Both music and myth, he said, operate in a continuum not limited by time. Both music and myth strike those chords in us which participate in that same inner awareness of timelessness. Timelessness is a favorite subject of Yehudi's. He often likes to say that there is no such thing as time.

I was surprised that Levi-Strauss sounded more mystical than scientific. He suggested that in myth and music man looks at the most profound unconscious, universal truths. He pointed out that anthropologists have been able to understand some of the mechanisms of myths as collective creations, but not those of music. According to him, "we know nothing of the mental conditions in which musical creation takes place. We do not understand the difference between the very few minds that bring forth music and the vast numbers which do not, although nearly everyone is sensitive to music. The musical creator is comparable to the gods."

In the Russian Jewish world of the late 19th and early 20th century, the violin became the vessel into which everything was poured, the Kabbalistic form of which universal life is the content. In one rush, in one of those eddies of history ill-explained by the academic world, came Elman and Heifetz and Milstein and Menuhin, all Jews from that part of the world where Jewish life was once again being murdered. The violin would become the ultimate Jewish instrument; better than any other it would express love and exaltation—and suffering.

Yehudi still judges a person by his knowledge of suffering, as conveyed by the eyes and brow. If he says you have suffered, that means he approves of you. It means, if nothing else, that you will understand where his music comes from.

I quickly saw the importance of Messianism in Judaism partly because I could feel the Messianic impulse in myself. It was enlightening to read the great Jewish philosopher Martin Buber, who insisted that the Messianic concept is the source of creativity in Jewish thought. There are always two forces seeking synthesis, he said, the prophets and the priests. The prophets are mystics and rebels; the priests and rabbis keep the laws.

Prophesy has always been the very special undergirding of Judaism. Prophets opposed the priests in Biblical times, proclaiming their revelations from Yahweh. The priests wanted to curb the prophets because they were troublemakers. They wanted to enshrine Moses as Yahweh's last prophet so that the rest of history could become the province of the clerics.

By the rules of prophecy, a prophet is answerable only to Yahweh. He need not spend years in proscribed religious discipline. Yahweh, after all, must encompass many even seemingly contradictory truths. He is the One. Yehudi's kind of precocity, and yes, Mozart's, must come, according to this tradition, from no less an authority than Yahweh. But child prodigies remain a mystery to modern science, which can only fall back on the well-worn phrase, "God-given talents."

Yehudi, however, tries not to see anything miraculous in his early triumphs. One can perhaps understand why he likes to ignore his precocity because it was partly that which made his life as a mature artist so difficult. "To achieve the miracle and prolong it a lifetime," he says, "means working daily with hands, heart and mind." After all, he continues, his own life "is the constant proof and realization" that he was no miracle, but simply a human being. "One cannot help the accident of his birth."

But whether you call it a miracle, reincarnation, genes, coincidence, or tradition, the Menuhin line reads like a prophetic "Who's Who" of mystical Judaism. And it is this line that I began to explore in depth. I was not able to fully understand the mysteries behind the Menuhin phenomenon, but I could no longer dispute that such mysteries were operating in my family's history, a history that can be traced back, according to Hassidic tradition, to David himself.

II
FROM MOTHER RUSSIA
TO THE HOLY LAND

SIX

A Spirit Nurtures the Family

WE HAVE SEEN THAT the family from which Yehudi came was the priesthood established by one of the greatest prophetic movements in Judaism, Hassidism. Basing itself on the mysterious Kabbalah, the prophet-created religious movement has lasted three centuries. The basic Kabbalistic secret was the merging of opposites into something whole— synthesis, a Menuhin specialty. In the case of the Lubavitcher dynasty, the synthesis revealed a schizophrenic duality. It was a hereditary priesthood, which is essentially conservative politically, yet its religious principles came directly from its rebellious prophets.

The first Schneersohn, the man from whom the hereditary first family of the Lubavitchers traces itself, was Schneur Zalman. His Hassidism, the movement he represented in his lifetime, was revolutionary; Zalman, though, was its conservative face. He carried the seed of revolution forward as the major disciple of a man named Dov-Ber. And it was this Dov-Ber who was accused by some of having invented the Baal-Shem, the great man whom Martin Buber compared to Jesus in terms of historical importance. The Baal-Shem was the great prophet of the Hassidic movement that swept the Jewish communities in eastern Europe in the eighteenth and nineteenth centuries. But a lot of what is known about the Baal-Shem was told by Dov-Ber.

Dov-Ber's disciple, Zalman, did an interesting thing, something that appeared to be little more than an exercise in Kabbalah. But it was an important act, because it was repeated by his descendants years later. God, it is said, created heaven by putting on a robe of primordial light, which he then harmonized with the darkness. Schneur Zalman took the Baal-Shem's prophetic light and merged it with the rabbinical establishment of the day. He was the great co-opter.

The basic truth that the Baal-Shem promulgated concerned, really, a state of mind; ecstasy or *Hitlahavut*. It is that state of mind to which Schneur Zalman was committed, and it is also more than evident in Yehudi. Through *Hitlahavut* the Messiah will be persuaded to come; *Hitlahavut* unites man with God in the wondrous state of concentration wherein ecstasy makes even the most oft-repeated actions fresh again. For the Hassidim, it was the quality of their prayers that made their relationship with God so powerful.

Yehudi has said it, the Baal-Shem said it: repetition is dulling and deadly, whether one is hearing the Beethoven Violin Concerto or seeking God. In the light of the ecstasy of *Hitlahavut*, the deadliness is gone, and each day rises as a new miracle.

The life of the Baal-Shem expresses the essence of *Hitlahavut*. Cognition in this state is quite the opposite of the kind of intellect measured by intelligence tests; it is much closer to the intuitive and the creative. If Yehudi is, as he insists, an "interpreter," and not a "creator" like Mozart, then his interpretations are imbued with that special quality, *Hitlahavut*, that renders the music alive.

The Baal-Shem was born in 1700 and lost both his parents while still very young. He was raised by the Jewish community in the tiny, obscure village of Okep. He lived at the *heder*, or school, which was central to Jewish life. But he rebelled against the *heder* and its musty rabbis and many arbitrary rules. The *heder* was dark and dank with earthen floors and wooden benches. The rabbis who taught the children sat on the benches with a bowl of snuff between their knees, dispensing Torah along with bits of food and stern punishment. They kept most of the food for themselves. Life in those Jewish communities before Hassidism was full of tales of the cruelties which learned men showed to common men, such as the old rabbis starving their students. It would be the Baal-Shem's role to challenge the power of these rabbis with his Hassidism. Talmudic scholarship, more than wealth or physical attractiveness, was power in those days.

In time, the Baal-Shem's mystics would tour the Russian countryside attacking abuses by the learned and teaching the common man that he could have power, much as Communist student revolutionaries would do a couple of centuries later.

Who was the Baal-Shem? What did he look like? No one knows. We don't know because he left behind so many legends that all sense of proportion, of reality, has gone from the man.

Buber says that the Baal-Shem is almost unique in Jewish history because he was one of the few prophets who ever emerged victorious over the priesthood. The Baal-Shem is the figure at the bottom of the Lubavitcher dynasty legend, and hence also at the bottom of Yehudi's legend.

The old men in the *heder* thought the Baal-Shem was stupid because he would not study Torah. Instead, he lazed around during the day and it was assumed that he was a loutish oaf who slept at night as well as in the daytime. But he wasn't sleeping at night. He was studying the Kabbalah and specifically *The Book of Splendor* (the *Zohar*). The Kabbalah had to be studied in secret because the false Messiahs Zevi and Frank had done much to discredit it, a fact that the traditional rabbis seized upon.

The Baal-Shem was anxious not to be regarded as a Messiah or a magician. His Kabbalistic universe was not filled with ghosts and demons. It was a kind, gentle, friendly place where even evil was benign because God watched over all.

The common folk in his village loved the Baal-Shem. He was a gentle man, and children always responded well to the special qualities in him. Later, adults came to see those same qualities, and even though he had no status at the synagogue, he did begin to gain a reputation as a wise man.

When he married, his wealthy in-laws tried to have scholars teach him Torah and they also attempted to find him suitable employment. But he was a failure as a coachman, and scholars could see nothing of value in this uncouth peasant. Finally the Baal-Shem and his wife went to live at an inn in the Carpathian Mountains. They were poor, but his wife was devoted. There in the mountains, Hassidism was born. The Baal-Shem spent many days alone in the wilderness, speaking the language of birds and trees.

A story is told that some bandits were waiting, ready to kill him as he walked precariously near a mountain cliff. He was so wrapped up in his thoughts that he was unaware of the chasm ahead. The bandits thought they would not have to do the evil deed after all; but then the mountain moved to bridge the chasm without the Baal-Shem's even being aware of it. The bandits realized then that he was a holy man.

After seven years in the mountains, the Baal-Shem began to travel from village to village. His fame spread rapidly. It is said that one day the Baal-Shem saw the Messiah in heaven and talked with him. Stories are also told about his travels, with the wind as his companion. When he had hundreds of miles to cover and not enough time, he traveled through the fourth dimension, making a joke of time and distance.

Once at his destination, he would begin by telling his tales to a solitary listener, and then a crowd would gradually gather around him. He told his tales the way an Indian musician improvises ragas. Even if one missed the beginning, he nonetheless would be immediately in contact with its totality. The stories were simple but profound and subtle, like parables. To hear him, they say, was to feel the magic of the sea and the stars, and to hear the soft stirrings of the air.

SEVEN

Early Generations
of Holy Prodigies

THE SCHNEERSOHN CLAN specialized in the production of genius children. The first of these holy prodigies was Rabbi Judah Liva, whose tombstone records his death in 1440. It is said that he was a direct descendant of King David. The next prominent child prodigy was the famed MaHaRal, born in 1512. By the age of seven, he was discussing Torah with the most learned men of the day.

Jews are divided into two main branches, the Ashkenazim and the Sephardim. The greatest Jewish thinker of all was a Sephardic Jew named Maimonides. Some claim that the MaHaRal was the only thinker the Ashkenazim ever produced who could rival Maimonides.

At ten years of age, the MaHaRal was engaged to Pearl, the daughter of a wealthy and scholarly man from Prague, from a family of so-called "court Jews." "Court Jews" were sought out by both the Gentile and Jewish communities of the time for advice and counsel. The MaHaRal's future in-laws sent him to a famed *yeshiva*, or Jewish university. By the MaHaRal's description, the school was a place where he mastered the fine art of "creating complete and intricate structures of ideas," a mental process common to both mathematics and music.

Now a curious and confusing thing occurred. The MaHaRal, an Ashkenazi, became fast friends with a young man his age who came from an old Sephardic family that had been driven from Portugal by the Inquisition. This young man was the son of the MaHaRal's greatest teacher, an old rabbi named Yitzhak.

The MaHaRal became a great master of Torah, but this Yitzhak was his tutor in Kabbalah. Yitzhak's son was to become a great Kabbalist, known by a name that sounded almost like the MaHaRal. He was called the MaHarShal. The MaHaRal and the MaHarShal became close friends. More importantly for our story, their common descendants produced the great Schneur Zalman two hundred years later. You see, the grandmother of Zalman was descended from old rabbi Yitzhak.

You will remember that Schneur Zalman, the first of the Lubavitcher rabbis, could find no peace in his soul between the forces that were then battling in the Jewish community, a battle that could be seen as a division of thought between the rationality of Torah study and the intuition of Kabbalistic inquiry. You might say that when the MaHaRal and the MaHarShal had disagreements, those were the same disagreements which their common descendant, Schneur Zalman, would attempt to synthesize into *Chabad* Hassidism two centuries later.

For now, however, let us keep to the MaHaRal (1512-1609). He is best known in history as the creator of the legendary Golem. The Golem, according to Kabbalists, was the secret of creation, the Jewish Frankenstein, if you will. This Golem was a clay figure that the MaHaRal had fashioned, and into whose mouth he had inserted a piece of paper bearing the mystic and ineffable Name of God, which had to be taken out before every Sabbath. As long as the paper stayed in the Golem's mouth, the Golem would perform various functions, not only for his creator, but for the whole Jewish community in Prague. He would, for instance, fetch water. He never got sick, for his creator insisted that he had none of that evil in him from which illness comes.

At the same time, as if to emphasize that the Golem was on a lower level than his human creator, just as Adam was subordinate to his divine creator, the MaHaRal created the Golem without a sex drive. Why? Because, said the MaHaRal, had he been given a sex drive, no woman would have been safe with him. Also, the Golem had no speech.

One day the MaHaRal went off to the great Synagogue of Prague for Sabbath services, forgetting to remove the slip of paper from the Golem's mouth. Suddenly the Golem grew to enormous size and rampaged through the ghetto, destroying everything in his path. The MaHaRal was summoned and, with a valiant effort, reached up into the Golem's mouth and tore out the slip of paper, whereupon the Golem turned into a lifeless clay creature once again.

The MaHaRal may have been the last Menuhin ever to play so lightly with the powers of creativity.

The MaHaRal became the chief rabbi of Prague during times that were very bad for the Jews. Both the nobles and the Pope himself called on King Ferdinand to expel the Jews. The MaHaRal called the first mass meeting of Prague's Jewry. He walked onto the speaking platform wearing *tallis* and *tfillin*, orthodox ritual attire, leading a procession of the Jewish community's high command. "Hear, O Israel, the Lord is our God, the Lord is One," he chanted. The moment he had uttered these words, the audience began to weep and wail, for they knew that calamity was afoot.

"Let us cease our weeping," the MaHaRal admonished them. "Let us show no weakness. Let us rather show how strong we are, and let all of us, men, women and children, young and old, sanctify God's holy Name. Let us all swear before *Sefer Torah* [the scroll of the Torah] that not one of us will go to hear the sermon of a Catholic priest. And in the event any of us are taken to their churches forcibly, we will stop up our ears, and we will not listen."

The MaHaRal was not unknown in local royal circles. His wife Pearl's father, Samuel Reich, a tough man with many enemies, had much influence in King Ferdinand's court. Every day the king told him that his enemies were becoming more and more insistent and that he would soon have to order the Jews' expulsion. Reich toyed with the idea of spending his own considerable fortune in bribes to prevent the expulsion. The MaHaRal advised against this, arguing that it would only leave the Jews open to constant blackmail.

The MaHaRal's advice was usually greatly respected. A story is told that once a young prince had been arguing with another about a perplexing mathematical problem in astronomy. They asked the court scholars for an answer but they received none. Reich, however, told the princes that they could go to the MaHaRal for help. "A Jew can answer questions that our greatest scholars can't?" questioned one of the princes. Reich, of course, was angry with the young prince's attitude, but he replied that the MaHaRal could most likely solve the problem. "Well, then, bring him to me," said the prince. "Oh, no," explained Reich. "One does not summon the MaHaRal. You must go to him." The prince did go to the MaHaRal, who answered his question with no apparent difficulty.

The Jews also had allies among the population at large. The Church's priests were not universally loved, nor were the nobles. Sometimes when priests came to harass the Jews or confiscate their property, their Gentile neighbors came to their defense by beating up the priests.

When King Ferdinand's expulsion order finally came, it gave the Jews two years to leave their homes. During that time the priests embarked on a major policy of trying to convert the Jews. For all their efforts, they were largely unsuccessful. Finally, the fickle tide of politics shifted, and the king was able to cancel his expulsion order, which had been his intention from the beginning.

After Ferdinand's death, Rudolph the Second came to the throne at Prague, and the MaHaRal became a frequent visitor at the palace. Rudolph was a freethinker, openly contemptuous of the Church. He was quite impressed by the brilliance of the MaHaRal and spent many hours in conversation with him. This was particularly galling to the Pope. In 1590, the Pontiff sent three cardinals to Prague to debate with the MaHaRal. King Rudolph laughed and went out of his way to stage the debate as publicly as possible, for he was convinced that his brilliant Jewish friend would easily get the best of the Pope's men.

So that there would be no argument about the outcome, King Rudolph put three sets of scribes to work taking down every word that was said. The discussion went on for ten days. By the end there was no doubt who had been the victor. One of the cardinals committed suicide in a back room of the church at Prague.

But the MaHaRal knew that the Church, which has never looked upon its enemies with much tolerance, would not take his victory well. So he voluntarily turned his post over to his son and went to another town. He died, in 1609, at ninety-seven years of age.

The MaHaRal's grandson, Judah Lieb, married a woman named Sara. Judah Lieb and Sara had a son named Moshe. Moshe had a son named Schneur Zalman, who was the grandfather of the legendary Schneur Zalman.

EIGHT

The Schneur Zalman Legend

THE GREAT SCHNEUR ZALMAN was born in 1745. His father began to teach him Torah when he was two, and by the time he was six he knew all his father could teach him. Two years later he had outgrown another teacher, and his parents began to search for still another.

They found what they were looking for at Lubavitch, a secluded place by the Dnieper River in White Russia, surrounded by great forests. It had been founded centuries ago, perhaps in the Middle Ages, by a Jew named Meir who was looking for a place to start a Jewish colony. It was only a square mile in size, a small place, but of great importance to Jewish history. "Luba" means "love" in Polish and Russian, and the place had been loved by Jewish mystics for centuries because of its great beauty. To have believed that they could see God in His creations would have been blasphemous, yet the Jews there felt close to Him.

Zalman spent only a year in Lubavitch and never settled there, but his son did, and thus the Lubavitcher dynasty began. The name stayed with them even after Joseph I. Schneersohn, the sixth generation Lubavitcher, evacuated the town during the First World War and moved his followers to Brooklyn.

Young Zalman studied not only Torah in Lubavitch, but also the laws of nature and mathematics. There is a parallel to the life of his descendant, Yehudi Menuhin. At the age of eleven, Yehudi went to Paris to study with the great Romanian composer Georges Enesco, rather than with some traditional German violin professor, as one might have expected. There were those who felt this was a mistake, for Enesco was not primarily a violin teacher. The musical education he gave Yehudi consisted of many happy days when neither of them even picked up a violin. Instead, they went to folk festivals where gypsies played music whose Oriental strains were unmistakable. Enesco believed that "real art comes from inside," and years later he resisted efforts to get him to explain Yehudi's genius. "You can't get me to do it, and you won't get him to, either," Enesco said. In other words, he taught Yehudi how to play the violin by widening his conception of music, just as the mathematical and scientific training Zalman received in Lubavitch expanded his horizons.

At eleven, Zalman was sent to Vitebsk. His reputation as a prodigy had preceded him, and his legend grew. The sun clock in the city center was not working properly, and none of the professors in the scientific institute could figure out why. Zalman did some calculating and found that the device was not working properly because of some bushes on a far-away mountain ridge. The governor of the province was so impressed that he insisted the young prodigy enter the institute. Such scientific talent would one day be of great importance to the world, he declared. He demanded that the young lad be brought to him. Zalman, however, wanted to devote his life to his people and not to science. He left Vitebsk rather than be forced into a life he could not believe in.

Zalman's times were torn by the conflicts between mysticism and the old orthodoxy, the poor and the rich, the villages and the larger towns. Zalman had roots in both streams of thought and ultimately abandoned neither side, but won over the old to some aspects of the new. Similarly, Yehudi looks at the world as involved in a great class struggle, although he prefers to describe the struggle as between "the demands of the moment and the requirements of the future." When he talks politics, one gets the feeling that he is torn between the two. He wants the masses to have food and shelter and freedom, yet at the same time he yearns to maintain traditions and continuity.

The rich and powerful hated the Baal-Shem and the Hassidic movement that grew from his teachings. But, as figures like Schneur

Zalman came out of the Hassidim, the movement gained more and more respectability. When Zalman was young, however, the forces of Hassidism were still subversive. They were tearing the old order apart.

At age fifteen Zalman was married off to a girl named Sterna, the daughter of a rich man who agreed to support him for the rest of his life. But after awhile his new in-laws came to regard him as an eccentric. When he studied late every night, they took away his candles. Then he resorted to studying by moonlight. They took away the heat, and he nearly froze. They tried to convince Sterna to divorce him, but she loved her new husband. Indeed, this pattern of arranged marriages, unhappy in-laws, genius and eccentricity survived for the next two centuries, down to the Menuhins' time.

Schneur Zalman's great contribution was a synthesis of the way of the rabbis and that of the Baal-Shem. The establishment in those days was represented by the *Gaon* of Vilna, a figure all religious Jews venerated, even the Hassidim. Even though the *Gaon* (meaning "genius of Talmud") was a sworn enemy of Hassidism, Schneur Zalman's attitude toward him had always been, at worst, ambivalent, despite the fact that the *Gaon* refused to confront Zalman in a face-to-face debate on the merits of the new religious movement. When the *Gaon* personally ordered Schneur Zalman's books publicly burned, the great philosopher ordered his forces to remain calm and to remember that even if the *Gaon* was wrong in his opposition to Hassidism, he was still the *Gaon,* a very great Talmudist.

Some have interpreted Zalman's attitude toward the *Gaon* as the result of his noble nature, but it is most likely that Zalman contained within himself much of what the *Gaon* represented. He was torn between the approach of the *Gaon* and that of the Baal-Shem. His conversion to the latter's philosophy resulted in a kind of Hassidism called *Chabad* Hassidism, popular today among young Jews, which synthesized the priestly and the prophetic. The word *Chabad* comes from the initials of the Hebrew words for wisdom, understanding and knowledge, attributes that a scholarly person would venerate.

Zalman had enemies within the ranks of the Hassidic movement who felt that, while his approach might win the battle, it would lose the war. Zalman led the forces of the Baal-Shem to triumph over the opposition, but the new movement that triumphed was a far cry from the one that this secret cult of mystics had been propagating.

This is not to say that some of the original spirit did not survive. One can see strong evidence that something of it lives even today. One fellow reported the strange sight in London's Waterloo Station of a Hassid who looked up, saw the sun streaming in through one of the high windows, and lost control of himself. There, while some of the reserved English population looked on, he threw aside his briefcase, removed part of his Hassidic "uniform" and danced and sang ecstatically until he slumped in exhaustion to the floor.

But Yehudi noted on a visit to a Lubavitcher settlement in Israel that although much of the original mystical spirit survived, it had become too slick, too professional even, and without real soul.

Schneur Zalman's great synthesis was philosophical, but its expression was in music. It was because of Schneur Zalman that music came to be regarded by the movement's *tzaddiks,* or wise men, as literally the access to the heavenly courts. Yehudi calls the Hassidim "musical yogis." The search for the ecstatic, rather than the dour and academic, was Hassidism's major characteristic.

This search could be carried on in whatever way best suited the individual. There are stories of Hassids who achieved heavenly bliss by eating, by stuffing themselves. Other stories, spoken of almost reverently, tell of Hassids who favored great sexual and drunken debauches. In the ecstasy that Hassidim find in their praying, dancing and chanting, communion with God is not meant to be merely intellectual.

Schneur Zalman definitely had an intuitive and mystical turn of mind, but his rational and scholarly side pulled him in another direction. At nineteen, Zalman had a choice to make. He could go to the Lithuanian capital of Vilna and study with the *Gaon,* or he could go to Mezeritch, where the Rabbi Dov-Ber, the Baal-Shem's heir, held forth. Dov-Ber was a great Talmudic scholar who had fallen under the influence of the Baal-Shem. Upon the Baal-Shem's death, he assumed leadership of the new movement the Baal-Shem had created.

Schneur Zalman decided to go to Dov-Ber, not to the *Gaon.* However, his first meeting with the Mezeritch Jews was a disappointment. All they seemed to do was pray; no one used intellect to analyze anything. Zalman sadly packed his bags and left Mezeritch. The world must have looked bleak as he trudged down the road toward Vilna. Finally, he decided to give the Mezeritch group one last chance. That was the turning point in his life, for he chanced to walk in just as Dov-Ber was in the middle of what struck Zalman as one of the most brilliant discourses he had ever heard.

While others were impressed by the miracles that occurred in Mezeritch, Zalman shrugged the matter off with the remark that in Mezeritch miracles were an everyday occurrence. Despite the fact that what appeared to pull him to Dov-Ber was the latter's intellectual powers, his conversion was essentially spiritual and mystical.

One day Dov-Ber's inner circle was gathered in a room, awaiting the master's arrival. They had been deeply involved in a discussion of the divine court where *En Sof*, the Divine Emanation, reigns. Soon the disciples were experiencing the pulsating, advancing and retreating motion of love and fear that is the constant rhythm of that place where only a thin veil hangs between the heavenly hierarchy (the angels, the Messiah, the prophets and the Baal-Shem) and the Infinite Light itself. Dov-Ber's disciples were in ecstasy because through their conversion they had nearly transported themselves right up to the palace gates. But their ecstasy was stopped by the approaching footsteps of Dov-Ber.

The master took his place at the head of the table and told them not to despair, that man was the ultimate reason for creation anyway. Zalman later wrote, "Two things I saw then: the sublime ecstasy of the Holy Society on the one hand and the remarkable composure of our master, Rabbi Dov-Ber, on the other, which enthralled me completely. That is when I became a Hassid."

Zalman's enthrallment with Dov-Ber was total. Dov-Ber was also impressed by the young lad. Although Zalman was the youngest of his disciples, Dov-Ber was quick to realize his unique mind. One night Dov-Ber walked into the room where his disciples slept, and holding a candle above Schneur Zalman's face, looked at his sleeping form, saying, "How wonderful that this young man, who is sleeping unaware on his little pillow, should one day become the rabbi of all the provinces of Russia, with multitudes of people listening to his voice."

Religion at this time, before the Enlightenment, was frequently the totality of a man's life. Everything served religion: economics, science, music and literature. The Jewish community within the Pale (the area in which Russian Jews were confined by the Czar) was a nation within a nation. Its internal life was generally untouched by the outside world. Its ruling class represented it to the Gentile courts. The religious leaders were directly associated, often by marriage, with the wealthiest Jews.

It is strange to think of mysticism as aligned with a movement expressing the anger of the poor against the rich, but that is what the Baal-Shem was doing. His mysticism was a shortcut whereby the masses could obtain the communion with God that the priestly class said could only be obtained in their manner, by their methods, for themselves. The Baal-Shem went further; he said that a simple man had a real advantage over an educated man, for his faith was uncomplicated by intellectualism.

It is not surprising that this anti-intellectualism caused such strong objections. There were many people who suspected that the very thing that gave Judaism sustaining power was its veneration of knowledge. The Baal-Shem's views seemed to strike at the very heart of the sacred Jewish belief that education is paramount in importance.

This debate was not academic. The battle between the Hassidim and the establishment was a virtual civil war, and families were split. The *Gaon* of Vilna believed strongly that the Hassidim were evil, that they were a threat to Israel. Those who had his ear were mostly strident opponents of the new movement, but there were others who tried to influence him to moderate his opposition to the Hassidim. They saw that the violence of the *Gaon's* feelings was splitting an already divided community. When these peacemakers heard that Schneur Zalman wanted a public debate with the *Gaon,* they urged him to accept the invitation. But when Zalman arrived in Vilna, the *Gaon* slipped out of town and said he would not return until Zalman had left.

Despite the *Gaon's* hostility, Zalman could not bring himself to fight him. Most of the time he counseled his forces to act moderately, and when the *Gaon* ordered Schneur Zalman's books burned on the steps of the Vilna synagogue, Zalman said, "Remember, this was the fate of Maimonides' works, too, and still they prevailed."

Schneur Zalman, the movement's leader and hero, also became

its martyr when the establishment twice caused him to be arrested by Gentile authorities. One of the complaints originated with a rabbi named Avigdor in the town of Pinsk. Avigdor denounced the Hassidim and Zalman to the authorities in 1797 because his own congregation was becoming more and more Hassidic. Both times Zalman was arrested he was charged with being a foreign agent, because he collected money to support a colony in Palestine. Palestine was under Turkish rule, and Turkey and Russia were, as usual, at war.

The Czar's police arrived on Zalman's doorstep with a detachment of soldiers and the big, black coach normally reserved for doomed prisoners. They were to take him to St. Petersburg for trial. It was a long journey, and one of the days was a Sabbath. Zalman asked the entourage to halt the carriage, but they refused. The next moment, an axle broke. It was still Saturday, however, when the axle was repaired, and so Zalman asked again that the carriage wait until the sun had set.

Again he was refused. This time the horse collapsed. There was another delay while a new horse was obtained, but the fresh animal could not pull the carriage. So Schneur Zalman was able to spend his Sabbath in a pastoral field. Years later, or so Hassidic legend tells, the spot was graced by a majestic and vigorous shade tree.

Schneur Zalman was frequently absorbed in other, more heavenly worlds. Similarly, audiences used to be amazed by the sight of the prodigy Yehudi, who would appear on stage, close his eyes, apparently enter another world, and then play his instrument. He still does that, and it is no affectation. His sister Yaltah always admires his ability to turn away from the multitude of distractions that fill his daily life, close his eyes and remove himself to that world he describes in his music. There need not be anything mystical about this. Like Zalman, Yehudi is a man with higher powers of concentration. It is the kind of concentration needed to transport one to another reality.

It must have been during just such a moment of concentration that the Czar's chief investigator entered Zalman's cell. Rather than question Zalman, the man looked at him and asked him to reveal what he could of his, the interrogator's, destiny.

Zalman asked him, "Do you believe the Scriptures are eternal, for every generation, that in every era God calls to every man and asks, 'Where are you in your world?'" The man nodded. "So many years and days of those allotted to you have passed," said Zalman. "How far have you gone in your world? God would say you have lived forty-six years. How far along are you?" The man trembled, for he was indeed forty-six years of age.

Legend has it, that his report so intrigued Czar Paul that he went to see Zalman incognito. Disguised as one of his own investigators, he was surprised to see the rabbi rise to his feet and greet his visitor with a benediction. "How did you know?" asked the astonished Czar.

"Our sages state that kingship on earth is a replica of the kingship in heaven. When your Imperial Majesty entered, I felt a sense of awe and trembling such as I have not experienced with any of the officials who have visited me. I knew you were the Czar in person."

On December 15, 1798, Zalman was cleared of the charges of political subversion, and his movement was practically given a stamp of approval. He became the chief spokesman not only for Hassidism but for the whole Jewish community as well.

Zalman undertook the role with reluctance. His inclination was to retreat into religious, literary or musical activities. Yet he also embarked on a series of political moves that made him one of Russia's most powerful men. He gained influence with estate owners. He was even able to buy large tracts of land on which Jewish families could settle and become self-sufficient farmers. His contacts at court were many, his spies everywhere.

Schneur Zalman proved his loyalty to the Russian government during the Napoleonic invasion. Napoleon had done his best to cultivate the support of European Jews. Where Jews had been in the forefront of the Enlightenment, he had been successful. But Zalman was not impressed. There were rumors that Napoleon was personally an atheist, and Zalman had no sympathy for the Enlightenment. While one would think that the ghetto Jews of Eastern Europe would have little for which to thank their Russian rulers, in the end Zalman was a supporter of the old order, and the Jewish community followed his lead.

This, then, was Zalman the politician. Of greatest significance in this story is Zalman the musician, composer of many *ningunim*, traditional Hassidic melodies. The most famous of these is the *"Ningun of the Alter Rebbe,"* the tune of the Old Rabbi. Zalman was still a disciple living in the house of Dov-Ber when he wrote it. Unlike the typical Hassidic melodies, his were less gay and melodious. To Zalman, music was not just a way of worship, it was the way from this world into the next. *Ningunim* bypassed words and speech, since they expressed only thought and emotion. To the "Alter Rebbe," as Zalman was known, music was the one expression of desire and purpose, and these are the *real* essence of the soul.

The *"Ningun of the Alter Rebbe"* was constructed to correspond to the four worlds around which Zalman had built his *Chabad* philosophy: emanation, creation, formation and action, all from the Kabbalah. The four parts correspond to the rhythm in heaven. The first helps the singer or listener to disengage himself from the mundane world and move to the next in order to ponder the state of his soul and meditate on his purpose and his desires. The second part yields one up to fervent hope. The third uplifts the soul. The last provides that ecstatic feeling that the Source gives each soul.

Sometimes in public debate Zalman would put aside all his philosophy and sing one of his *ningunim*. It is said that he was sometimes more successful with his songs than his arguments.

One lad who knew the power of those songs was Zalman's son, Rabbi Dov-Ber, named after Zalman's mentor in Mezeritch. The son said that his father's songs could penetrate the soul of any Hassid. The lad, whose relationship was especially close to his father because his mother died when he was very young, revered the man. For Zalman was the young Dov-Ber's teacher as well as his father.

As one can see in the relationship between Moshe and Yehudi, this father-to-son transmission of culture continued through the generations. Moshe would take Yehudi into the countryside and talk for many hours of philosophy. Then Moshe would sing Hassidic songs. Perhaps one of those songs was the *"Ningun of the Alter Rebbe."*

If it is true, as composer Felix Mendelssohn said, that music is much more precise a language than words, and thus, what music expresses can *only* be expressed by music, then perhaps music, even more than something genetic, might have been the way genius was passed down to Yehudi.

Martin Buber tells this illustrative story: Zalman, in his old age, was driving through the countryside with his grandson, and the birds were chirping very loudly. Zalman bid the driver stop the carriage. "How fast they chatter," he said, turning to his grandson. "They have their own alphabet. All you need to do is listen and grasp well, and you will understand their language."

Schneur Zalman's grandson was Menachem-Mendel Schneer-sohn, the third of the Lubavitcher dynasty and the first to take on the surname of Schneersohn. He was born in 1789. A hard-working fellow, Schneersohn studied eighteen hours a day, taking to heart everything his grandfather said. He learned to be systematic at three and orderly at five because orderliness is fundamental in all matters of intellect and emotion. Not surprisingly, Schneersohn became an excellent organizer. In 1844 he created a Jewish community of 300 farmer families on 1,700 acres, one of the earliest Zionist experiments.

Schneersohn was persecuted by the Czar's secret police, and his house was searched. But he was also one of five committee members of the Ministry of Culture, and fought there for Jewish rights. He survived a trial on the trumped-up charge of drinking Christian children's blood, only because the Czar was warned not to make Schneersohn a martyr. He returned to Lubavitch a triumph.

Schneersohn was not as great a figure as was his grandfather, but he lived in a different time. His grandfather had been concerned with building a new religion against the forces of the old. Rabbi Schneersohn was concerned primarily with consolidating Hassidism, which by then had become the established orthodoxy of religious Jews. Napoleon may have lost the wars, but the winds of Enlightenment were blowing vigorously.

In Judaism the forces of Enlightenment were called *Haskala*. They had gotten their start from a brilliant hunchback named Moses Mendelssohn, who emerged from the German ghetto. The Menuhin family represented quite a different force in Judaism than did the Mendelssohns. Both Schneur Zalman and his grandson Schneersohn spent their lives bitterly fighting everything Mendelssohn stood for.

Mendelssohn wanted the Jews to leave the ghettoes, if not physically, then mentally, so they could participate in the revolutionary changes then beginning to sweep across Europe. Schneersohn saw only evil in the attempts of the hated assimilationists to send Jews to schools where the language and customs of the larger nation were taught. Mendelssohn was as much the enemy as were the Gentiles, who were always trying to convert the "chosen people" to Christianity.

Schneersohn's position hardened when he saw the assimilationists cooperating with Russian authorities. These assimilationists, many of them from Germany, hated the old rabbinical order because they felt it encouraged supersitition rather than the new god, science.

Centuries of experience in the old feudal order had convinced Jews that the less they had to do with the uncouth and barbarous Gentiles the better. Still, Gentile and Jewish lives were bound together, and ways of relating had been worked out over time. As the old feudal order began to crumble, in the early nineteenth century, the particular niche Jews had carved out for themselves was disappearing. As the revolutionary changes known as the Enlightenment were sweeping away the power structures of the Gentile world the Jewish microcosm was affected.

To Schneersohn, Gentiles were always suspect. The German Jews came to Russia talking of the new Enlightenment that they said would free their people, but instead they worked closely with the same old anti-Semitic authorities. Czar Nicholas was a known Jew-hating Christian, and conditions were getting worse for the Jews under his reign. Conscription into his army was much higher in the Jewish community than in the Gentile. And once a Jewish child was spirited away for the army, he would seldom return. Special taxes, physical violence and innumerable economic sanctions were making Jewish life intolerable. Thus, when the Russian government and the assimilationists began talking of special schools for Jewish children, Jews were naturally suspicious.

Schneersohn's fears of the Gentiles were not unfounded. His own descendants' lives proved that the outside world insisted on pounding down the ghetto walls. The most savage form of this were the pogroms, and pogroms stalked the lives of the Schneersohn descendants.

NINE

Moshe and the Pogroms

WHEN MOSHE, YEHUDI'S FATHER was born in 1893, it was into an age of pogroms. Pogroms were the policy of Czar Alexander III, a vicious anti-Semite, whose answer to the "Jewish problem" was to kill a third, convert a third, and force the remaining third to emigrate. And emigrate the Jews did, by the millions, in an exodus the size of which the world had never seen before. Moshe spent his earliest years growing up in the small, mean world of Southern Russian winters, when the great snow curtain descended on the poor little classrooms of the *heder* where students and teachers alike shivered. The teacher was as ragged and thin as his students, since his sustenance came only from what the parents of his five or six students could spare, which wasn't much.

For centuries, however, Russian Jews had learned to survive awful deprivation—as miserable as this world was, the inward religious one was glorious. They read their prayer books and the writings of Moses, other prophets, and Tenasch. It was a narrow world, but one with deep roots back to the moment when Moses received the Word of God and the Jews became His chosen people.

Life may have been intolerable for Jews because the Gentiles were cruel, but the specifically Jewish ritual gave one the strength to cope. In Moshe's *heder* religious expectations were so high that Moshe wouldn't have been surprised if the Messiah, or at least Elijah himself, had walked through the low door. In the classroom, one learned Jewish ways of life. Outside, well, outside . . .

Moshe tells the story of the day when he was playing with a stick and a rock. The rock went sailing across the street and shattered the glass in the front window of a Gentile's home. Moshe was gripped with fear, the fear of an age of pogroms, for of such incidents did the authorities create pogroms.

In a few minutes the Gentile emerged from his home. He appeared on the doorstep and asked to see Moshe's mother. He apologized for disturbing her and then said to the trembling woman, "Keep calm. I am a father, and children are children. I know it was an accident. I forgive him. You will, of course, fix the window. But don't tell anyone about this." Then his voice grew lower and he declared, "If there will one day be pogroms in Gomel (the town where Moshe was born), and there may well be, it will not be the fault of people like me. There are still decent people in Russia."

It was Christmas evening. The man who was hired to pick up the students in Moshe's classroom came to take them to their homes for dinner. He drove through back alleys, and at first, the young Moshe did not know what was wrong. Everywhere they turned that night, priests were stirring up angry mobs. The priests were holding up giant wooden crosses and chanting, "Kill the Jews! Kill the Jews!" The children got home safely, however, in time for dinner.

Later that same night, the children went back to the *heder* and began delving into the laws of the Talmud. There was something exciting about those evening classroom sessions, something that brought Moshe closer to the unlocking of the most secret world, the passionate dream-world where those long, hard hours in the dreary *yeshivas* were supposed to lead.

It took only the snap of cold air bursting in through the open door to bring Moshe back to the world of his ragged, thin teacher and the cold, bleak classroom. That night, when he had returned to the classroom after dinner, dodging the pogromists marching through the streets of Gomel, he was not able to get into the old religious reverie at all. The terror must have been overwhelming. It may have been that terror which changed his whole life.

Later, the man his parents had hired took him by the hand, and again they slipped through the darkened streets to the Jewish part of

Gomel. They did not want to be the first victims of the angry mobs. Once at home and in bed, Moshe shook with fear, for he could hear outside his window the odious chanting of the priests and their mobs. "Kill the Jews. Kill the Jews," they chanted. Their torchlight danced satanically on Moshe's bedroom wall in red and yellow patterns. "Lights I will never forget to the end of my days," he says.

In his youth Moshe remained a conscientious and orthodox Jew. He remembers his grandfather telling him that the more he prayed the better. In the course of a day, there were at least a hundred and twenty prayers. One went not only to *heder* and the *yeshiva*, but also three times a day to the synagogue, morning, afternoon and evening. It was a life right out of the Middle Ages, nay, Biblical times. It was the way of life since time immemorial until the First World War ended time immemorial.

Although Moshe's orthodox ways came to an end, he still admits picking up the *Ethics of the Fathers* in his spare moments. Such deeply ingrained habits are hard to change for a man who remembers that the highlight of his early years in Russia was when the *Maggid* came to town. The *Maggid* was the traveling preacher and story-teller. Stories and legends would pour from the *Maggid's* lips for hours. It was an intoxicating brew that made the Jews swoon. One was always seeking the clear, clean feeling of redemption, of again being made new by visions conjured up with words, by dialogues with God.

Shortly before Moshe's father, Isaac (Yitzhak) Mnuchin, died in 1897, Moshe's grandfather, Judah Lieb Mnuchin, migrated to Palestine, where he became the chief Lubavitcher rabbi in the Holy Land. After Mnuchin's death, and with no one left in Moshe's hometown, Gomel, Moshe's mother, Sara Liba, had to turn to her Schneersohn relatives. She went to stay with the fifth-generation chief rabbi in Lubavitch, Sholom Dov-Ber, the grandson of the great Menachem-Mendel Schneersohn.

The summer that Sara Liba had taken her little Moshe and boarded the train to Lubavitch must have been a nightmare for her. For Moshe, however, it was a dream. Moshe did not know that human fates were being decided there in his "grandfather's" palace.

Moshe believes today that Sara Liba was a sister to the great rabbi, but my research would indicate that she was a first cousin. Still, Moshe can be excused for that mistake, for he was treated like a grandson. Too young to really have felt the pain of his father's death, he knew only that he was going on a grand adventure.

The train ride that night was very special. Little Moshe was riding on a shelf high in the car next to a window. It was cramped in fourth class, but he could see the moon glittering through the pine forests as the train slowly wound its way up the mountainside. As the train swayed and jerked, he fought off drowsiness. In the distance the cold Dnieper shimmered. Sometimes its moonlit surface was highlighted through the birches and pines.

Lubavitch was a small town with rivers bordering on three sides. One was the large Dnieper; another one, a very small rivulet, started out as a spring from one of the oldest gravestones in the ancient cemetery, dating back to Lubavitch's prehistory. No one knew how old the gravestone was, or whose it was. But town tradition forbade anyone to wash in or drink from the Gravestone River.

In Lubavitch's center was a marketplace, and from the marketplace three streets, Brom, Shilova and Chachuliuka, led to other hamlets. One of the streets led to the Lubavitcher Court.

Sara Liba and Moshe were greeted at the train by the rabbi's fine coach, with its Gentile coachmen in livery, pulled by a team of spirited horses. The rabbi himself greeted the party. His house was a court as royal as any king's, with acres and acres of flowers, fruits and trees and a grand house. Officially, Jews were not allowed to own property, so it is possible that the Lubavitch estate was only rented. But it had been occupied by Schneersohns for several generations, and Moshe and his mother stayed there most of the summer.

The life was grand, especially the meals. Twenty people would sit down at the dinner table, and it was the one daily event where everyone present would be Jewish, even the servants. God forbid, says Moshe, that the people who handled the food weren't Jewish.

Oddly enough, it was in Lubavitch that Moshe began to discover the non-Jewish world. One was not supposed to talk to a non-Jew, and a good Jew could not play with a dog, or pet a kitten or, of course, eat anything not kosher. "But I was a strange fellow," Moshe says. "I liked doing all those things." And "all those things" were done in Lubavitch, in the great rabbi's court.

Often, Moshe would sneak out from the walled estate and run free with the Gentile children and their dogs. For Moshe, it meant freedom because it was not proscribed by a million different blessings and rules of behavior.

At the same time that he played and ran and sang in the hot summer air, and tasted the forbidden joys of the non-Jewish world outside the walls, he was pampered within by the entire Hassidic court. Since he was in the line of succession, he was treated as a special person. They would always put five times as much as he could eat on his plate so that left-overs could be stolen afterwards. The loyal Hassidim would put these left-overs in their pockets or in boxes to take home and show to their wives and children—left-overs from the plate of a "good Jew." Today, Moshe laughs at his image as the "good Jew."

It was at these dinners that Moshe first heard the *ningunim*. The big feasts, at which little Moshe was loved and spoiled by everyone, were always accompanied by song. The songs were sung with hands extended and eyes uplifted, stretching to God as the singer's soul engaged in dialogue with Him. Moshe says he had never heard songs like these in Gomel. There were no women at these feasts, only men. And each night the feast was not so much a dinner as a great party with God as the guest of honor. The men would put their arms on each other's shoulders and dance around the table. They would sing back and forth in exalted joyous rhythm.

Those festivities have remained in Moshe's memory. But he insists that his happiest moments were those spent outside with his Gentile playmates. He did not know much Russian, but the children seemed as fascinated by him as he was by them.

After spending that first summer in Lubavitch, Sara Liba went to live with a husband that Sholom Dov-Ber had picked out for her, a well-to-do agricultural broker named Israel Asher-Libo. Asher-Libo had five children of his own and lived in a town some distance from Gomel. Moshe's first memories of this time are not bad ones.

It was again summer and cantaloupes were abundant. Asher-Libo bought the cantaloupes from the Gentile farmers and sold them in the cities. Relations were good at this time between Jews and Gentiles, and young Moshe used to watch the peasants come up to his stepfather's house, their carts loaded with produce. Because the prices were good, everyone was friendly.

The following summer, however, when the peasants brought their produce to Asher-Libo to sell, they could not agree on terms. Hour after hour they haggled over prices. Voices rose, and the words "dirty Jew" were in the air. Then Moshe remembers Asher-Libo being carried up the iron staircase of their home. He was bloody and unconscious, and was put to bed. Moshe crept up to the top of the stairs where his stepbrothers and -sisters had gathered. They were hovering over their father and crying, for he had been beaten by the angry peasants. Moshe began crying too, and the eldest of the brothers turned and stared at him. Then he aimed his fists at little Moshe's head and shoved him down the stairs. "Don't you dare cry for our father," he yelled at Moshe. "Get out of here."

Moshe must have again run to his bed, too confused even to beseech God and ask Him why this had happened. This time there weren't flames on his wall from the Gentile mobs. The pain that throbbed in his head was from the blows of his own Jewish stepbrother. He pulled the blanket over his head to block out the world that had gone insane.

Sara Liba had not wanted to marry Asher-Libo. She did not want to give up her own children to become the mother of another man's. Most especially, she did not want to give up Moshe, her youngest. But she was a weak person, and Rabbi Dov-Ber took special pains with her because she was a Hassid and, more importantly, a member of the family.

So Moshe was born into the very heart of the ruling mechanisms of one of mankind's most bizarre religious manifestations, Hassidism. For six centuries the family had been producing prodigies, as we've seen. Sons were trained from birth to succeed the fathers in hereditary positions of intellectual leadership. And every other generation or so, a real prodigy would appear. The process was reinforced by the fact that the brightest students in the community were matched in marriage with the Schneersohn women, and this helped build a genetic pool of intelligence. To the extent that this inbreeding is no longer done, the possibility of great prodigies in the future is lessened.

Moshe was a child of this tradition at its end. The Schneersohns were a priestly royalty, and royalty of any kind is increasingly an institution of the past. In Lubavitch, Moshe had tasted the life of royalty. No wonder he sang those Hassidic tunes with such an unearthly fervor throughout his life. Those tunes were his son Yehudi's first taste of music. Although Moshe had intellectually rejected Hassidism because he found the proscribed way of life oppressive, he sought out its prophetic qualities. The prophetic was represented for him by certain recurring themes in his life. He expressed these themes in the constant retelling of tales, and continues today, no doubt, even in his declining years. The most important tale is how as a young man in Jerusalem he yearned to play the violin, only to find his desire to perform on the instrument thwarted by his grandfather. When Moshe tried to sneak away and play the violin, his grandfather would catch him at it and forbid him. He would say that "as long as your people are in exile (i.e., not in Palestine), you have no right to fiddle." So Moshe put down the gypsy instrument. Yehudi would have to become the prophet on the violin that his father never was, thereby living out the expression of his father's deepest yearnings.

Moshe himself never found a way to synthesize the two opposing movements: the one, a religious aristocracy whose authority came directly from the heavenly courts; the other, an escape into what he saw as the twentieth century enlightenment. It was not just coincidence that Yehudi would later in his life sponsor the merging of Eastern and Western music, while noting that Hassidism was the only Western philosophy close in spirit to the Orient. "Both share a sense of the Divine order of things, rather than some human order," says Yehudi. This idea squares remarkably with Martin Buber's observation that the Jew's alienation stems from the fact that he came out of the crossroads between East and West and that he has always been uncomfortable in his wanderings across the Occident.

TEN

A Stranger
in a Strange Land

MOSHE'S MOTHER, SARA LIBA, married Asher-Libo around the turn of the century. She was following the wishes of the Lubavitcher rabbi in her new marriage, but she was disconsolate. One of the things that bothered her was that she would have to give up her own child to take care of her husband's children, the very ones who treated Moshe so badly. Her own child would have to go live with his grandfather Mnuchin in Palestine. It is said that Sara Liba sailed back and forth between Odessa and Jaffa, the old city next to what is now Tel Aviv-Jaffa, four or five times to visit with Moshe, who was not only her youngest child but also her favorite. Finally, after a trip to Palestine in 1904, she returned to Russia, never to see her son again.

Mnuchin, the chief Lubavitcher rabbi in the Holy Land, was also a wealthy man. Moshe loved his grandfather and his grandfather loved him, but the grandmother was a terror. Mnuchin was also old and weak and couldn't really be a father to the little boy. Moshe, who stayed with his grandfather until the old man died, seemed more like an orphan, and ran free in the new land as he had tried to do in Lubavitch. He often went hungry, and he actually began to identify more with the Arabs than the Jews, since most of the population in Palestine was Arab at that time.

Moshe now wanted to escape from the Jewish world. It seemed that his sisters and brother, who had come to Palestine earlier, were always giving him advice and orders, but never seemed to love him. He blamed them for the death of his favorite sister, Sonya. Sonya had a lover in Russia, and she wrote to him, but he never answered. She did not know that their sister Mussia took the lover's letters and kept them from her. Sonya ended up marrying a man she did not love, and committed suicide soon after. Without Sonya and without his grandfather, who had died, Moshe felt truly alone, unloved and unwanted. The Sonya episode would be Moshe's excuse in later years for keeping Yehudi and his sisters ignorant of the existence of the aunts, uncles and cousins in Israel.

Moshe found a new kind of Jewish youth in Palestine. As he stood before them, he was ashamed of his shrunken size, his earlocks and his Hassidic uniform. One of the Jewish youths, named Yosphe, came to symbolize much of what bothered Moshe. Yosphe, tall, dark and strong, came from South America. His family had been wealthy enough to buy a great deal of land in Palestine, which they had turned into orange groves. Yosphe's family was not religious; they were Zionists, who had not grown up inside the dank, cold ghetto walls of Russia where mysticism had inbred upon itself, where the sun seemed less real than the imagined eerie glow from heaven.

Moshe has said that everyone who ran with Yosphe admired him. He was so strong and so athletic that he once even won first prize in a horse-riding contest in which the other contestants were primarily Arabs (who have always been known for their fine horsemanship).

Moshe's spirit must have blossomed as he roamed the hills and valleys of the Holy Land. He says that he traveled over every square foot of it and loved it all, from the blue Galilee to whitewashed Jerusalem. He played on the dunes of the sun-drenched Mediterranean in the places that Zionists were then trying to purchase to build their Tel Aviv.

It was, and still is, an odd and beautiful land. In the early 1900's about thirty-five thousand Jews lived there, and nearly half a million Arabs. The Holy Land was officially a part of the Turkish Empire, but the Turks had lost control of it after the First World War.

Moshe's first encounter with the Arabs came by accident. There was a particular way to get to the Jewish butcher; his grandfather had, in the past, sent him there. It was a twisting route that he had to take to avoid the dark, narrow corridors and alleys where the Arabs lived. He had often been warned to stay away from them, which he gladly did. To the young Moshe, the Arabs seemed like moles who lived in dimly lit places full of strange smells. One terrifying day, he stumbled into one of the alleys, quite by accident, and was lost in the myriad of corridors. His heart beat so furiously that today Moshe is convinced that his present heart condition was the result of that experience. The Arab faces seemed menacing and leering, and a group gathered around the boy. "Are you lost, little Jewish boy?" one asked kindly. And they took him by the hand and showed him the way out.

No doubt part of Moshe's terror about the Arabs in that sector came from the fact that they worshipped the outcast figure of Jesus. One night during Moshe's first winter in Jerusalem, a rabbi had called a halt to the study of Torah and Talmud. He began telling a disparaging tale about the *Acher*, Jesus (*acher* means "strange one"). The Jews did not love Jesus. How could they love the person in whose name the Jews had been persecuted? It was even easy to forget that Jesus had been a Jew. But the kindness of the Christian Arabs jolted Moshe. To be sure, he still said all his prayers, but he was also beginning to become interested in and to investigate the remnants of the holy places revered by so many of the great religions in the Holy Land. This was the beginning of his lifelong attempt to discard the "they and we" of being a Jew, the process of climbing out of the ghetto mentality.

Moshe, born into the beginnings of the turbulent twentieth century, could not help but be a product of its confusions. His memories seem absurdly simple, his greatest joys almost nothing. He remembers sitting for hours in the train station at Ramala talking to the Arabs. He spoke Arabic fairly well, and this, he says, made him something of an oddball. The Zionist spirit was taking hold of the offspring of the old religious Jews who had settled in the Holy Land. Don't go to an Arab butcher or an Arab cobbler, the Jews were telling their children. Yet Moshe's emotional life compelled him in exactly the opposite direction.

He often spent his summers with his uncle Mnuchin, who owned a large estate near Rehovot. Most of his uncle's workers were Arabs.

He began living with them and spending more time with them than with his own family.

Still, of course, he was a Jew. One does not stop being a Jew even if one tries to. He could not become an Arab. So he took the more conventional way out of the suffocating atmosphere of his orthodox background. When his grandfather had grown old and weak, it was easy to sneak out of the house at night to Zionist meetings. These were not the old worshipful, gentle Jews, whose only defense was their sharpened wits. They were nationalists, as angry at their religious forefathers as at the evil Gentile world. They were ready to fight, to grow up strong, to eat well, to think fiercely. Many of the famous old Zionists became Moshe's teachers and friends. The orthodox little boy must have found the slogan "Our Nation, Our Homeland, Our Land" heady stuff.

Moshe's grandfather preached a universalist Judaism of brotherhood. He often used to say that when the Messiah came, he would come not just to save the chosen people, but all mankind. Yet Moshe remembers that after dinners to which his grandfather had invited the American and English consuls, the old man took away the undrunk bottles of wine and threw them out, because they had been handled by *goyim*. This struck Moshe hard because he knew how gentle and kind his grandfather was.

Rabbi Judah Lieb Mnuchin was a well-to-do man and generous with his money. Many poor brides obtained their dowries from him, and then, of course, he was the honored guest at the wedding, which he also subsidized. These weddings usually ended with a discussion of Jews, Judaism and God. Moshe claims that the seeds of his anti-Zionism were sown on one such occasion. The conversation had turned to the subject of Dr. Theodor Herzl, the Viennese journalist and the patron saint of Zionism. Rabbi Mnuchin was asked his opinion of Herzl.

Rather than answer the question directly, he told a parable. The Czar, he said, wanted to meet a real Jew, a God-fearing rabbi. He gave orders to the Minister of the Interior to find such a man and bring him to the St. Petersburg palace. Finally a small-town rabbi was found. He and his congregation were overjoyed. The first thing they decided, in light of the occasion, was that God wouldn't mind if the rabbi cut off his beard and earlocks and wore a business suit and top hat, rather than the long black dressing gown and fur piece.

Secondly, the rabbi learned as much Russian as he could, the better to talk directly to the Czar. All this accomplished, he arrived at the palace with his hat, cane and business suit. The chief of the guards was aghast. "You are not a rabbi," he said. But the rabbi showed him the written invitation and insisted that he be presented to the Czar. Before the rabbi had a chance to say a single thing in his newly-acquired Yiddish-flavored Russian, the Czar spat in his face and called him a pretender, adding, "I wanted to meet a pious Jew. Swine like you I have millions of. Get out. Get out!"

At the time Judah Lieb told his tale, Theodor Herzl was traveling around Europe having audiences with various potentates, wavering between one plan and another to find salvation for the Jewish people. Many of his actions made him seem as though he had delusions of grandeur. One moment he had a plan to save the Jewish people by making them all socialists. Next he contemplated in all seriousness obtaining the Pope's help in establishing a national homeland for the Jews provided they would all convert to that particular gentleman's faith.

Judah Lieb had a different concept of Jewishness than Herzl's. If it was not stated thus, it was nonetheless apparent in his manner that Jewishness, with its poetry and music, was somehow gentleness in a world of violence. On religious holidays, Judah Lieb would go from house to house begging his neighbors' forgiveness. That, to him, was Jewishness. He would even say to his grandson, Moshe, "Mischele, if there is anything I have done to hurt you, please forgive me."

So Moshe saw the contradictions in his grandfather and excused them. "Few men can rise above their times," he is fond of saying, "unless they have divine inspiration and are really prophets."

At sixteen, Moshe made his first attempt to run away. His destination was America. For Moshe, America was the Promised Land, not Palestine. Mussia, the sister Moshe blamed for the death of Sonya, had wired ahead of him, however, and he was picked up at Crete and returned. Yet another time, he got as far as Marseilles and went to see Paris. But the ticket he had purchased in Jaffa would not take him all the way to New York, as he had been told. So again he had to return, this time as cholera was raging in Jaffa, and it took him another four years before he succeeded in getting to New York.

During the remaining time spent in Palestine, Moshe became part of the extended family of Zionists there. He was considered by them as one of the bright young lads in whom they saw potential leaders for the nation they were trying to form. Moshe's only previous education had been the classic orthodoxy of Hebrew and Talmud study. Now, at the Herzlia Gymnasium, he began studying history and math, French, geography and, most importantly, boys and girls.

The embarrassed little orthodox Moshe, who still wore his earlocks, had begun reading Emile Zola and racy French novels. In his years at the Gymnasium in Jaffa, he never once met a rabbi, never once attended any religious services. Most of the Zionists were agnostics or atheists.

During the summers he worked on the early kibbutzim in the Galilee. These were the very first work communes of their kind, and Moshe, despite his virulent anti-Israeli feelings, admits to much admiration for these "collective farms." He also delights in pointing out that some of these great socialist institutions were literally stolen from the Arabs, who had owned the land in the lush Jordan valley.

Thus was Moshe slowly weaned from the Hassidic background he had been raised in. And thus did he begin to turn against the chosen people concept that fed the Hassidim.

There was no love lost between the Hassidim and the Zionists. The latter were purely nationalistic and almost totally irreligious. The former were spiritual and principled to the point of fanaticism. Today Moshe's whole prophecy, to which he has rather self-consciously committed himself, decries the very notion of a chosen people. "The world has had enough of chosen people!" he bellows. It is because of this exclusivism that mankind has been madly committing genocide, he says. To hear Moshe one would think that the people most guilty of this sin of nationalism are the Jews. Indeed, he wrote and published this thesis in a book called *The Decadence of Judaism in Our Time*. The book's argument is that Zionism took the old prophetic and universal values of Judaism, emphasized the narrowest, most archaic nationalistic ones and created a monster every bit as evil as the times it was rebelling against. The book was self-published and then issued for a second time by the Institute for Palestine Studies in Beirut. Moshe is not the most popular man in Israel today, nor with many Jews in this country. Although some of his points are well taken, I have never been able to accept the hatred and bitterness of Moshe's prophetic rantings.

Moshe likes to describe Jeremiah standing before the temple, surveying the corruption of his time and crying with bitter sarcasm "The Temple of the Lord, the Temple of the Lord, are these?" Moshe sees himself as just such a prophet. Indeed, perhaps the Baal-Shem's ghost was meant to inhabit his son's violin!

Most of the Jews in Palestine before the war were *schnorrers.* *Schnorring* is a word Moshe spits out with great disdain. It is a Yiddish word meaning begging, and to him all those poor but pious Jews who lived in the Holy Land and spent their time praying while subsisting on the contributions collected from throughout the Diaspora were despicable *schnorrers.* He claims he never met a Jewish mason or a Jewish worker in the vineyards of his uncle, who was a man rich enough to wear a pressed shirt with his suit and tie, and shoes that had been polished by an Arab. His uncle used to spend most of his day reading Yiddish novels and wondering when Baron Rothschild would send more money to the Zionist movement.

There were in those days Jews called *shomers.* These were the first military Zionists. Tall, dark and handsome, they rode out on horses to protect the kibbutzim against the invading Bedouins. The Bedouins attacked not for any ideological reason, but because they had no food or water. Moshe resented the *shomers* perhaps because they were dashing figures and the ones that girls were the most interested in.

Undoubtedly the most important event in Moshe's young life was that of his encounter with the Arab dentist. How many times and in how many different versions has Moshe told this story? It became part of his stock repertory, dragged out as regularly as a milkman delivers milk.

In Russia, Moshe had never been to a dentist. Tooth extractions were something one performed at home. But while in Palestine, a tooth grew out of Moshe's mouth, a big, terrible thing that extended beyond his lips. His grandmother didn't dare pull it because, she said somberly, he would go blind. And certainly being blind was a fate worse than having an ugly fang.

As Moshe got older, the problem grew worse, especially now that he was an adolescent and becoming aware of girls. The tooth cut his lip continually, making it ugly and raw. He was fifteen, virtually an orphan, but a member of the Zionist "extended family." There in his depressing little room he would look in the mirror. By now he was shaving with a real razor, and that made him proud, but the prouder he became the more the tooth bothered him, and the uglier it seemed.

The only money he was getting now came from his older brother Louis in New York. Every month Moshe would go down to the Zionist bank to see if Louis had sent five dollars. Sometimes the money came, but often it did not. One day, finding no money, Moshe emerged from the bank and spotted a sign across the street for the first time. It said, "Dentist, English spoken."

Moshe had been studying English secretly because his dream was still to go to America. It was three in the afternoon when he went into the dentist's office. There was a full crowd in the waiting room, but he just sat and waited until finally, three hours later, the room was almost emptied. The dentist emerged, an Arab who asked the young Jewish boy if there was anything he could do for him.

"I would like to ask you something," said Moshe. "May I?"

The dentist looked at him. It was probably quite obvious to the dentist what Moshe wanted to talk about, but with a straight face he said, "Certainly, certainly."

Moshe looked around to see that no one was watching. Then he made his plea. He pointed at the tooth. "It bothers me," he said. Then he told the dentist what his grandmother had told him. Moshe looked very unhappy.

The dentist laughed. Moshe thought he would never stop laughing. "Are you a little Jewish boy?" he quizzed Moshe.

"Yes, I am," Moshe replied, explaining that he attended the Herzlia Gymnasium.

"Oh, that is where they teach you to hate us."

Moshe nodded. "In a way you are right, yes," he agreed. "But I have come to have my tooth extracted."

The examination took more than an hour. Not a word was spoken. Finally the dentist was finished. He looked down at Moshe and said that he could extract the offensive tooth in two minutes, and that Moshe would not go blind. He added in a serious tone, "No wonder, my child, you are so small and thin; there's pus all over your mouth. You haven't had one tooth extracted. You must have at least fifteen extracted and a good many of them filled, and you must drink lots of milk and eat lots of fruit. Have you no family?"

"No," said Moshe. "My mother is in Russia. My brother is in America, and he is often too poor to send anything. I am often hungry, so I teach younger children at the Herzlia Gymnasium, but that doesn't bring in much."

"Listen," the dentist told him, "you come here every day at 4:30 when I am done with work. I will extract your tooth right now."

The work took nearly two months, and the same fillings are still in Moshe's teeth today. One day, Moshe actually had eight dollars in his pocket. He wanted to pay the dentist the money, but the dentist said no. "Look," he said, "you buy milk with this money, and you buy fruit. I don't want to be paid. I am paid by my conscience. But when you grow up, try to get out of yourself this hatred for Arabs. Remember that there was one good Arab. And there are thousands of them."

Moshe has never been bashful in telling the obvious epilogue to this experience. He claims that the dentist, his fabled dentist, was most probably killed, or if he is alive, he is someplace in a camp. At the very least his children are Palestinian guerrillas. He claims that the Zionists, backed by the most evil forces of the status quo in the West, have been out to destroy the Arab way of life that exists there. To listen to him, one would think the Arab way of life was idyllic, that everyone was kind and loving. "Who says the insane pace of modern society is the right path?" Moshe asks today.

During the years he spent at the Herzlia Gymnasium, Moshe was still extremely religious. He excelled first in Jewish and Hebrew studies, and later in mathematics and physics. Somehow his orthodoxy and his still ardent Zionism had found a way to co-exist in those years prior to his move to America.

In those days, Moshe would visit his sister Mussia at her house outside Jerusalem, near what is now an Arab village on the freeway between Tel Aviv and Jerusalem. Today, the village is littered with the burned-out jeeps and tanks from the War of Independence. During those long-ago summers, Moshe would take Mussia's son, Hochy, for long walks; he was trying to convince Hochy to become a doctor. (The boy later became an engineer). Usually, they went to the beach, which was segregated sexually. As they walked, Moshe would teach Hochy Zionist songs.

On other occasions, Moshe, along with his two buddies at the Gymnasium, Moshe Sharett (who later became an Israeli Prime Minister) and Dov Hoss (founder of the Israeli army) would kidnap students from other schools and take them down to the beach at Tel Aviv for Zionist indoctrination. Once the three youths threw a stink bomb at the feet of a writer named Shedlovsky because he was opposed to the Zionist attempts to resurrect the Hebrew language.

Today, Ben Yehuda, another of Moshe's buddies and a former director of the famed Gymnasium, is convinced that Moshe's criticism of Israel has much in common with such far right-wing religious fanatics as the Satmarer of Brooklyn, who believe the national State of Israel is a gross perversion of the Messianic ideal.

Moshe's fury at the State of Israel sometimes goes past being reasonable. Indeed, when he was writing letters to Israel, he kept saying that the person he was writing to would receive the letter only if the censor, who examines all the mail going in and out of Israel, let it through. "They'll probably decide my thoughts are not good for Jewish ears," he said, "and won't let this letter in." The anti-Zionism has grown in his later life until it has become an obsession, and his fury against Israel extends far beyond such issues as mail censorship, which probably exists to some extent in Israel today.

Still, while Moshe may be irrational about Israel, there is no question that Israel is a militaristic society. One can argue effectively that it has to be, for its own survival. There is no way of answering those victims of the holocaust who had nowhere to go after the war. Certainly Moshe's children reacted to his obsessive hatred of everything in his past by trying to trace back their own roots through his history. What else could they do?

The circumstances of Moshe's departure from the Holy Land are not easily ferreted out because he obviously had no great fondness for those years of late adolescence spent there. At eighteen, he was given a choice of scholarships either in Constantinople or New York to pursue his strong interest in mathematics and science.

Four years earlier, as I've described, he had tried a couple of escapes to the New World. Thus, this time, he had no trouble making the choice once again. His only real unhappiness on leaving the Old World was that he wouldn't be able to see the blue-eyed, fair-skinned girl he pined away for—a piano teacher named Marutha. But then that was an unrequited love anyway. She was very popular with men and rarely gave Moshe any encouragement.

He still wrote Marutha letters when he got to New York. But most of his time was taken up with the impoverished life of a Jewish student on scholarship. He began straight away as a sophomore at New York University. A year after he arrived in New York, Marutha appeared—though not exactly in quest of a great reunion with Moshe. But she did know him, and did spend time with him. Just the fact that he could be with her without being crowded out by the competition must have endeared him to this New World.

III
A NEW LAND

Marutha at fifteen. Exotic costumes would become her passion

ELEVEN

New York:
A Marriage and a Child

MOSHE MENUHIN AND MARUTHA SHER were married in New York City, five years after their first meeting in Palestine. The official version of the marriage has it that Moshe pursued his Ruth (Marutha's real name) to New York. Some dark rumors hint that she had gone off to America to marry a "mystery man," and for one reason or another did not find him. Whatever the circumstances, the marriage came about in 1914.

A son was born to them on April 22, 1916, whom they named Yehudi. Marutha allowed Moshe the privilege of siring this Messiah, for that was the one thing that really mattered, the one great reason for the union of man and woman—a child. It was clear from the beginning that the first child of these two regal people would be something special.

I often wonder if there was genuine love between the couple in the beginning. One does sense that there may have been some abandoned nights long, long ago, for Moshe and Marutha did share something—he and this grand, haughty woman with her self-obscured origins. For better or for worse, she had chosen this intense little man as her husband. Then, throughout those cold winter nights, as Marutha's stomach grew large with child, they kept warm in their bed, reading all the great Yiddish writers.

Looking back on his childhood, Yehudi has told me that his parents were blissfully happy. "My first four years were real heaven, and it was only with a growing family and growing responsibilities that we strolled out of our Garden of Eden." Yehudi says that Hephzibah began life in some of that bliss, but that Yaltah came along after it had passed.

One thing is certain: In good and bad times, the basis of the Menuhins' union was Jewishness. Regardless of how they felt about it, this Jewishness was a God-given quality, transmitted through one's family. Both Moshe and Marutha felt they had been abused by their families. So now, as the child approached, they shared some of their terrible doubts in the intimacy of their New York apartment at 207th Street and Broadway, so far away from all they had left behind in Jerusalem.

The young married couple kept a large apartment and paid the rent by taking in boarders. Marutha characteristically says that these were all boarders "with terrible Brooklyn accents." The young Menuhins liked it when they could get away from the apartment. Their happiest moments were on the weekends, when they would escape across Harlem Bridge to Bronx Park. Marutha would fill her skirt with apples that Moshe picked from the trees, while he discoursed on the beauties of nature, long a Menuhin passion. It is part and parcel of the old Hassidic way of looking at things.

A serious, intense and rather humorless fellow was Moshe in those days, the kind of man who is an easy mark for a woman like Marutha. People who take themselves overly seriously often fall prey to those who know how incapable such people are of seeing beyond their own delusions. By all accounts, and according to the photographic evidence, Marutha was very beautiful, and she used her beauty as a weapon to keep Moshe, who was always insecure about his own appearance, in his place.

Later, the Menuhin children saw the same pattern work over and over again. Moshe, for instance, would bring his beautiful princess some flowers he had lovingly grown in his precious garden. Marutha would look at the offering and rebuff her husband. To know how effective her remarks must have been, one only had to watch Moshe working in his garden hour after hour, caressing his plants with soothing words and gestures. It was the same kind of devotion he yearned to give his wife.

Their marriage may not have been unusual for their time. In the traditional Jewish marriage the man often pondered and thought and dreamed of the world to be, while the *balabusta*, the wife, took care of reality. Indeed, it was an old, old tradition from which Moshe and Marutha made their variation. The men were typically meek and studious and other-worldly. The women were strong, ambitious and thoroughly realistic and practical. In some cases, according to Moshe's own testimony, such women not only ran the household but made the living as well.

Marutha was definitely something more exotic than just an ordinary wife. Anyone foolish enough to question her strange claim to being a Tartar, for example, would quickly discover this. For Marutha would inflict punishment by sticking pins in a doll that looked like the transgressor. Presumably, in true Voodoo fashion, horrible things would then happen to this person. Certainly Moshe did not question his wife's claims to Tartar ancestry, though he must have known better. Even today he will publicly insist, though sometimes privately admitting the contrary, that Marutha's father, Nachum Sher, was a Tartar who converted to Judaism and knew his Judaism better than many Jews.

The more one gets into the mystery that surrounds Marutha's background, the more exotic it seems, perhaps because there are so few hard facts.

One fascinating possibility is suggested by the name Frumkin, which is written on the back of a picture of Moshe's and Marutha's mothers taken in Palestine. Amazingly, both mothers' first names were Sara Liba. I have not been able to determine Moshe's mother's maiden name, but Marutha's mother's maiden name was written Frumkin. Frumkin, according to one of my relatives in Israel, is one of the names of a branch of the Schneersohn clan. Thus it is possible that Moshe and Marutha were related, and maybe even knew that, and perhaps that was why in later life Moshe defended his wife's patently absurd claims to being every kind of aristocrat there was, as long as there was nothing Jewish involved. My mother showed me a picture of the two Sara Libas taken in Palestine at the turn of the century. They obviously knew each other, Sara Liba Sher and Sara Liba Mnuchin.

The Schneersohn family tree includes a number of first-cousin marriages. When an intelligent and preferably wealthy Jew was not available for an eligible Schneersohn, a marriage inside the family was sometimes arranged. Moshe's own nephew Hochy, for example, married his first cousin.

So intermarriage was not rare. Sonia Miller, Marutha's only known living relative (Sonia's mother Edie was Marutha's second cousin), suggested to me that Marutha may have come from Rostov-on-Don, a Gentile town. Sometimes the Czar allowed a few Jewish families to live outside the Pale (the Southern part of Russia which Jews were confined to) because they had specific skills. When six or seven of these families lived in a town where there were few other Jews, they began to deny their Jewishness. They felt themselves to be superior to the Jews who lived within the Pale. Sonia, who has lived in England all her life, suggests that Marutha may have come from a family most of whose neighbors were anti-Semitic. That is why she is so anxious, says Sonia, to disown her Jewish background.

The life of a Russian Jew in pre-World War I New York was difficult. The German Jews hated the Russian Jews, and the Gentiles hated both, although it was the Gentiles who shamed the Germans into helping their desperate brethren survive in the new country. The word "kike" was invented, not by Gentiles, but by Jews. It was what German Jews called Russian Jews because so many Russian Jewish names ended in "-ski" or variations thereof.

But after all that he had seen and lived through, New York must have seemed a haven to Moshe. He threw himself into his new life with abundant energy. He attended New York University, from which he eventually graduated with degrees in political science and mathematics. His intention, which in itself showed how far he had come, was to teach mathematics. He was not anxious to become a "professional Jew," as he called them. Nonetheless, when he was unable later to get a job as a math teacher, that is just what he would become.

Moshe was still a Zionist in 1916 when his son was born, although he was already beginning to make a distinction between political and spiritual Zionism, with his vote going for the latter. On Friday nights he visited the Lubarsky home, where poor Jewish students from Palestine met for tea and conversation. He was staunch enough in his Zionist convictions to write a piece for one of the movement's newspapers retelling the exploits of Judas Maccabeus of the second Commonwealth of Judea. Maccabeus fought against Judea's Greek and Syrian overlords, losing a noble battle in 162 B.C. Moshe's prose on the subject was florid.

The occasion when he and his new bride first started looking for a place to live became the subject of an often-told tale. They found an apartment on 165th Street where the landlady bragged about its exclusivity. "I don't rent to Jews," she said proudly.

There are several versions of what followed. According to Hephzibah, Marutha loudly proclaimed, "But we are Jews." And the landlady replied, "You don't look Jewish."

She had no doubt meant this as a compliment, for she indicated that she might be willing to rent to them. She never got the chance, however. Marutha rocked back on her heels and angrily cried out, "I will name my child Yehudi (the Jew), so the whole world will know he is Jewish."

Yehudi himself is acutely aware of the uniqueness of his name, and although he himself followed in the tradition of naming his offspring after grand and glorious things, he has been known to suggest wistfully that his parents might have chosen some less dramatic, less prophetic name for him. His full name is even more dramatic. It is Yehudi Sinai Menuhin. It might well have been Mnuchin but for the fact that the immigration officer convinced Moshe to Anglicize his name somewhat.

To support his young wife, Moshe undertook a variety of laboring jobs. For a short time he worked on the New York waterfront, although he was really too small to do the work well. He did not last long on the job, but it made a deep impression on him. Although it appears rather incongruous, his nostalgia for those days runs so deep that he even praises the old Industrial Workers of the World, the radical union that ran the waterfront. What is incongruous about Moshe praising the Wobblies is his present-day conservatism. His best friend, for instance, is a banker who is convinced that Franklin Roosevelt was a Communist. Moshe's patriotism for his adopted land is almost a mania.

The Wobblies and the anarchists were the scapegoats before the Communist menace came along. Yet Moshe's impressions of the

Wobblies seemed to have been more favorable. His brush with the revolutionary proletariat left an indelible mark. Most of the Wobblies were Swedes. When Moshe talks about them, he speaks with genuine respect and admiration. He likes to recall the large, hulking Swede who came up to him and declared, "You might be a little Jew, but if you are a good, loyal member of the working class, you're one of us."

With his eyes bulging and his hands gesticulating even more than usual, Moshe would explain how hard the work was. To his everlasting shame, it was too hard for him. He felt he was physically inadequate, especially when he compared himself to his work-hardened, muscular comrades. It became one of the themes of his life. The Russian Jews had rarely been proletarians. They were often tiny and soft from years of starvation and restriction from normal occupations. The stereotype of the Jewish ragpicker did not come about without reason. So if people who did hard, brawny work were often Moshe's idols, it is not surprising. This brawn-worship was also an old theme of Zionism. Jews of the ghetto sought redemption in what they considered real, hard work.

To be sure, Moshe did not go out and join the industrial proletariat, and certainly neither did his children. Yet he consistently urged some of his grandchildren (myself included) to become carpenters and ditchdiggers, even when they were still in elementary school.

Upon graduation from New York University in 1917, when Moshe could not get a job as a mathematics teacher, he became the principal of a Hebrew school in Camden, New Jersey. Marutha taught there too. Moshe had always wanted to be a professor, Yehudi says, and for a while Marutha was planning to teach to support the family while Moshe went back to school.

Instead, while Yehudi slept in a basket on the billiard table in the recreation room of the New Jersey Hebrew School, his parents attempted to make Hebrew a living language, a language for everyday life, not an anachronistic "holy" language. Moshe believed at this time that the place to fulfill his people's destiny and bring forth the Messiah was in Israel, and thus Hebrew must be taught as the language of living Jews, not of Jews dwelling in the past or in heaven.

The school principle would often take his students on walks through the park rather than continue studying in the classrooms. And as they walked, he would remember the mountains and valleys of the Holy Land and tell his students of the Jews who lived there. Moshe would describe it all in a forceful Hebrew, for that was the best language in which to conjure up the image of the New Jew for his students.

Moshe and Marutha became the students' favorite teachers. They were the least popular, however, with the old rabbi who was in charge of the school. The students hated the severe, bearded old men around the school. Moshe and Marutha were young and alive. Unlike the old men, they had not been worn down by years of what the students saw as pious delusions traditionally accepted as reality, simply because reality itself had been so ugly.

One of the Menuhins' young students was Sammy Marantz, now a New Jersey airplane parts manufacturer. Sammy became very attached to the Menuhins and was a frequent visitor to their tiny apartment, crowded with books, a piano and a cello.

"Moshe was a bit of a revolutionary," Sammy told me with a laugh in London in 1973. These days, Sammy is one of the few friends the elder Menuhins still have. He certainly does not say that Moshe's politics are more reasonable than they appear at first. Moshe had been an opponent of political Zionism since Sammy had known him, and Moshe did not want to see a Jewish political state created. Moshe's sympathies lay with the spiritual Zionists, such as Asher Ginzberg, whose pen name, Ahad HaAm, meant "one of the people". Ginzberg was an agent of a tea company and a Zionist hero until he was supplanted by Dr. Theodor Herzl. If Herzl was the Stalin, Ginzberg was the Lenin; the ruthless supplanting the visionary. To some extent Yehudi concurs with his father's opinion of Israel, but his views are tempered by the fact that he did not share Moshe's bitter childhood experiences and hence he does not hate his own people in the way Moshe obviously does.

Moshe has spent the last four decades pursuing his anti-Zionism. During the 1973 Mideast war, he said "a true Jewish people would be meek and be killed." Many people began to feel that Moshe himself was an anti-Semite when, just before World War II, he undertook to criticize his beleaguered people for demonstrating too much nationalism. It took a certain kind of incredible insensitivity to bring up the old debate at such a time, even if Ginzberg was right in his opposition to a Jewish political state.

Moshe's new view of Zionism grew out of the fact that he was obviously disillusioned with the past. He felt that the Lubavitchers' fifth rabbi had meddled in his family's affairs and had made him an orphan. Outside his family, outside the ghetto over which they presided, was the spirit of the new age. Now was the time for Judaism to cease being just the religion of the chosen people. In Moshe's view, the Schneersohns exercised an evil influence. They used superstition to manipulate the great mass of "ignorant, naive" Russian Jews.

Moshe still talks as if Jews today were really those same ignorant, ghetto-bound Jews he hated so much in the Russia of his youth. When Moshe rails on against Zionists and the evil, power-seeking rabbinical priesthood, it is obvious his anger is as much personal as political. His family represented evil. Moshe was the equivalent of a Jewish anti-cleric, only the clergy were his own family. No doubt this is why even when Moshe is saying perfectly reasonable things, there is an unusual personal stridency in his tone.

TWELVE

Feud in California

To SAMMY MARANTZ IT HAS always been a mystery why the Menuhins suddenly left New York for California. One day, Sammy went to visit the Menuhins, and they were gone. Everything had been cleared out. Sammy suspected that the Menuhins' increasing conflicts with the old rabbi at the school had caused the abrupt move. But Yehudi has explained to me the true reason. One cold morning Moshe had a vision of California "while seated on that more-than-shared democratic throne that every Westerner knows," which is Yehudi's way of describing the toilet.

It was, as usual, Moshe's vision and Marutha's action. As Yehudi has said, "My mother's decisions were always immediately carried out. They were off before anyone could say how, why or where." Sometime later, Sammy heard from Moshe, who wrote him a long letter once they were situated in California. The letter urged Sammy and the other students to "keep up the good fight."

Moshe's vision coincided with Marutha's. She liked the idea of California because it's climate resembled that of her native Crimea, or so she said. Moshe was eager to join his older brother Louis who lived on a ranch in Hayward, across the bay from San Francisco.

The Menuhins—Moshe, Marutha and young Yehudi—succeeded in getting to California only by a fluke. They went to New York's Grand Central Station with all their belongings. Moshe pulled their life savings from his pocket, about $165. It was not enough to get the three Menuhins across the country. But the ticket agent took pity on them. First he pieced together a series of day coach fares via a complicated route that cost less than the simple cross-country fare. They were still short, so he lent them six dollars. The Menuhin family walked onto the train with, strangely enough, a snow shovel and ten dollars for food. They arrived at the Oakland terminal with 32¢ to their name. Luckily, Louis was there at the station to pick them up in his farm wagon.

For a few stormy months, Moshe, Marutha and Yehudi lived with Louis and his wife Batja. They would sneak across the bay to San Francisco whenever they could. It was a place they felt they must have spent their whole lives waiting to run to. Here, on California's sunlit shores, they felt they had found deliverance from torn families and crumbling social orders. Suddenly they themselves were parents, clinging to life in a new land, a magic land, a *holy* land, if you will.

Certainly San Francisco was the catalyst that freed something in these Europeans. The sun was like an all-powerful hand from heaven that could release human souls from their European bondage.

Today, San Francisco is no longer what it once was. The bay is only two-thirds its original size. The buildings that weigh it down, those monsters of commerce, do not seem to belong at all. When Moshe and Marutha arrived at the Oakland train station, they looked across the foggy bay at the city. San Francisco was a marvelous island, now sunny, now foggy, that one reached only by ferry.

The City had always been a difficult place to figure out. It had been built by a motley assortment of souls during the Gold Rush, and it has remained a haven for the world's most restless people ever since. For Moshe, San Francisco became "the New Jerusalem" he had been looking for. During those early days in San Francisco, the city was working a special magic on the Menuhins. Perhaps the use of the frustratingly vague 1960's word "vibrations" fails to explain what was going on, yet something like that was happening to the young Menuhins.

San Francisco has always seemed rather boorish and gaudy to me, but Yehudi, always looking on the other side, once responded, "But what beauty, color, variety, excitement, freedom, health and elegance" it has. I answered Yehudi that spit-swollen, plank-floored saloons with swinging doors were its beginnings. The spirit of the grand old European castles or even the highly-evolved spiritualism of Jewish wise men are alien to the more superficial realities of Baghdad-by-the-Bay. And that may have been just the very reason why the Menuhins took to the place so.

The great Martin Buber insisted that Jews have had to endure a special suffering because they have had to exist in the Diaspora, cut off from their ancestral homes, their primal link, in the Holy Land. If so, Moshe didn't feel that pull for the Holy Land. He felt it instead for California, for that strange mixture of natural beauty and human chemistry that was especially San Francisco's in the early days. It is a feeling many people have had for San Francisco, yet among the Europeans, Africans and Orientals who live there, who can claim any primal link to the area?

The problem is that when you talk about primal roots, you are talking mysticism. And the vagueness of mysticism can make it most obscure. Yet San Francisco poet Kenneth Rexroth has described mysticism rather well. He says mysticism is merely the invisible chain that binds husband to wife, parent to child, friend to friend and individual to society. When all these relationships become too complex to be easily analyzed, they grow mysterious. This is all "mystical feelings" ever were—that sense of awe that comes with contemplating the mysteries that abound.

Whatever the reason, Moshe suddenly felt his primal link being forged not with the land of his ancestors in Palestine, but with California. It is no doubt significant that while his children would grow up and themselves succumb to the pull of another "New Jerusalem" back in the Holy Land, Moshe never left California after his children left home.

The first weeks in California were not auspicious. Perhaps it was inevitable that even in California, there would yet have to be one more trauma—one more breaking away from the clutches of Moshe's family.

There had been a time when Moshe revered his older brother Louis, whose name had actually been Levi-Yitzhak, after his famous Hassidic ancestor in Russia. Louis was blond and blue-eyed, like Moshe, but despite the physical similarities, the two brothers were quite different. Louis had come to Palestine from Russia in his teens. The change to a new situation in new lands was less traumatic for him. Also, Louis had had the advantage of spending the greater part of his childhood free of the trauma that had filled Moshe's. Isaac (Yitzhak) Mnuchin, their father, had become a wealthy man as a supplier for the Czar's army. According to family tradition, the family house in Gomel was so large it had fifteen servants and a fine horse-drawn carriage. But Isaac died when Moshe was hardly out of infancy.

Before World War I, Louis left his little brother in Palestine and came to New York. In the middle of a particularly bad winter he was sleeping in doorways and selling matchbooks for an income.

One day a customer of his said, "Louis, don't you recognize me?" It was the former manager of the Mnuchin household in Russia. He looked well-dressed and comfortable, while Louis was starving and freezing. The manager took Louis home and eventually helped him go to an agricultural school.

Finally, Louis went back to Palestine to fight the Turks in World War I, and when he later returned to America, he did so with a wife, Batja, who shared his two great interests—agriculture and Zionism. For a while Louis worked as a milkman in Los Angeles, living in Echo Park, close to downtown. Then he and Batja moved to Hayward, where they purchased a ranch.

Superficially, one might have thought that these two young Jewish families would have found the ranch in Hayward something to share. Louis was a very practical man, while his brother was more of a philosopher. Moshe was still something of a Zionist in those days—albeit a "spiritual" one.

But neither brother had counted on the fact that Moshe's young bride had no intention of allowing her beauty, her brilliance and her considerable charm to be wasted on the soil all in the name of some half-baked ideological notions. Also, Marutha and Batja were bound to conflict, for Batja was a down-to-earth woman who shared her husband's Zionism. Many years later, after Louis' death during the Depression, she returned to the Holy Land, where she established herself as one of the foremost poultry experts in the Middle East.

Louis, as might be expected, possessed all of the traditional Jewish virtues. His family was his life. His sister Mussia, still in Palestine; his mother, Sara Liba, still in Russia; and now Moshe, living with him in California; these relations were the central concerns of his life. Louis kept up a steady stream of correspondence to Sara Liba in Katerinoslov, which is now Nepresetinov. Not so long ago, Vera, the half-sister of Louis and Moshe, who now lives in Tel Aviv, told me of her memories in Katerinoslov when news from Louis in far-off California would be read at the local Hassidic meeting. The memory of those packets of news from Louis was brought back to her during an interview with yet another Menachem-Mendel Schneersohn, the present Lubavitcher rabbi, who was visiting in Israel. Schneersohn told Vera that he was the little boy who would run to their house to pick up the envelope each week and carry it back to the Hassidic meeting.

The final act of weaning Moshe from his brother and thus from the whole family was accomplished by Marutha and the fabled case of the scrawny, dead chicken. Both Moshe and Marutha thought the chicken in question, a scraggly beast if there ever was one, was too unappetizing to eat. The two Menuhins, especially Marutha, protested having to eat the thing. Louis replied, "In this home we do not waste." Not long thereafter, Moshe found work in San Francisco, and the two young families separated, and their differences continued to grow. To Marutha, the line "in this home we do not waste" became almost as funny as the old orthodox refrain "next year in Jerusalem." She thought that both were hilarious jokes.

Separated now by the bay between San Francisco and Hayward, the final scenes of Moshe's estrangement from his family were being carried out—now by letter. Sara Liba, the mother of Moshe and Louis, had, as you may recall, married an agricultural broker. Moshe felt no allegiance toward the new family; for one thing, his stepbrothers had treated him so badly before his exile to the Holy Land, that he felt loyalty was out of the question. But Louis adopted Sara Liba's new family as his own. Beginning in the 1917 Russian Revolution, things went badly for Sara Liba and her family. Both Louis and his sister Mussia in Palestine were sending packages of food, without which Sara Liba's family would not have survived. They were also looking for ways to get Sara Liba and her brood to Palestine. Louis asked Moshe to contribute to these efforts, not long after Moshe and Marutha left Hayward. Moshe—no doubt with Marutha's backing—said no, and the great feud between the brothers was launched.

The younger Moshe wrote across the bay to his older brother to tell him that he wanted nothing to do with his irresponsible Jerusalem plans. He wanted to be left alone and threatened to return any further correspondence his brother Louis might send him. Then Moshe proceeded to write a series of letters to Russia, advising his mother to join the attempts to create a new society there instead of running off to the "land of the *schnorrers*." To this day, Moshe's half-sister, Vera, cannot bring herself to forgive her half-brother for those letters. They were nearly starving to death, and instead of food or money, Moshe was sending his mother advice on world events.

So Louis insisted on clinging to his family ties despite the distance of oceans and continents, despite wars and revolutions. Moshe, on the other hand, rejected his family. He was bitter toward his sister Mussia because of Sonya's death, among other things, and Marutha did not try to discourage that bitterness. She certainly did not attempt to get along with Louis, to whom she would refer in later years as "that Yiddish socialist".

In any event, Sara Liba, Asher-Libo and Vera did not follow Moshe's advice, and it is well they did not, for by the time they were able to leave Russia, their only possession was a large Torah. They took it with them to Palestine.

Which of the two Menuhin brothers was the real heir to the family traditions? Today Batja, who lives in Israel on Kibbutz Maagan Michael, which she helped start, says she thinks it was Louis. Louis was a real Hassid, not in his religion but in his being. He was like old Levi-Yitzhak himself, she says. To her, Moshe was some sort of monster sired by the tradition but not reflective of it. Yet there is, even today, something of the Hassidic tradition in Moshe. If there is little of the Hassid's peculiar sense of social and political relations, Moshe's sense of nature, his love of the soil, particularly the soil of Rancho Yaltah, bought in 1936, gives the evidence that Moshe's spiritual Zionism, born out of his Hassidic background, survived. Even in his seventies, when cancer and other infirmities forced Moshe to move to a smaller home in Los Gatos, he made sure it had a plot of land to cultivate.

But in 1918, as the two young parents of Yehudi rode the hilly streets of San Francisco in cable cars, watching the fog curling its fingers through the city's remarkable, bay-windowed Victorian houses, connections with land and family seemed permanently severed. They ate crab at Fisherman's Wharf, and that was where they met the Kavins, the marvelously jovial Russians the Menuhins quickly befriended. Moshe and Marutha looked around San Francisco and liked what they saw. Their little boy, Yehudi liked all the sunshine, too. The sun on the golden California hills is a childhood memory that stays with him.

California had cut the ties that bound. Or so it seemed then.

THIRTEEN

The Miracle

FROM ALL INDICATIONS, Moshe Menuhin was going to be a great success. He found a job in San Francisco serving as the director of the city's Hebrew schools, and he was a good teacher. While his brother Louis was plucking chickens, Moshe was wooing both the best of teachers and the wealthiest of patrons. In 1920, the Menuhins purchased a house on Steiner Street, a few blocks from the orthodox temple, now a part of the black ghetto.

Batja, Louis' wife, tells an amusing story that she believes reveals Moshe's double standards. Even though Moshe was the director of San Francisco's Hebrew schools, he had a wife with a hankering for bacon, which is, of course, a taboo food for Jews. It was a craving that Marutha could only satisfy secretly. Yehudi remembers that his parents would load the family into the Chevrolet and drive to one of the outlying San Francisco districts, and there they would feast on the forbidden fatback. Yehudi laughs, "That was our equivalent of the speakeasy."

While the Menuhin family established itself in the Jewish culture of San Francisco, Yehudi was beginning to show an amazing attraction and aptitude for music. His early precocity is often described by stories that could be dismissed as a Jewish *mamaleh's* tales about her son, the genius; but since Yehudi proved to be a great genius, they should be recorded. A few weeks before Moshe and

Marutha left Hayward, Louis was feeding one-year-old Yehudi. Suddenly and inexplicably, the boy burst into tears. Moshe came running, and so did the women. No one could figure out why the lad, normally so good-tempered, was crying, until Moshe finally noticed that the spoon Louis had been feeding Yehudi with was much duller than the one usually used. When the spoons were changed, Yehudi quickly returned to his normal, contented gurglings. Moshe suggests that his son was so sensitive that the difference in brightness in the two spoons had upset him.

Three months later in San Francisco, another such incident occurred. Yehudi had a little girlfriend named Lilli Edelmann, who, incidently, grew up to be Pearl Buck's secretary and a writer herself. The two youngsters took their naps together in a bay-windowed, sunlit room. On this occasion, Lilli had fallen asleep, but Yehudi stayed awake. Somehow his child's mind had been able to grasp the essentials of melody, either from the records that Moshe played when Yehudi was napping, or from the beautifully mournful old Hassidic tunes his father hummed. In perfect intonation up and down the scale, Yehudi began to chant, "Lilli has fallen asleep. Lilli has fallen asleep." He was, of course, singing the words in Hebrew, for that was the only language the little boy knew until he was three or four years old. He sang the same tune over and over again, and each time he sang it, he embellished it with variations.

The next sign that the boy was unusual occurred in a neighborhood park. Yehudi screamed and smashed a toy violin that a guest had brought him. It wouldn't produce music. It looked like a violin, but it wouldn't sing.

It was just a few months later that Moshe and Marutha started taking the child to the concerts of the San Francisco Symphony, conducted by Alfred Hertz, at the Curran Theatre. The Menuhins could not afford a babysitter. Besides, the parents were convinced that if Yehudi did not sleep through the concert he would probably just listen quietly. Members of the audience looked annoyed when the Menuhins walked in with their baby, but the symphony members were so used to him that when he didn't show up, they enquired after him. Moshe and Marutha noted that Yehudi was particularly animated when the concertmaster Louis Persinger played the violin.

Yehudi was a little past four years old when, pointing at Persinger, he announced that he wanted "that man" to teach him to

play. But it was some time before Yehudi would get his chance to
audition for him. When he did, however, Persinger said he
recognized Yehudi as a frequent audience member the moment he
walked in the door.

Yehudi had begun pestering his parents for violin lessons a few
months previously, but they had not taken his desires seriously.
They shrugged off his first requests as a passing fancy, and it was
only Marutha's mother, Sara Liba Sher, in Palestine, who seemed to
take the matter seriously. Marutha, who filled her letters to her
mother with all the details of everyone's daily lives, sometimes even
including descriptions of the child's digestive processes, had
mentioned Yehudi's desire for a violin. Sara Liba sent money to buy
one. Half of it went for a down payment on the family's Chevrolet,
and the rest for a small violin.

Just what was the source of Yehudi's determination to sing on
the violin? Were the old Hassidic songs a call from destiny? Schneur
Zalman had said, "For the song of the souls, at the time they are
swaying in the high regions and drinking from the well of the Al-
mighty king, consists of tones only, free and unencumbered with
burdensome words." Music, we have noted, was the chief vehicle of
the mystic's approach to God.

Obviously, Moshe's songs awakened something in Yehudi's sub-
conscious mind. Although Yehudi muses that perhaps the mysticism
of the Hassidim might have been more Russian than Jewish, it was
the uniquely Jewish quality of his father's tunes that remained with
him.

When the five-year-old Yehudi drew the bow across the strings
of his first real violin, and, to his chagrin, it did not produce song, he
never quit until it did. And, as the frustration reached the breaking
point, the uncannily determined Yehudi would merely redouble his
efforts with a single-mindedness that astounded even his teacher.

Yehudi's first few lessons with Sigmund Anker were a disappointment. Yehudi made no more progress than the other students.
That especially surprised Anker because he was quite taken aback by
the boy's unusual determination.

Sometimes, in complete frustration, Anker would yell at
Yehudi, and Yehudi would hardly be able to hold back the tears. But
then, almost suddenly, he began to make the violin sing. Six months
after he had been studying with Anker, Marutha accompanied him at

Anker's annual student recital, and two months before he was six, Yehudi gave his first real concert. It was still not a major event, but people were taking notice. He played Paderewski's Minuet before the Pacific Music Society, his mother accompanying, once again, on the piano. Only a few months after his sixth birthday, it was predicted by Redfern Mason, music critic of the San Francisco *Examiner*, that Yehudi would become "a master among masters."

Yehudi soon got his chance to study with Persinger. Persinger had reluctantly agreed to hear Yehudi, for he was constantly approached by parents and friends of parents promoting the cases of various prodigies. But from the moment Yehudi began to play, all doubts were gone. Not only audiences but musicians wanted to hug him. Yehudi's playing seemed proof that there was a God who could still work miracles.

Persinger's approval was aroused not only by the boy's playing, but also by his hungry enthusiasm. Yehudi's haste would later come back to plague him, but it could not be held back. As a teenager, Yehudi was already a veteran of the concert stage, yet he still had not ırned scales.

A few years later in an article in *The Etude*, Persinger recalled 's first audition and his attractively grave demeanor.

ımn little lad with a serious expression. Quietly
ınder his chin and began to play. He was
oed him. I shall never forget the fury
interruption. It was an insult to him
enough. There was no doubt in my
idden there. His feeling for rhythm
utely true. There was more besides,

looks at the printed score and tries to
n in the composer's mind. To do this he
sory perception. And to interpret, he
to its historic period as well. He
ıstruct of the past, which is part
conservative image. For to
ust have a view of
he present and

Underwood & Underwood
WASHINGTON

Yehudi and teacher Louis Persinger

into the future. The interpreter's mind must be, in this sense, broader than the creator's.

And the interpretive genius by itself is as valid and necessary as is the creative genius. It is well that there remains the man or woman who can look at a Mozart passage and see that Mozart is beginning to slip into the depths of despair but who in the next moment can sense how he has found the strength to twist the threads of his life and music around in order to survive with genuine hope.

That kind of genius is akin to the creative, and is indispensable to the performance of real music. The interpreter senses his audience and then, hopefully, takes his listeners on the intellectual and spiritual journey which the recreation of a piece of music should be. Perhaps the great recreator is really a very different phenomenon than the creator. Yehudi believes this is so. Although he is drawn to improvising, for example, he deprecates his own ability to do so. "Perhaps if I had been trained differently," he says, but one gets the feeling that in his heart he believes his greatest creativity is in recreating.

Certainly that was the emphasis in Yehudi's training. All Yehudi's ancestors who interpreted Torah, in a sense, helped define what it was for their times. But essentially the laws were already given, and to interpret them one began by giving them great reverence, and one also made the assumption that they were holy. That is the way Yehudi approaches music, too. The interpreter approaches the music with a sense of awe, devotion and humility, and reinterprets it for the listener.

Perhaps that very humility kept Yehudi from having the boldness which creation requires. Perhaps the difference between the creater and the recreator is the difference between prophet and priest. But there is something quite powerful in the ability to believe wholeheartedly in one's teacher, one's God, one's faith, to allow the teacher to mold one's imagination. Yehudi had the ability to accept his mentor's context, and then to live in it. During a particular Lalo passage, Persinger asked his student to express voluptuousness. But Yehudi did not know what that meant. Persinger told him to put down his violin, and they went for a walk.

Here is how Persinger conveyed the meaning of that grown-up term. Imagine, he said, Cleopatra floating down the Nile in her gorgeously outfitted boat; the indolence and grace of her posture; the rich tapestries surrounding her; the luscious fruit on which she nibbled. Yehudi and Persinger spent most of the day talking about voluptuousness, and when Yehudi picked up the violin to play the passage, the tones were voluptuous.

Presumably a great master does not impose his teaching but develops what is already in his student. Yehudi's mind was not a blank waiting to be filled by whatever came along. To recreate one must bring one's own mind to it. His initial reaction to Ravel, for example, bordered on disgust. Ravel made him think of a sticky octopus, he said. But Mozart, ah, that was a different thing. Yehudi admits that his greatest early kinship was with Mozart. Mozart's style had crystallized early, and he was the composer with whom Yehudi felt most at home for many years. The beauty of Mozart's music, Yehudi has said, is its utter simplicity, which has richness and maturity yet keeps its childlike innocence.

It was easier to identify with Mozart than with Beethoven because to play Beethoven, "one needs to have lived," says Yehudi. To play Beethoven, the young Yehudi had to transpose himself into something he was not. He had to feel big and powerful and understand love. Today, Yehudi does not agree with this, saying, "I have always been in love." But still, spontaneity and innocence were the magic bonds between the young Menuhin and the young Mozart. Yehudi uses the words "tender sorrow" and "angelic anguish" to describe his view of Mozart.

FOURTEEN

Successes and a Final Farewell

IN 1922, YEHUDI, A SIX-YEAR-OLD boy, was already becoming famous. He was an appealing youngster, blue-eyed and pink-cheeked, who loved to scooter down the hill outside his house at ninety miles an hour, or so he says. He also looked forward to a rosy future when he would become, he believed, the greatest violinist in the world. But Yehudi was already a diplomat. "I've heard Jascha Heifetz and Mischa Elman. They are wonderful, but I shall play even better when I am a big man."

Moshe observed that Yehudi was actually two people. On the one hand, he was often a sweet, even-tempered boy. But when he picked up the violin, he became an intense and even stormy youth. Sometimes, however, the sweet-tempered boy exploded even away from the violin, and became a raging tyrant, strong enough to stand up to his formidable mother and throw back at her all the qualities she had instilled in him.

Yaltah remembers how a friend of the family once gave Yehudi a present. Presents were being offered more frequently to Yehudi, and most were turned down. But this happened to be a present from someone who had, for whatever strange reason, found favor with Marutha at the time. So Marutha wanted Yehudi to accept the present. Yehudi, however, could not stand such a double standard. It was not something he wanted or needed, and he saw no reason to say

"Thank you" for the gift. Marutha insisted that he do so. Again he refused. Marutha lost the battle—Yehudi never thanked the giver.

Could Yehudi's amazing talents and moody, rebellious maturity be interpreted as the House of Schneersohn re-establishing itself, this time in San Francisco's Jewish ghetto? There certainly was an uncanny parallel between the Lubavitcher's royal court in Russia and the Menuhin household. People came to visit Yehudi as if he were true royalty. One woman's letter reprinted in a national magazine suggests the power the Menuhin court had for visitors. The letter begins, "One Sunday afternoon my mother dressed my brother and me in our very best clothes and announced that we were going to visit Yehudi Menuhin." Her Russian Jewish parents lived just a few blocks from Yehudi in the neighborhood already astir with his fame. She attended the Hebrew school which Moshe ran. Marutha greeted the family at the door and showed them into the parlor, but she said Yehudi could not be disturbed for the next couple of hours because he was practicing. The girl never got to meet Yehudi and grew up convinced that he was merely a mystical figure invented by Jewish parents.

Meanwhile, two-year-old Hephzibah wanted to play the violin just like her six-year-old brother, but that was refused. Then she cast a longing look at the cello in the corner, but the cello was soon sold. It had been Marutha's instrument, but now, with children and household chores, she had no time for it. When Hephzibah was finally allowed to play an instrument, it was the piano, and her talent was obvious. Soon she was good enough to accompany her brother. Only one sister could be Yehudi's accompanist, however, which put Yaltah, a year younger, in the difficult position of trying to justify her existence, an important consideration in the Menuhin household.

Yehudi's existence was getting all the justification it needed. He started making money after he had been studying with Persinger only a few months. He was awarded checks of $25 for ten successive months after participating in a contest. One of the judges was Alfred Hertz, the San Francisco Symphony's conductor. At the contest, Yehudi had begun playing the second movement of the Mendelssohn Violin Concerto in an extremely accelerated tempo.

Hertz stopped him and enquired, "Why such a rapid tempo?"

"I'm afraid there won't be any time left for the third movement, and I must play it. It sparkles so." Hertz assured Yehudi he could slow down; the judges would listen.

A short time thereafter Yehudi made his first professional appearance at the Oakland Auditorium, on February 29, 1924. He played with the San Francisco Symphony conducted by Hertz. Two weeks later he performed for six thousand youngsters his own age.

His first major San Francisco appearance came on March 25, 1925, at the Scottish Rite Hall. It was attended by almost every musician and music critic in town. It must have been an impressive performance, because its repercussions affected many lives. Cheap violins were sold out overnight, and the San Francisco air squawked with their screechy sounds. How many unhappy hours of horsehair tickling catgut would have been spared McAllister Street and the other streets of the Jewish district if there had been no Yehudi? There might also have been no Isaac Stern or Ruggiero Ricci, both of whom emerged from San Francisco not long after Yehudi had blazed a trail across the world's concert stages.

The social pressure on the Menuhin court was growing steadily. The most memorable pests were the society ladies, who would pull up in front of the Menuhin home and announce that they were bringing their children over to play with Yehudi, Hephzibah and Yaltah. If they happened to see any of the Menuhin children, which was rare from the ladies' standpoint but all too frequent from the children's, they would pinch them on the cheek and even plan their marriages. The Menuhins became deeply resentful of all this attention, however well-meant. The Menuhin parents resented it because it smacked of patronage, something, as Yehudi says, "their independence and pride could never, ever stomach." Yaltah still has a fear of returning to San Francisco, her native town, because of all those memories. "We couldn't walk down the street without those awful women coming up and pinching our cheeks," she says.

There was one wealthy San Franciscan about whom the Menuhins would come to feel differently, but even his initial attempts to help were turned down. Sydney Ehrman, a wealthy businessman, was first approached by a colleague of Moshe's, Dr. Samuel Langer, director of the Pacific Hebrew Orphan Asylum. Dr. Langer wanted Ehrman's permission to use some of his funds for Yehudi's musical education. Ehrman declined, saying he did not think that the money he had contributed to the asylum should be diverted from the orphans. Instead, he offered to give Yehudi's parents $500 directly. The offer, to Langer's chagrin, was turned down.

The Menuhins were somewhat overwhelmed by all the sudden attention. Had there been no Yehudi, his parents would never have left their positions as educators in the schools of the Jewish community. All doubts that plagued them would have been suppressed as they immersed themselves in their work. But with all the fame and attention, they went out of their way to hide even such minor matters as their break with the orthodox (kosher) eating customs.

Increasingly, the Menuhins went to Petaluma on weekend retreats to visit their friends the Kavins. During one of these visits, Yehudi and Hephzibah went out to play. They chanced to wander across the property line, and there stood Louis' wife Batja, for Louis and Batja had moved next door to the Kavins.

"Hello, Yehudi," said Batja.

Yehudi looked up. "How do you know me?" he demanded.

"I'm your aunt," replied Batja, a little sadly.

Yehudi and Hephzibah went rushing back to the house to tell their parents they had discovered their aunt. Moshe looked down at the pair and sternly declared, "She is not your aunt. You don't have an aunt. Everyone wants to be related to you."

As it happened, that was the last year that the two Menuhin families saw each other. Louis died unexpectedly from appendicitis, and Batja was left alone with her two girls, Tikva and Leah. Moshe came to his brother's funeral at the Oddfellows Cemetery on Geary Street, but he hung in the background wearing dark glasses. He did not venture forth to make even the smallest kind remark to his sister-in-law or nieces.

Batja went back to Petaluma to try to make a go of the chicken ranch without Louis, but it was impossible. She had to work a full day in a packing shed just to keep herself and her daughters alive. She soon decided that there was no future for her in America and returned to Palestine.

Batja did make one attempt to contact Moshe after the funeral. Her daughter Tikva was showing quite a talent on the violin and had impressed a violinist in the San Francisco Symphony enough that he suggested that Tikva should pursue the instrument as a career. So Batja wrote a letter to Moshe and Marutha asking if she could leave

Tikva with them. She never received a reply.

Moshe had not completely forgotten Batja, however. A short time after the funeral, a teacher from Moshe's school came to woo Batja. She quickly discovered that the fellow had been sent by Moshe as a potential suitor, and she chased him off her property.

Batja was well-acquainted with the old Jewish passion for music. As a child in Palestine, she spent half her salary for piano lessons once a week at a convent. The teacher was bad and the piano was worse, but it was worth the price to her. It was one of her life's great disappointments that Tikva gave up the violin. Tikva, unlike Yehudi, had no drive. When she was supposed to be practicing, she was reading books instead. Books were her passion. Eventually she married, and she now lives a quiet life outside London.

Perhaps it was the falling out between Moshe and his brother that turned the young father away from the outside world in order to totally devote himself to his family. Yehudi describes it this way:

> Marutha took care of social deportment and conscience in the practical world, Moshe politics and social problems in the more abstract. Within that framework, the roles were severely worked out. All centripedal activities were Marutha's. Centrifugal belonged to Moshe. And I was definitely Moshe's. The girls were Marutha's.

The world Moshe created was self-contained within his own family. He must have turned to his own family with such a vengeance because he was making his final filial farewells in San Francisco at his brother's funeral. After that, he would never again have any contact with his own family. No one can know exactly what was going through his mind as he watched his brother's funeral through those dark glasses. Probably even Moshe has so twisted those thoughts of long ago that the moment will never be recaptured. But undoubtedly, in some way, he knew that moment was very much a final farewell.

FIFTEEN

Marutha and the Sara Liba Incident

HAVING CUT HIS TIES with his family, Moshe went on to make a fatal mistake with his own wife. Moshe was possessive and jealous when it came to his Marutha, and not without apparent reason. "Maruta," as he pronounced her name, was a flirt who wrapped men around her little finger with ease. She had not only beauty but charm, the charm of a highly complex and intelligent woman who had woven a fabric of fantasies about her father's ancestors, claiming, among other things, that they were fierce Tartar tribesmen.

It is clear that she loved her mother, Sara Liba, and hated her father, Nachum Sher. She was always telling the children that her mother would do something this way or that, and this was supposed to be enough reason for everyone to do it that way too.

Marutha and her mother shared a love for all things Italian. Even her ancestry became Italian, for one of the many things she hinted at was that her grandmother on her mother's side was actually an Italian princess by descent. Her mother was like a mythical creature to the three Menuhin children, but the grandmother was nearly a goddess whose origins were undetermined, but so exotic that it is doubtful mere mortals could be told of them. Her aristocracy was of the great blue sky, from the other side of the world, on the dark side of the moon, in Xanadu. She had come directly from the Heavenly courts.

The name of Marutha's pet poodle was Giamela. The goat that she loved and cared for as a pet was named Italy. The last time Marutha left Palestine, she and her mother promised each year they would one day meet in Italy. How both dreamed of going to Italy together! But they would never see each other again.

Sara Liba and Marutha had finally made a tentative date for a rendezvous in Italy. It was near the end of 1922 or the beginning of 1923. Marutha was talking more and more about the trip and each time she talked about it, Moshe became more adamant in his opposition to her going. Finally, he absolutely refused to let her go, and they had a tremendous row. A few months later Sara Liba Sher died.

Marutha went about, pale and drawn, for days. She said nothing. She did not complain. She carried on her chores as if nothing had gone wrong. Yehudi watched his mother suffer and wished he could go out, find Sara Liba and bring her home with him. He could not accept the idea of death.

Yehudi says that after the Sara Liba incident, Marutha developed a genuine aversion to watching her husband eat at the dinner table, even though the family always ate together. Moshe wolfed his food down, like a Russian peasant. Marutha meant to be dainty and noble.

Many years later Yehudi began to suspect that the greatest evil of Sara Liba's death may have been what it did to his parents' marriage. Marutha never forgot that Moshe had denied her the last chance she had to see her mother alive.

As mentioned, Marutha hated her father. But she never admitted that he was a *shokhet*, a kosher chicken butcher. Marutha insisted he was a Tartar, but in actuality he was merely a pious old Jew. He left Sara Liba and his young daughter in Russia to go to the Holy Land. He lived there with a woman who was more a housekeeper than a wife; living alone was a sin to an orthodox Jew like himself. He also lived in the United States for a while, collecting money for the Holy Land and ministering to Jewish families as a *shokhet* in order to make a living. He was miserably poor and lived while in the United States with a woman who had a mute son. No one is sure who that woman was or even if she was perhaps the same one with whom he had lived in Palestine.

A portrait from the twenties of Marutha and Yehudi

Once, while Marutha was still a young girl, she went to visit her father in Waukegan, Illinois. She arrived with a big steamer trunk full of fancy clothes and no money. She impressed some of the local girls in that small town, not only because she knew ten or so languages, but also because she could discourse on art and music with great sophistication. When it was suggested that she get a job as a salesgirl, she said with horror, "Me, a shopgirl?" The idea was instantly dismissed. Yehudi says "Marutha must have certainly been a remarkable meteor, traveling at so young an age between Tel Aviv and London and Waukegan." Marutha didn't stay long in Waukegan. She returned to Palestine to be with her mother.

The insistence that there is Tartar blood in Marutha's family line has always been the cornerstone of her strength. Her husband could never match her vanity, pride or ruthlessness. The word Marutha used was "Cherkess", or Circassian, a warrior tribe of Tartars who rode out of the Caucasus Mountains. These warriors had incredible strength; legend says they were almost superhuman. Marutha thought she had that strength, for she announced that she would be capable of having a baby at eighty, if she wanted one. Once, when Yaltah was sick in the hospital in New York, the first thing Marutha said to her on coming to see her was, "True Menuhins don't have such illnesses."

Where did Marutha get the idea that she was a Tartar? That is one of the puzzles of the Menuhin family. Perhaps during one of their genocidal raids the Tartars visited some poor Jewish village, and a Tartar warrior had raped and then spared a pretty Jewish girl. Marutha's insistence that her father was a Tartar may have stemmed from a desire on her part to inflict some sort of perverse psychological punishment on her father for having left her and Sara Liba in Russia when he went to Palestine.

At first, various relatives of Moshe's were amazed that any Jew would claim to be a Tartar, since they were one of the peoples who would swoop down and murder Jews by the score. Still, there may have been more truth to Marutha's claims for her father's Tartar ancestry than it might appear at first. During the Dark Ages in Russia there was a tribe of Tartar Jews who were called Khazars. Not much is known about them, and much of their story appears to be legend. They were partly Asian and lived in an area of the Ukraine in the Caucasus between the Volga and the Don. For two hundred years, they remained the most important independent state outside the Byzantine Empire. In the eighth century the Khazar ruling class had become Jews. By the eleventh century, however, the Khazars had disappeared. There is a current theory (Arthur Koestler's) that Khazars are the ancestors of modern Eastern European Jews.

Perhaps it was from this legend that little Marutha in Rostov-on-Don imagined her own legendary Tartars. She never tired of telling Yehudi about the great Cherkess tribe. All the Menuhin children were raised on that tradition.

Nonetheless, Moshe's relatives in Israel today knew Nachum Sher and insist he was simply not a Tartar. One relative said, "The Tartars were our killers, and when one Jew wanted to insult another Jew, he'd call him a Tartar." The relative smiled and added, "Unless, of course, that is the very reason why Marutha wanted her father to be a Tartar." Once Marutha even engaged the famous Zionist rabbi Stephen Wise in a debate over Yehudi's Jewishness. She argued that he was not Jewish since she was only "half Jewish."

Marutha claimed to be not only a Tartar, but a Tartar princess. Tartar princesses must be a determined lot then, for not only was she aristocratic, combining fierceness with elegance and determination, but she expressed these virtues by wearing corsets even though she had a slim and attractive figure. Another quality of Marutha's is, according to Yehudi, that she never forgets or forgives. Fierceness, along with great virtues, were somehow united in Marutha's scheme of things and in the values she impressed on her own children. It was only later in life that the children began to suspect that the peculiar code against which their parents judged all things might not be the epitome of universal wisdom after all.

But even if, in their moments of adult reassessment, the Menuhin children have become a bit cynical about the unusual value system their parents had given them, that system must be given some credit. As regards the relatives outside the immediate Menuhin clan, it is not surprising that they, like Marutha, cannot forgive or forget their treatment by the elder Menuhins.

SIXTEEN

Patronage and Politics

I N THE SUMMER OF 1925, after two years as Yehudi's teacher, Persinger announced that he had to go to New York for a few months, for professional reasons. This presented a crisis. Yehudi was an unusual phenomenon; everyone was quite aware of that. But Moshe and Marutha had not yet realized how much his precocity would affect their future. Moshe was running his schools with a great deal of energy and success, and Marutha was establishing her natural hegemony over the home and the children. Then Persinger dropped his bombshell.

This time Marutha said she was going to go. The Italian episode would not be repeated, she vowed. Moshe would not give up his job, so Marutha packed her three children and their belongings, and on a cold, rainy night, the four of them boarded the train for New York. Moshe looked as if all the world were coming apart, and he was powerless to do anything about it. His wife and children were leaving against his wishes.

Moshe was not anxious to give up his career for his son's. He was not even sure his son should have a career. To this day Yehudi is convinced that it was his mother's courage prevailing against his father's indecisiveness that gave him the chance to develop as he needed to. Whatever the truth may be, it happened that Moshe's chance to truly test his own educational theories would come, not with other people's children, but rather with his own.

There were brief attempts at public education for Yehudi and Hephzibah. These, however, were resoundingly unsuccessful. Hephzibah was an even worse failure in public school than her brother was. Yehudi reported feeling terribly out of place, but Hephzibah (who had started to play the piano when she was four) was sent home by the teacher, who had concluded that her intellect was subnormal because she would do nothing but sit and stare.

The decision was made to make the children's education a family affair. Judging by some of Yehudi's responses, the parents knew what they were up to. When Yehudi was once asked what his favorite game was, he answered, "Oh, handball and arithmetic, but I like history, too." What educator could feel displeased with such a remark from one of his students?

In model Summerhill School fashion, the oldest child was allowed to put his energies where his own mind directed him rather than into the forced, "rounded" molds public school officials impose on their students. Yehudi has said that he thought about little other than the violin. At first Persinger would not let him practice more than half an hour a day. Eventually he was allowed four hours, but Yehudi didn't consider even that enough.

Was this the right way to do it? "I am not sure, even now, that this is a sensible regimen for young musicians," Yehudi says. He seldom went to movies or listened to the primitive crystal set radio, or read the funnies. There were exceptions. "Blue Sunday", a jazz tune that was the rage (people actually committed suicide over it), was popular with the Menuhin children. Yehudi also attended the first movie with sound shown in San Francisco. He believes it featured Al Jolson, which would have made it "The Jazz Singer."

He attempted to read the funnies on three consecutive Sundays, but ended up deciding that they were an alien element. He satiated himself with them quickly, "somewhat," he says, "in the same way one eats truffles and then stops."

I was a violin player; I heard that everything had to come from within; there could be no escape for my emotions except in making music. And so I had to live on a constant level of emotional containment and await a performance to blow off steam.

Perhaps this is not the way to grow. But it was the path that had been marked out for me. In due course I was to have a very full and very happy life, but I wonder if, well . . .

Here Yehudi's voice dropped off.

Perhaps part of the reason Moshe had such terror on his face as the train pulled away from the station, aside from the thought of losing his family, was his belief that there were thousands of potential Yehudis. The key was in how they were taught and raised. If he ended up following his family to New York, and eventually forsaking his own career, his chance to prove some of his ideas would be gone, or so he believed.

In New York, Sammy Marantz, the Menuhins' dear friend and former student, tried to make up for Moshe's absence. Sammy, who had grown up considerably in the years since the Menuhins had gone West, read to the children and played chess with Yehudi, who had learned the game from Persinger. Sammy was always willing to play hide-and-seek on the regular dewy morning walks the family took through Morningside Park. On most weekends Sammy slept in the front room of the Menuhins' apartment, between two chairs that always seemed to separate by morning. His back has never been right since then, he says.

Moshe's appearance a few months later, joining the family in New York on a short leave of absence, was welcomed by everyone. It also served to get Yehudi's career going again, for he gave the impetus to get Yehudi's New York debut on January 17, 1926, at the Manhattan Opera House. Moshe objects to biographers who say he had arranged the concert. He points out that there was a professional manager involved. But he and Sammy spent several nights before the concert folding and sending out programs.

It is hard to guess exactly why Moshe was so upset at the mention of the large role he played in that debut, save that he did not want to be revealed as a master mechanic in the legend trade. His Hassidic ancestors had had an ideology of Divine Rights that would have made a mere monarch blush, and certainly Yehudi deserved his acclaim.

Moshe must have been rather galled by the fact that his son's debut rated only a three-paragraph story on the back page of the

New York Times. But the concert was far from a failure. The audience responded enthusiastically as Yehudi played a Handel sonata in E major, the first movement of the Paganini D major concerto, and short pieces by Bloch, Sarasate, Lalo and Dvorak. Still, the *New York Times* story had the feel of something dashed off by a tired, cynical rewrite man who was reporting on a miracle that had taken place somewhere far away. The *Times* noted that the audience was composed of curious musicians, who seemed quite impressed. It did not mention that the fathers of violinists Elman and Heifetz were present. So was Walter Damrosch, the conductor of the New York Symphony Orchestra, who was a kind of early-day Leonard Bernstein.

The Menuhin family did not feel that New York was a very friendly place. There were good times, of course. Moshe and Yehudi spent considerable time at the home of Dr. and Mrs. Garbat. Mrs. Garbat had been the Rachel Lubarsky of Moshe's student days, when Moshe and Marutha used to visit her home with other students from Palestine for tea, in 1916. Now the Garbats were continuing that tradition. Not only were the Menuhins frequent visitors, but other musical luminaries such as George Gershwin were often present.

Yehudi was becoming well-known in New York. He had played for Mischa Elman and the great violinist had called him a genius. People came by most evenings to visit, but usually Moshe would come in and usher everyone out of the house quite early with the simple, firm comment that it was Yehudi's bedtime, and nothing must disturb his rest.

As soon as Persinger was done in New York, the Menuhin family happily packed their bags and went home to San Francisco. Moshe, who had wrangled only a short leave for himself, was back at work for the time being. Yehudi was back impressing large audiences. Redfern Mason of the San Francisco *Examiner* declared:

> This is not talent; it is genius. It is the combination of vision with a nature magnificently normal... He is just a boy, but such a boy as we may imagine the prophet Samuel to have been, who heard the voice of God in the night watches.

Various San Francisco patrons and patronesses decided to give a tea for Yehudi, where he would perform. They offered the purse for his musical education of $5,000. The plans were cancelled and tempers raised when the Menuhins refused to attend. They declared that Yehudi was no itinerant musician who needed to play in people's homes.

And once again Sydney Ehrman approached the Menuhins. This time he did so in person, right after a concert. Ehrman came with his daughter Esther, with whom Yehudi immediately fell in love. Succeeding where others had failed, Ehrman convinced the Menuhins that they should accept his help. Marutha said she thought that being a prodigy might ruin Yehudi's life. Besides, she continued, she had two other children to raise. Ehrman emphasized that his offer was for the whole family, that they really could not say no because the boy's talent belonged not just to them, but to all the world.

Finally, after further talks with Ehrman and then Persinger, the Menuhins accepted Ehrman's offer for complete support of the family. They would go to Europe for further education.

Oddly enough, about the time that the nine-year-old boy was the talk of the town in San Francisco, a cousin of his, Joseph I. Schneersohn, the sixth generation Lubavitcher rabbi, was being released from a Soviet jail. The grand Jewish patriarch was leaving Russia and migrating via Paris to Brooklyn. People still remember the rabbi's arrival there. He was an important man, and the fact that he was coming to Brooklyn was an historic event.

No one took any notice of the fact that the little boy causing a similar excitement in sunny, far-off San Francisco was the rabbi's relative. Moshe certainly wasn't going to mention it. If anything, Moshe was a socialist, and his heart was more with the Revolution. No doubt he would have preferred the rabbi to languish in the Soviet jail. Moshe wrote in a now defunct San Francisco daily that his son was "a socialist humanitarian at heart, who can suffer vicariously for others."

The Menuhins' stubbornness in at first refusing to accept patronage was, at least superficially, related to politics. Even the young prodigy was political. One day he and a friend were walking through foggy Golden Gate Park and his friend suggested that Eugene Debs was a notorious lawbreaker and anarchist. Yehudi strongly contradicted his friend, saying that Debs was "not only a lover of humanity but a lover of human individuals."

Today Yehudi insists he belongs to no "ism" because "plans induce a blind, uncompromising following who become pedantic, didactic and eventually brutish." Yet he was becoming increasingly aware of the world's woes and he had dreams of saying things that needed to be said in order to help produce universal happiness and goodness. As a youngster, Yehudi fantasized it thus: he would awaken late at night, dress and sneak to the front door, where he would slip away from the house and run through the darkened streets of San Francisco until a new light would dawn. It would be in that daylight that he would rally the world to a new state of con- sciousness where evil was gone and good prevailed. But Yehudi never really opened the front door. He stood behind it and projected in his mind that search through the darkened streets, somewhat the way poor old Diogenes went looking for an honest man. Then, suddenly, "reality" would return, and Yehudi would slink back to his bedroom and become very, very depressed. The nine-year-old prophet would never find words quite as powerful as the sounds he could bring forth from his violin.

The young genius' sense of a mission in his life obviously came from Moshe, and Moshe's resistance to patronage was rooted in that sense of mission. A tale told by Ernestine Black of the *Call-Bulletin* goes as follows: She once trailed Moshe, without his knowing it, to the San Francisco office of Yehudi's manager, Alice Seckels. Hiding outside the door, she heard the excitable Moshe indignant at the manager for even mentioning a ten thousand dollar offer she had received that would merely require Yehudi to put in an appearance at a vaudeville show. "No, not even if we needed bread; Yehudi will never be exploited. Tell them no!" Moshe's voice, says Ms. Black, "sounded like the voice of the prophets crying out against the sins committed against children." Moshe knew of sins committed against children.

As the Menuhin children grew older, they became very aware that some nation was expelling or killing some minority somewhere in the world at any given moment. They knew of such things because their parents had been among those expelled. And that is the fact that made Moshe's and Marutha's lives ultimately so Jewish, even if neither was anxious to claim their heritage. Throughout Jewish his-

The three Menuhin prodigies in the early thirties

tory, the theme of exile is the one recurring motif. Refugees are a constant refrain in Yaltah's speech—it's as if my mother is always seeing long lines of refugees with nothing but a few belongings on their backs, making their way to who knows where. Moshe's obsession is the Palestinian refugee, a ghost stalking the Middle East, dispossessed, miserable.

A story my mother often repeated is a scene from her childhood. She, and her brother and sister were taken deep into a diamond mine in South Africa. The mine owners where showing the famous children where diamonds came from. But instead of diamonds, the children remembered only the gaunt faces of the black miners. My mother learned that you don't have to be a refugee to be oppressed. The blacks were the indigenous population in South Africa, after all.

Moshe drew the political conclusions for the children—conclusions that helped mold their thinking. Moshe would go out of his way to point out some of the inequities in the things they were seeing. That's how they got such a sense of social justice—Moshe had it. Marutha's sensibilities were different. It is a little ahead of our story, but when the Menuhins later lived in Europe, Marutha would buy the most beautiful tapestries from Armenian refugees from the Turkish holocaust who literally carried all their possessions on their backs as they spread out over the face of Europe, and later America. My mother has always been disgusted by the fact that to Marutha, who had herself once been a refugee, the misfortunes of the Armenians meant no more than the fact that they enabled her—Marutha—to obtain such beautiful things for so little money.

IV
CITIZENS OF THE WORLD

SEVENTEEN

Enesco and Carnegie Hall

WITH THE HELP OF Sidney Ehrman, the Menuhin family arrived in Europe in 1926. Persinger hoped that his prize student would study with his old teacher in Brussels, Eugene Ysaye. Yehudi, however, had heard Georges Enesco play the violin in San Francisco, and his heart was set on having him as a teacher. Since Marutha had raised Yehudi to believe that he was a Tartar, and since "Tartars don't run with the crowd," he was encouraged to trust his own judgement.

In retrospect, many people have suggested that Yehudi would have been better off with Ysaye than with Enesco, who, while a brilliant musician (he was, of course, a brilliant composer as well as a pianist and violinist), was less concerned with fundamental technical matters. Later in life, as I have indicated, the fact that Yehudi had learned so quickly in his youth would come to haunt him because no one insisted that he then learn fundamentals. His teachers felt that to have had him learn scales would be like asking an advanced mathematician to study multiplication tables. Yet after hearing him, Ysaye warned Yehudi, "You would do well to work on your scales and arpeggios." Yehudi hardly took notice, however, so set was he on Enesco. He had merely gone to Ysaye out of deference to Persinger.

Ysaye had been quite willing to meet Yehudi, but luckily for Yehudi the Menuhins were prudes—they considered Ysaye too colorful to be a teacher for the boy. Ysaye's house in Brussels was on a lovely tree-lined avenue, but they found it to be in total disarray. Ysaye himself was in an advanced state of aging, and his young wife was very much in evidence. He was a weary man with hardly enough energy to lift his massive arms. But when Yehudi played Lalo's "Symphony Espagnole," Ysaye sat up. Yes, this was great playing. Ysaye was impressed, and pleased too, for Yehudi was the student of one of his own students, Persinger. He asked Yehudi to become his student, but Marutha said she would first have to discuss the matter with Moshe back in Paris. Mother and son quickly left the depressing surroundings.

Back in Paris, Yehudi saw a poster on a wall advertising an Enesco concert at the Salle Gaveau. Yehudi's parents took him to the concert and afterwards the small, plump boy, not yet eleven at the dawning of 1927, went backstage and approached the great Enesco by himself. "I would like to study with you," he said simply.

Enesco, always a gentleman, looked down at the boy and said, "I'd love to teach you, I'm sure, but I travel a lot and have very little time. In fact, I must leave Paris tomorrow at six in the morning."

"All right," said Yehudi, "I'll come at five."

Yehudi was at Enesco's apartment at 26 Rue de Clichy the next morning, and when he played for Enesco, he was accepted as a student then and there.

Also as a result of that early morning audition came Yehudi's first European engagement. Cellist George Hekking had been present both the night and morning of Yehudi's first meetings with Enesco. Enesco and Hekking stared at each other in amazement as the boy played. Enesco left that morning on a month-long tour, but Hekking went to talk to his friend Paul Paray, conductor of the famed Lamoureux concert series. Paray's initial reaction was that he did not want to hear another prodigy. Finally, though, Paray agreed to hear the boy "for Enesco." Two weeks later, Yehudi played his first concert in Europe.

It was not well-advertised, but it was a complete triumph. Yehudi came onstage beaming, pink-cheeked and clad in a white sweater and black pants. At the end of the first movement of the "Symphony Espagnole," the audience burst into applause. Even the orchestra members lost themselves, and some were weeping. Paray, normally a very shy man, snatched up Yehudi after the performance in an uncharacteristic outburst and kissed him on both cheeks.

After his performance, a newspaper tried to start the legend that the boy wonder from the wild West had been taught by an American Indian. The editors assumed that Louis Persinger was an Indian because he had been raised in a Colorado mining town.

Back in San Francisco, the news of Yehudi's European triumph reached ready ears. An expatriate pianist named Mallory Dutton wrote home to the newspapers about the phenomenon:

> His face changed as if by magic to a face completely absorbed in the concentration of his art. The audience broke loose in a frenzy of wild applause after the first movement. We have heard Heifetz, and although Paris worships his perfection, his success was not comparable to Yehudi's.

On Enesco's return, his first suggestion was that Yehudi study harmony, fugue and counterpoint. He also began to emphasize something else to the boy: "Do not imitate me, but hear and consult other artists as well, so that your own vision will not be unduly influenced by one of us. And above all," Enesco counseled Yehudi, "don't listen to criticism or praise. Do not look level; look above the adoring crowds to a remote star."

The lessons began with Yehudi playing while his master sat in a large chair in the corner of the room. Sometimes Yehudi would stop because he had caught a glimpse of disapproval in Enesco's eyes. Enesco would smile and say, "Ah, there!" but he would not tell Yehudi what he thought was wrong. Yehudi would have to find that out for himself. He did.

Their lessons knew no time schedule. Often they would simply play chamber music for hours, discussing the works at great length. Enesco wanted Yehudi to learn to keep in mind the personalities and the aesthetic tendencies of the composers. He advised Yehudi to read biographies of the composers, to understand what each work meant to them and what they wanted it to mean to humanity.

Enesco would advise him:

> Absorb deeply the ideas and the moods of these composers to try to impart their spirit to the audience with the self-effacement required for the projection of the ideal pursued by them. Read about the history of music, its evolution, the part played in that evolution

by different masters, but remember all books are incomplete and biased.

Yehudi learned his lessons well. Years later he would say:

The task of the interpreter is to strike a balance between the work of the composer and his own conscience. He is ever trying to fill to the utmost with his own essence another man's form. In no circumstances may he distort the form, yet in order that it may re-live, it must contain the reality of his own convictions and his own emotions.

Although Enesco taught him how to be an interpreter, he did so by imparting the very secrets of creation. For that very quality of improvisation that Yehudi describes in Enesco's playing has always been his. Yehudi says that when he first had seen Enesco play in San Francisco, it was as though he were improvising the music; and that is what Enesco taught Yehudi—that to play he must recreate the music out of the nameless void where all creativity begins.

Yaltah remembers Enesco as a man who could play any music at a glance and remember it instantly. Once when Yehudi was having a lesson with him, Ravel burst excitedly into the room and wanted Enesco to play a piece of his music right then and there. The publishers wanted to hear the music. Enesco asked Yehudi if he would not mind the interruption, then sat down and played the Ravel composition perfectly. When he had finished, he asked Ravel if he could play it a second time, and did so without the music.

Yehudi says that Enesco could perform such feats with all kinds of music, right up to Schoenberg. He could play any opera, symphony or chamber piece "in the most inspired fashion on the piano using various auxiliary means such as whistles, grunts and singing to convey the full impact and breadth of the score." He orchestrated the horns with his grunts, the violins with his singing and whistles.

Enesco's playing had a gypsy quality, an "impetuous, emotion-filled expressiveness." Again it is interesting to note that Yehudi could just as well have been talking about his own playing, and the music of his Hassidic ancestors. Rumania, where Enesco came from is on the very border of East and West. Enesco also had a fascination with Oriental music and had even sat in on sessions of Ravi and Udi Shankar in the thirties. In Paris, Enesco took Yehudi to hear Balinese music at the great Colonial Exhibit.

Georges Enesco spoke of the way Yehudi played Mendelssohn: "He can give free reign to the Oriental something which is in every Jew, but that won't do with Bach and Beethoven. They're emotional, too, but in a restrained, classical way." Enesco was the reason Yehudi was drawn to Europe; he wanted to study with the great Rumanian composer, perhaps because that man represented the Oriental influence Yehudi was searching for. To the child that Yehudi still was, Enesco must have looked like a Roman emperor. In Yehudi's words, his head was topped by "a shaggy crown of black hair," and he was "tremendously tall and romantic-looking." To Yehudi, Enesco could have been one of his mother's Tartar horsemen, yet his soul was mystical and musical, not violent.

On one of the trips that Moshe and Yehudi took to Enesco's Sinaia (Rumania's summer capital in the Carpathian Alps), they visited a gypsy camp. Yehudi remembers being fascinated by "the absolutely natural way the music spoke, by the way it imitated bird song and other natural sounds." But Moshe was listening in amazement because the gypsies were playing the "Jewish melodies" he had sung as a child!

Marutha, too, was a carrier of the Eastern influence, and it most showed in her trunk of costumes. She was fascinated by ethnic clothing, and costumes were a part of her abundant fantasy life, the theme of which was a hunt for the exotic. Marutha had always wanted a Chinese grandchild, for instance, and Yehudi's daughter, Zamira, provided her with a great-grandchild by marrying (and later divorcing) the Chinese pianist Fou T'song, by whom she had a son.

Of course this Oriental essence that all Jews carry and that Yehudi seemed to express so well, has been noted before. The great Martin Buber said that if you peer into the soul of any Jew, you would find there an Oriental element. In Yehudi's case, the Oriental influence came primarily from his mother. The intellect came from his father.

Toward the end of their stay in Europe, the family moved to Sinaia, where Enesco had his home. One of the first things Yehudi noticed was that everywhere—in the marketplace, the monastery and the forests—there were pictures of Rumania's boy king, Michael.

Yehudi knew, of course, that Queen Marie, Michael's grandmother was beautiful and had been generous to Enesco.

But one day on the castle grounds, Michael's carriage, pulled by two white horses, came thundering down the narrow path at great speed, obviously expecting that anyone on the path would jump out of the way. The Menuhins were picnicking on a slope above, and Yehudi picked up a stone and threw it at the carriage. He says now, "It was more a symbolic gesture than in earnest." He not only resented the boy's haughtiness, but he was also jealous of the king's horses, toys and servants.

On another day, a guard was showing the Menuhins the throne where only the king was allowed to sit, and Yehudi could not resist the urge to run up and throw himself down into the great chair. An outraged guard and an anxious Moshe removed him.

A few days later, an invitation came from Queen Marie herself. She asked Yehudi to come and play for her and have some tea. Moshe and Marutha rejected the invitation because they thought it beneath their son's dignity to jump at royal command.

But the Queen finally did get to hear Yehudi. She arranged with Enesco to show up at his home, Villa Luminisch, while Yehudi was having his lesson. She stayed on the floor below him, but she could still hear him quite clearly. When he was done, Yehudi came down the stairs and saw her. He did not bow or kiss her hand—he merely shook it. Yehudi had probably been reading Mark Twain, most especially *A Connecticut Yankee in King Arthur's Court.*

"This is probably the first time, Yehudi, that you have met a real queen," Queen Marie said laughingly.

"Oh no," he replied quickly. "In America every woman is a queen."

This is a good demonstration of Yehudi's democratic spirit, but he also had strong aristocratic instincts. His great ancestors had mustered the dignity, glitter and mental presence to present themselves on equal terms with the Czars. Yehudi may not have been overly impressed by the Queen, but after he played, and when they began talking, he found himself a ready admirer of hers nonetheless.

If Yehudi was not overwhelmed by Europe's monarchy, America's Presidency was even less impressive to the boy. One fine afternoon some months after his experience with the Queen, Yehudi and Moshe were guests of that great and most profound gentleman,

Calvin Coolidge, the President of the United States. Who can say what banalities he directed at the boy, all instantly forgettable, no doubt. But it is recorded that as Yehudi and Moshe and congress-woman Florence Kahn left the White House, a conversation took place. The congresswoman turned to face the building, over which the sun was setting. Wasn't it a beautiful sight? she asked the young violinist. Yehudi pondered her question. Yes, indeed, sunsets are always most beautiful sights. "But," he said, "don't you see the pale, fatigued faces of hundreds of men and women leaving those offices for home?"

The reports out of Europe about the young prodigy were just not believed in New York. Many technically proficient youngsters had sprung up. They played a few times and were quickly forgotten. They were novelties, to bring in the audiences, much like electronics is the novelty used to bring audiences into concert halls these days. Fritz Busch, conductor of the New York Symphony, had himself been a prodigy, and he was something less than enamored of the thought of having to perform with Yehudi, "another prodigy." No, he was not looking forward to having to conduct a concert with such a monster. But on November 25, 1927, he did so at Carnegie Hall.

Meanwhile, while still in Sinaia, Moshe had rather rashly promised Yehudi that he could perform the Beethoven Violin Concerto as part of his program at Carnegie Hall. The concerto is a piece of music often regarded as the most profound in a violinist's repertoire. But Busch, on hearing this heresy from the Menuhin camp, wired back that he was not going to allow Yehudi to play the Beethoven and noted rather dryly that he also would not allow Jackie Coogan (the popular child actor) to play Hamlet.

When Busch and Yehudi met face-to-face, it was in full view, with all the attendant indignity, of a corps of screaming, scuffling press photographers, bawling at "the kid" and the conductor to stage various poses. Busch barely contained his disdain for the photographers and for Yehudi. The only reason he was submitting himself to the concert at all was because Walter Damrosch insisted.

Damrosch was the orchestra's permanent conductor, and he had been at that ill-attended but increasingly famous New York recital Yehudi had given a couple of years previously. He told Busch that

Yehudi was no typical prodigy, that there was real greatness in his playing. Damrosch too, however, tried to talk Yehudi out of playing the Beethoven. Yehudi had not heard of the Jackie Coogan reference yet because Moshe had not shown him the telegram. So Damrosch asked the rather cruel question—could Yehudi imagine Jackie Coogan playing Hamlet? Yehudi agreed that he could not, but he insisted that he could do the Beethoven.

Busch was upset at the boy's arrogance, as were various New York critics who had heard of Yehudi's desire. Damrosch warned Yehudi that if he could not live up to the work, it would mean the end of his career. Yehudi just nodded stubbornly. He did not care about a career, he just wanted to play the Beethoven.

That evening Yehudi went to Busch's hotel room, violin in hand. The rest is history. After he had played awhile, Busch threw his arms around Yehudi and said, "You can play anytime with me, anytime, anywhere!"

Olin Downes, the *New York Times'* music critic, came to the Carnegie Hall concert intending to stay for no more than the first movement. He was in an apathetic mood and expected merely another attempt to launch a child prodigy. He ended up rewriting his review three times that night. He tore up the first copy because he thought it was too exhuberant. The second—well, he knew the boy deserved better. He let the third one go through, but he feared it would make him the laughingstock of his profession. He simply could not believe what he had heard. "It seems ridiculous to say that he showed a mature conception of Beethoven's concerto," Downes wrote, "but that is the fact."

Other critics were even more lavish in their praise. The audience was hysterical. Orchestra members were weeping at the sight of the chubby little fellow in short pants, playing with a golden tone touched with a brightness and, it has been said, a resonance no one has matched since, not even Yehudi himself.

EIGHTEEN

The Sisters
Follow Their Brother

AFTER CARNEGIE HALL, YEHUDI'S success story became almost monotonously magnificent. Where once the family had been afraid even to pursue Yehudi's career because of money problems, they were now turning down more engagements than they accepted.

Yehudi began his first tour with fourteen cities on his itinerary. Joyfully, Moshe was able to tell the Ehrmans that their kind support was no longer needed. In 1928 alone, Moshe turned down some two hundred thousand dollars in concert fees. Some of those came from the Soviet Union, and they apologized for offering only six thousand dollars per concert. Yehudi, however, hastens to say that the newspaper figures were quite exaggerated, admitting that his father sometimes fell victim to a tendency to aid the process. Yehudi says that with a few unusual exceptions, his highest fee was twenty-five hundred dollars a concert.

In the year 1928, another Menuhin, eight-year-old Hephzibah, played her first recital on October 25 at San Francisco's Scottish Rite Hall. She had been a student of Lev Shorr and Judith Blockley for eighteen months. Then, in Europe, Marcel Ciampi had become both Hephzibah's and Yaltah's piano instructor. When Marutha had first approached Ciampi, he was annoyed with this woman and her two oddly dressed daughters. Marutha's announcement that Hephzibah was already, at seven years of age, a three-year veteran of the keyboard, did not prove to be the right thing to say. But when Hephzibah sat down to play, and then Yaltah, who was a year younger, Ciampi turned to Marutha and pronounced his fabled words: "Madame, your womb is a veritable conservatory!"

Hephzibah's first concert came about because she asked why she shouldn't have one. After all, she argued, her brother had given his first concert at an even earlier age.

Hephzibah was an immediate sensation, not only on account of her playing but also because the press saw that the Yehudi Menuhin phenomenon was being repeated. The little girl was obviously quite intelligent. There are those who insist to this day that her influence over her brother equals that of Marutha or Yehudi's wife, Diana. On the eve of twelve-year-old Hephzibah's first New York recital, newsmen were invited in for tea and were treated to a royal dose of the little girl's uncanny coolness. She asked what all the commotion was about, and suggested that the recital was really only another evening of practicing with Yehudi. "Yehudi and I are going to have a lot of fun tomorrow night," she announced.

Two years later Hephzibah and Yehudi played in London at Queen's Hall. There, for some reason, Hephzibah was less self-assured, according to some critics, who said she clung to the hand of her brother. But then, says Yehudi, she always held his hand onstage. Her playing was at first nervous, but then she gained confidence. She did not look at the audience, gazing only at her brother in mute devotion. The audience, some of whom had paid up to ten pounds for a ticket, hardly got a glance from her. After the concert, Marutha quickly ushered her away from the crowds, saying, "Darling, home to bread and milk."

The world also waited for Yaltah, for it was known that she, too, was a fine player. At the time of Hephzibah's first concert, Yaltah had been playing for five months. Many critics were becoming aware of Yaltah's talent, and there had been predictions that she too would soon be concertizing.

There was never any suggestion in the Menuhin household that Yaltah could play publicly, for while her brother and sister were being groomed, Yaltah was told that two Menuhin performers were sufficient. If she were going to give a concert, that would only be exploiting the name of her brother and sister. She was told, "Make yourself useful."

Yet many old family friends said Yaltah was the most talented of the children, the most temperamental and spontaneous. Today, as I've said, Hephzibah believes Yaltah is the most intelligent of the three. Whenever people were at the Menuhins' house and Hephzibah played for the guests, little Yaltah would always run in and say she could play, too. With great persistence she kept practicing despite her mother's objections, and she made her debut with the San Francisco Symphony at ten years of age.

Marutha's third pregnancy was unwanted, and this fact was to affect Yaltah's entire life. Her brother and sister did not always treat her well, either. After all, Yehudi and Hephzibah were still children, and, despite all the attempts by their parents to cordon them off from the outside world, they were aware of the adulation heaped on them. Yehudi never read reviews of his concerts. He was kept unaware of the extent to which he was adored, except that he must have felt his power to move his vast audiences.

After the Carnegie Hall performance, Yehudi quickly became the biggest attraction on both American and European stages. He was the child every parent wanted to have, and still he could be mean to his baby sister. While Hephzibah was a prim and proper young lady with a cool, appraising manner, Yaltah was always the unlucky one.

No, the three children may have been miracles, but they were not angels. Not only did they tease each other unmercifully, and still do, others got that treatment as well. They teased poor Ernest Bloch, the great Jewish composer, half to death, though he did not realize it. Once on shipboard, Bloch spent two days looking for the Menuhin children, who were making a game of avoiding him. Although they were all quite friendly with one another, as Bloch had lived in San Francisco for a goodly part of his life, he could be an insufferable bore about his problems. "He was much easier to take in death than in life, I am afraid," Yaltah remembers.

A number of times Yaltah tried to get her career going and has received something less than encouragement from her brother and sister. They may love her, but they still regard her as the little one. Yaltah's life has been difficult, but her love for her brother has overcome whatever jealousies might have otherwise been expected. She has always been overshadowed by her brother and even by her sister, yet her own playing is indisputably fine. She is quite aware of

SONATA RECITAL
Presented by
MIRIAM ROSENTHAL CONCERT MANAGEMENT
SUNDAY — 8:30 P. M.   JANUARY 7, 1951
DAYTON ART INSTITUTE MUSIC HALL

Yaltah concertised many years with violinist Israel Baker

the attendant psychology. Anyway, Yehudi was a difficult person to be jealous of. The sturdy little boy responded to the applause of thousands with little sign of conceit.

Audiences and critics soon learned to stop thinking of him as a child prodigy. Increasingly, once they were accustomed to the novelty of one so small playing so profoundly, his actual age became irrelevant. The overworked word "prodigy" became meaningless. He seemed a mature musician, who not only struck people with his violin virtuosity, but also with the depth of his musical understanding. He also had an invigorating effect on the world around him, for suddenly there were prodigies everywhere, and some really great ones, such as Ruggiero Ricci. A nine-year-old boy violinist named Grisha Goluboff played in Manhattan in 1931, but soon disappeared. In Berlin that same year, a six-year-old girl pianist named Ruth Slenczynski made a big debut. When she was one and a half, her father used to sit her at the piano and make her pray, "Please, God, make me the world's greatest pianist." She did make for herself a modest musical career.

What was different, the very real miracle of Yehudi's playing, as Bruno Walter recalled of Yehudi's April, 1929, Berlin debut, was his "spiritual mastery and maturity." It was at that same concert that Albert Einstein went backstage and hugged Yehudi, saying, "Now I know there is a God in heaven."

Yaltah thinks that Yehudi's aptitude for the violin was something of a reaction to the "Talmudic traditions that circumscribed his personality." For him, Yehudi says, music was an escape. Perhaps had he been encouraged to follow more typical boyhood patterns, such as going to movies and brawling with neighborhood kids, the violin would not have been so all-consuming. But that might not have been possible for Yehudi, even if his parents had wanted it. The parents, however, wove a cocoon from which none of the Menuhin children seem to have escaped even in their rebellions. The musical career of Yaltah, especially, never matched her talents because of the tightness of her parents' weaving.

NINETEEN

Moshe and Yehudi's Mentors

MASTER THOUGH HE SEEMED at such an early age, Yehudi still needed to learn more. He was really to have only two great teachers. From Enesco he received a depth of musicianship, but not discipline and technique. For that Enesco recommended Adolph Busch.

Moshe did not like Busch, just as he disliked Toscanini (who would, not so incidentally, return the favor). The Menuhin family moved to Basel, Switzerland, during Yehudi's stay as a student of Busch, the tall, blond master violinist, who was very much of the German classical school. Busch's concern with his students was often very personal. He wanted them to join his household, and that Moshe would never tolerate. When Busch "discovered" pianist Rudolf Serkin, Busch's wife Frieda encouraged Serkin to marry their daughter. He did, and it turned out to be a good marriage.

Moshe and Busch had a strong disagreement. Moshe, Enesco and Busch's brother Fritz all argued that Yehudi should be concertizing. Busch felt that concerts and repertoire were not important. He instead wanted Yehudi to return to the original manuscripts of the great composers in order to understand their intent.

Yehudi spent two summers with Busch, and although he had to unlearn much of what he had already learned, he felt those years were absolutely essential to his development. But to him the difference between Enesco and Busch was the difference between poetry and prose.

Yehudi was not particularly upset when he left Busch, however much he felt he may have gained from him. Moshe may not have been entirely unhappy either.

Moshe was the reason Yehudi would see little of Toscanini after their great friendship began at a meeting aboard the S.S. Rex in 1932. Toscanini had heard Yehudi's Carnegie Hall concert, and the two spent all their time together during the voyage. Whenever they were on deck, crowds gathered, so they locked themselves in a stateroom, had the stewards bring plenty of coffee, and spent hours playing music and discussing the classics.

"Just imagine our trunkful of scores, all of Bach's works, Mozart's, Beethoven's, Schubert's, laid out on the tables. We are the happiest people on board, and I believe Toscanini is happy over this unlooked-for meeting," wrote Moshe, who sat in on the sessions and perhaps embellished his accounts. These music sessions began at eleven and ran well into the afternoons. Yehudi would beg Toscanini to criticize him without hesitation, for those would be "my most precious lessons," he said.

But after he played the Kreutzer Sonata, Toscanini had only this to say:

Yehudi, *caro, bravo! Bravissimo!* This is perfect. This is real music. How you have grown since I heard you three years ago; your heart, your mind! Oh, how little good music I hear in my life! Come, my child, play, play. Go on and on. Your singing is so natural, so fine!

One can see how close was the feeling between the two. Yehudi offered him much in return, including introducing Toscanini to the little-known Mozart Concerto No. 7. The cruise ended with Toscanini giving the lad a bronze, inscribed medal; Yehudi presented the maestro with a picture of himself and Busch. Yet the two ended up spending no time together afterwards because Toscanini was one of those who did not get on well with Moshe.

Marutha also entered that fray when Toscanini invited Yehudi to come see him in his country home on Lago Maggiore at the base of the Italian Alps, a short distance away from the Mediterranean coast where Yehudi was vacationing. Yehudi was delighted, but Marutha insisted that if the maestro wanted to see Yehudi, he should come to Yehudi. She reminded Yehudi not to forget his dignity with Tos-

The literal translation of this autographed photograph from Toscanini reads: "To dear Lionel with wishes that he grow up handsome, healthy and strong in the love of his mother. (signed) Arturo Toscanini, February 26, 1945"

canini, for he, Yehudi, was also a great maestro, she said. A flurry of letters was exchanged, but the reunion did not take place for another two decades, after Toscanini had retired.

Moshe was always present, and not always unobtrusively. Once he took conductor Thomas Beecham aside at a rehearsal and rebuked him for having made a rather innocent remark about a woman in Yehudi's presence. If something offended his strong moral sense, nothing could keep him from being outraged—not kings, queens, conductors or agents.

Moshe had made a great commitment when he gave up his own career as an educator and undertook to devote himself solely to his children, and he was jealous of what little was left of his role as an educator now.

As they traveled together on concert tours, Moshe would take a red pen and mark out the stories in the newspaper which he thought his son should read, none of which ever happened to be on the sports page. Many, many years later in Israel, Batja was telling me about Moshe, her "former" brother-in-law, and she said that she felt he had had a diabolical influence over his son. She thought that keeping him from reading such things as the sports page kept him from growing up as a well-balanced boy.

Yet another observer of the father and son together said that Moshe's influence on his son was magical. He would wave his hands over Yehudi's eyes to make him take a nap. Was this hypnotism? "It wasn't a deliberate act; it was rather a joint submission to an age-old injunction." Yehudi gave this response when I asked if he thought his relationship with his father was peculiar. This injunction originates, perhaps, in the unstated Jewish tradition of the father's absolute authority over his children.

Concertgoers at the Royal Albert Hall in London used to swap stories about the sight of Moshe glowering at his son from his little seat right behind the curtain. The legend was that Moshe hypnotized his son into playing well, and that were he to go away, Yehudi wouldn't play that way any longer.

This wasn't quite so. But to Moshe, everything was an excuse for a moral. If he was explaining to you how to handle a chicken or learn the multiplication tables or pull weeds, it was always accompanied by a lecture illustrating the relationships he saw in things.

He wasn't so much a Svengali as he was a philosophical dictator.

TWENTY

A New Life in the Old Country

I N THE FIRST HALF OF THE thirties, the Menuhins lived and traveled in Europe. Their home base was Ville d'Avray in a pleasantly wooded but sometimes cold and foggy suburb of Paris.

Yehudi and Moshe ventured forth from there on tour and a legend of an "Einstein of the Violin" was being created, along with legends of the hypnosis variety. Naturally, the world was curious about what went on at Ville d'Avray. Moshe explained Yehudi's genius as the result of perfect harmony reigning in his immediate surroundings. The notion was mystical. "Show me a perfect union and I will show you a perfect child," he said.

But life at Ville d'Avray seemed more strange than perfect. For one thing, there was Marutha, who acted out her exotic fantasies with her costumes, which to the two girls, who had to wear them, seemed more like old rags. "It was Marutha's sense of style, not economy," Yehudi explained. Clothes were much more than just clothes to Marutha.

More than one person had the experience of being led to a bath-tub by Marutha at the end of the day and being ordered first to take a bath and then a nap. She would then take the victim's clothes and insist that the victim (always female) wear one of her, Marutha's, costumes around the house. The two sisters loathed this habit, and so did the few girlfriends who came to visit them at Ville d'Avray.

"We looked like the original hippies," Yaltah explains. Being garbed by Marutha meant you certainly would be colorful, if nothing else.

Marutha always seemed to have the house in an uproar over this or that crackpot theory of nutrition. One such diet—no doubt the rationalization for it was as fanciful as was Moshe's theory of precocity in children—consisted of eating two foods, spinach and bread.

Another one of Marutha's quirks involved the benefits of shaved heads. She, who had been plagued with baldness and subsequently wore wigs, shaved her own head and wore a turban. She also thought it appropriate to shave Yaltah's head. Yaltah herself believes it was more as a punishment than it was for the supposed benefits. Moshe claims it was because Yaltah had tried to cut it herself and had botched it, so Marutha decided to cut it entirely. Whatever the truth, Hephzibah and Yehudi cut theirs off, too, to protest Marutha's actions.

Meanwhile, the children were growing more political. Marutha referred to her three children as "my little Bolsheviks." Once on a train Yehudi turned to his cousin Sonia, who was traveling with him and Moshe on a concert tour, and said, "Isn't Communism wonderful?" Marutha recommended a good, long trip to Russia for her brood, where, she said, they would discover that no "ism" means anything, "not so long as the individual stays selfish, greedy and stupid."

One starlit night Yehudi, still an adolescent, was given his first taste of love. Marutha locked his cousin Sonia in a bedroom with Yehudi and supplied both of them with Emerson's "Essays on Love." Marutha, peeking into the bedroom through a crack in the door, called over her cousin Edie, Sonia's mother, and said, "Isn't that sweet?" But Edie was not amused, thinking the whole thing too absurd. "Don't they look innocent?" Marutha asked. Edie replied that she didn't feel right looking in, and walked away.

It was innocent, of course. Yehudi read the book, and Sonia listened attentively. Neither knew what it meant, and they felt awkward.

Later that night, Yehudi and Sonia out on the balcony were

Marutha and her daughters in Paris in the early thirties

staring at the stars. Yaltah sneaked up behind them, kept quiet for a while, and then, very loudly, exclaimed, "Why, you two aren't doing anything interesting at all! Why don't you kiss?" Yaltah may have been the most sensitive of the children, but she was the one always getting into mischief.

Sonia is one of those many people who has spent her whole life loving Yehudi intensely. Her mother, called "Aunt Edie" by Marutha, was famous for her parties in London. In her Baker Street apartment, one could often find writers, musicians, actors and politicians. Her husband, Sonia's father Jack Miller, had made his money in the last century controlling the tobacco shops in the London subway stations.

No one is sure of the actual relationship between Marutha and Edie. Edie grew up a wealthy girl in London; Marutha, the poor cousin, visited her there. These must have been the "rich relatives in London" of whom young Marutha boasted to the impressionable girls in the small Midwestern town when she came from Palestine to America to visit her father, Nachum Sher.

The Millers and the Menuhins became quite close. Jack used to buy Yehudi's clothes, which Moshe ordered with instructions to buy only the very best. Moshe was a firm believer in the economy of quality and workmanship. Moshe and Jack seesawed back and forth for years over buying the tickets to Yehudi's concerts. Jack would offer to buy tickets for his family but Moshe would invariably give them to him gratis. Sometimes Jack would bestow a gift upon Moshe, such as a fine watch. Moshe wrote back to Jack that he had become a convinced and walking advertisement for that particular brand of timepiece, and that Jack could make a million selling them.

Moshe would often ask Jack and Edie to send clippings, or to deliver his letters about Yehudi to the press. Moshe and Marutha's letters to Jack and Edie, the only living family the children were ever told they had, were full of talk about the day-to-day problems of concert life, of arranging hotels, of whom to trust, of what the itinerary was, of what the reception had been.

Sometimes Moshe would include what he called "Jewish news" in his letters to the Millers. "I find myself too aggressive...I should hate to become an object for the WORLD SOCIETY AGAINST JEWISH AGGRESSIVENESS," he wrote in one letter written during the thirties before the holocaust, as Nazism was on the rise in Germany.

Another constant theme of Moshe's concerned his wife. "Poor Marutha, how tired she is from all her work." While it was true that Marutha worked hard, and was always the first up and the last to bed, so busy was she with running the house, Moshe's talk of his gallant, weak little woman "just didn't answer," to steal a quote from Mark Twain. "My own aim in life from now on, ideal and purpose, is to see my Marutha happy and healthy, and there will be no compromise of any nature on this," Moshe said.

Yet Moshe's main interest in life remained his son's career, of course, and that meant guarding against prying outside eyes. Sonia often traveled with Yehudi and Moshe on tour, and Moshe worried about how this might look.

> I have been watching the scandal sheets for "stories", and they would be missing their Calling if they were not to exploit their LAST chance to Tell some new story about the "innocent" Yehudi Menuhin who is no more a child, as he was seen, Sir, with a nice young girl, at his Intermission, in his car, and in the hotel room.

In Edinburgh, as so often happened, the car carrying Moshe, Yehudi and Sonia was mobbed. Photographers hung on the running boards. Moshe made Sonia get out of the car and make her own way back to the hotel, but nonetheless the next day the newspapers blossomed forth with speculation about "the woman in young Yehudi's life."

Sonia came to love Yehudi, but it was never romantic. It was philosophical love that Marutha felt she was teaching when she locked them up with the Emerson essay. The hint of anything beyond Platonic love was cause for alarm. Sonia remembers trying to make a date with a young man for a tennis game at Ville d'Avray. Marutha heard about it and made Sonia call back and cancel the date.

Sonia says that Yehudi's playing in his younger days was different than it is now because Moshe was a perfectionist, and valued "clarity of mind above all else." She says that the parents provided that for their children who were then "three happy children." Later, that over-protectiveness may have felt like a prison to the youngsters as they became adults and looked back on their childhood. But then, that protectiveness may have been beneficial and perhaps even the key to Yehudi's powers of expression. Maybe there was something, after all, to Moshe's version of why his children were prodigies. The irony might be that by being so successful with his prodigy children, he was sowing the seeds for problems in their adult life.

Yehudi's cousin, Sonia Miller, did these sketches of Yehudi in London in the forties

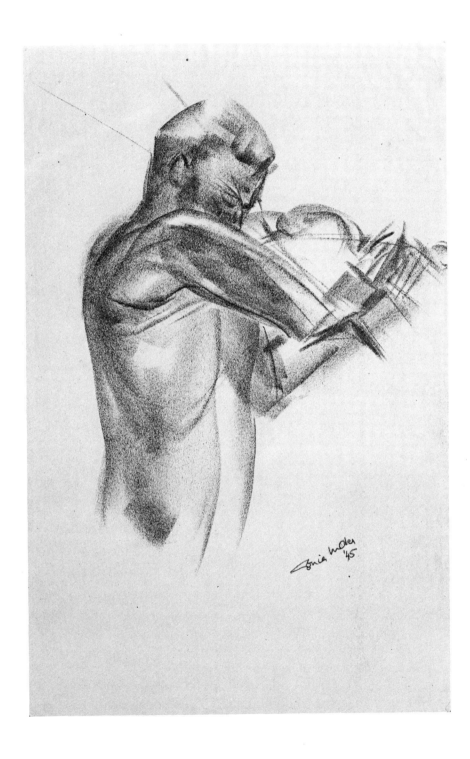

TWENTY-ONE

The Maturing Artist

ONE OF THE PRIVILEGES and joys of being a young Menuhin was to grow up with some of the greatest minds in the world. If Moshe denied his children a "normal" childhood, still they were given much of genuine value. The Menuhin "court" may have had some fakers within, but there were also some great human beings.

One of the most famous intimates was Willa Cather, author of *Death Comes For The Archbishop*, who, although raised in Nebraska, went to Europe to seek her roots. She became fascinated by the Menuhin children, and they by her. Moshe and Marutha loved her, and Willa was one of the very few people Marutha allowed to become very close friends with her children.

Moshe, too, approved of Cather. He liked the book she was then writing, *Shadows on the Rock*, because its heroine is a woman who commits suicide. Moshe identified with that very much because of his sister Sonya's suicide. Willa Cather had intended to dedicate the book to Yehudi, Hephzibah and Yaltah, but changed her mind after Sammy Marantz told her that the parents were overly sensitive to unbecoming attention being paid to their children.

As I've already said, the elder Menuhins felt their greatest job to be guarding the children against intrusion, and it took the concert agents in London considerable persuasive effort to convince Moshe and Marutha that their children should be "introduced." It was done at carefully arranged parties, where the guests would come in one at a time and talk with Yehudi.

Aunt Edie was honored when allowed to invite "a few people" to meet Yehudi. Her Baker Street parties became the object of envy for other London hostesses of the period. So jealous was one such hostess that she barged into one of Edie's parties and tried to convince everyone there to come over to hers. She was unsuccessful.

Yehudi was already beginning the worldwide concert tours that would fill the whole of his life. In fact, he was booked for three years' worth of concerts at the height of the great world Depression. When he and Moshe would return from these concert tours, they would find the household in full swing. In a sense, the two girls may have had a better education than Yehudi, who, in looking back on those days, says that his only real interest was his instrument.

That is not quite true, of course. Willa Cather spent hours with Yehudi and his sisters. With extra money coming in, all the Menuhins began traveling, and Willa sometimes worried that with all their traveling and speaking so many languages the children would never have a good grounding in English. She organized a Shakespeare club for the girls and for Yehudi who asked to be included. It was Willa who provided the children with their first real instruction in literature and philosophy.

There were many hours of music. At Enesco's suggestion, the famed duo of Yehudi and Hephzibah began. In about 1933, they gave a few concerts, but Marutha made such a point of insisting that a woman's place is baking bread and raising children that there were far fewer concerts than either wanted.

Still, they spent hours playing chamber music with Enesco. Sometimes Yehudi would play second violin, and the music-making would go into the wee hours of the morning.

Years later the great Gregor Piatigorsky was to report having been shaken on his first meeting with the Menuhin children in Europe. Later, as I was growing up, my mother would take me often to Piatigorsky's home in Brentwood, a small suburb of Los Angeles. They would play chamber music. Piatigorsky has said that meeting Yaltah was a great experience. It's hard for me to think of Piatigorsky and imagine such a huge and magnificent-looking creature as he was being shaken by anything. When he first met Yaltah, he had wondered what the conversation should be about with a five-year-old child. Yaltah didn't give him time to think of something trivial to say. She asked him what he thought of Schopenhauer and then plunged into a philosophical conversation, which the great cellist thought very astonishing.

During this period, around 1935, Yehudi, who was almost twenty years old, was practicing two or three hours every day. But there would always be some time in the open air. Once there was even a month-long auto trip when the violin was left behind. Yehudi began to find a life-long fascination with mechanical gadgets, and he would blacken himself with grease fixing things. He was especially fond of Dusenbergs and bicycles.

He would also sometimes suggest to his mother that knowledge gained through experience might be better than that from his ivory-tower existence. But Marutha retorted that one learns best from the mistakes of others, not one's own.

These were especially heady times for Yehudi. In Switzerland, on holidays, the Menuhins lived in Madame Prevosti's house in the Fextal near Sils-Maria, a thick-walled, two hundred year-old farm house. They had three cows and five goats that were looked after by local peasants. All the milk and cheese the family could eat was provided, and everyone, especially Moshe, had an enormous appetite.

At a nearby lake, Yehudi would swim out about half a mile and stay there for perhaps half an hour, testing his endurance. Then he would come back and sit with his sisters on the beach, where they would read Dante.

Other musicians—Horowitz, Piatigorsky, Bruno Walter—and the author Emil Ludwig, also lived nearby. They would have serious discussions of the great political and philosophical passions sweeping across the globe in those innocent prewar days. Yehudi was increasingly concerned with moral and political problems. He drew an elaborate diagram in which principles of good and evil, perils of the flesh and beauties of the spirit, were all represented in geometric form. He also became a life-long devotee of Spinoza.

He was quoted in the newspapers as declaring,

Some day, maybe not in my lifetime but some day, people will live in a world where machines take the monotony out of life. There will be no stupid tasks, such as driving taxicabs, working in mines, doing any sort of thing because of the necessity of existing...Above all, there must be education, education in how to employ leisure time in a world which will offer mostly leisure hours...Life would not be so terrible if it weren't forced, and it is not fair that any human being should be forced to work set hours, day after day. If such a system marks civilization, it would be better to return to the wild life.

Yehudi also began, in his quiet way, to see something of what was happening to his people in Germany. "What will they do with Heine?" he asked. "They're burning his poems, but they will still remember him." Marutha added, with irony, that the Nazis were going to substitute the German pagan god Wotan for Yahweh.

In 1934 Wilhelm Furtwängler, the director of the Berlin Philharmonic Symphony, had asked Yehudi to "restore the breach between Germany and the world of music and art" by coming to play there. But Yehudi, who had loved the Berlin he first saw as a child, discovered that politics is a very real component of art. Furtwängler had asked him to separate politics from the arts, and he begged Yehudi to come and play in Germany to prevent "Germany's descent to the dogs musically." Yehudi replied that as long as there was a ban on the great composer Mendelssohn because of his Jewishness, he could not play in Berlin. However, after the war, Yehudi defended Furtwängler from charges that he was a Nazi.

Furtwängler was sincere in his beliefs. He had defied Joseph Goebbels by defending such famous Jewish artists as Bruno Walter and Max Reinhardt, and he would come to save the lives of most of the Jewish members of the Berlin Philharmonic. Nonetheless, he remained at his post under Hitler while his Italian counterpart, Toscanini, spat in the face of Mussolini.

Shortly after Yehudi told Furtwängler he could no longer play in Germany, the family made ready to return to the United States. Yehudi looked forward to going home. For one thing, he was bothered by the news from California that his very own San Francisco Symphony was letting musicians go. There were other purely American things that he missed. He said he disliked jazz, although now he doesn't know why he thumbed his nose at it. He actually liked "Blue Sunday." Yehudi was going to come home and even try to play the saxophone—in private.

America was beckoning the Menuhins homeward.

TWENTY-TWO

Alma and Mother's Year

THE YEAR I WAS FINISHING this book, 1976, which was the year of Yehudi's second sabbatical in half a century of performing, Alma was sold. Yehudi's original intention had been to someday retire to the hundred-acre estate in the Santa Cruz Mountains, about sixty miles south of San Francisco.

Over a long and tortuous history, all the dreams for Alma never came to pass. Moshe long ago conceived of Alma as the home of the Menuhin "court," and there he would live, attended by his grand-children and their spouses, who would also reside there. But this was not to be.

When the Menuhins returned to the United States from their world tour in 1936, they purchased a large house in the orchard- and grapevine-covered hills next to the Sacred Heart Novitiate in Los Gatos, near Santa Cruz. The place was to be a temporary home while Alma was being built. But Alma would somehow never work out right for the Menuhins. Rather than becoming a court of culture, with great musicians from around the world coming to live and work there, the big house has remained virtually unused, full of furniture, yet with the windows covered and the interior in mothballs. Yaltah calls it a cursed place. Alma was to be the consolidation of a dream but marked its crumbling instead.

Alma was purchased for a mere $30,000 in those terrible Depression years. The chemistry went wrong for the elder Menuhins from the first, when artists Frank Ingerson and George Dennison, who lived next door to Alma in a place aptly called Cathedral Oaks, agreed to design the house. The Menuhins first stayed with the couple as house guests in 1935, but the elder Menuhins did not get along with the easygoing, civilized (and homosexual) pair. The children, however, loved them. They would walk up to Alma's adjoining acreage where the artists were designing the grand house, Villa Cherkess, which would be Alma's main house, named in honor of Marutha and modeled after the great house Marutha insists she was born in.

When Frank and George finished the plans for Villa Cherkess, Moshe had second thoughts about the cost of building the villa at $60,000. Eventually, though, the villa was built for Yehudi and his first wife to live in. Except for a brief while with each of his two wives, Yehudi has hardly ever lived there. The man with some of the best memories of the place as a music center is Adolph Baller, who for many years was Yehudi's accompanist. He says that he loved all the Menuhins, but that he is convinced they are all people "with strange nervous systems," and difficult to be around. The guest cottage at Alma is called "the Baller Cottage" in his honor.

Realizing that Alma would never live up to their dreams, Moshe and Marutha settled in at Rancho Yaltah, their comfortable five-acre Spanish-style home in Los Gatos. Here Moshe would putter among his plants and flowers, chickens and goats, and write his bitter, anti-Zionist letters and tracts.

The retreat from Europe to America had culminated with the family dropping out of public view. Marutha wanted the Menuhins to live together for a year as a "normal family" before each went out into the world again. She called it "Mother's Year."

It was obvious that the children were growing up, and Marutha wanted her offspring to have early marriages. All sorts of carefully screened young men and women were to be found in the house next to the Novitiate.

Yaltah's older brother and sister were more ready for marriage, as she was just beginning adolescence. To her, 1936 was different

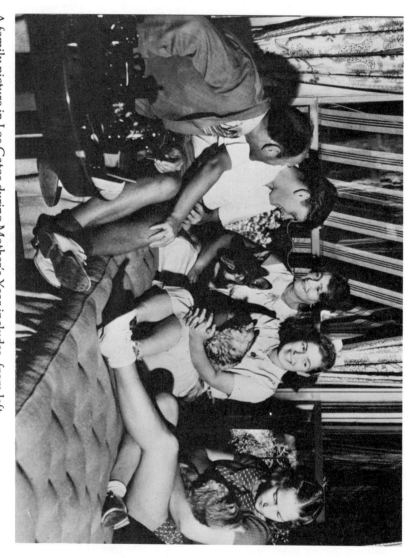

A family picture in Los Gatos during Mother's Year includes, from left to right: Moshe, Yehudi, Marutha, Yaltah and Hephzibah (plus pets)

only in that concertizing stopped. Music was not totally put aside, but hiking, reading, swimming and political discussions became routine. (Moshe was strongly for Roosevelt, a gentleman Marutha considered little better than a Bolshevik.)

Yaltah's relationship with her brother and sister remained unchanged; she was an awkward third. Yehudi and Hephzibah would take long walks, often on a rather dangerous water trough built on the sides of the hill next to the Novitiate up towards Alma, a few miles away. The two would walk hand-in-hand reciting poems about nature and man, picking flowers along the way. And always Yaltah would bring up the rear.

Yehudi's first sabbatical, "Mother's Year," attracted a lot of attention from the press. The *New York Times* said of twenty-year-old Yehudi that he would

> devote himself to spiritual exercises, as young squires did before being admitted to the order of knighthood. The decision is wise, and those who derived pleasure from his meteoric appearance as a precocity (sic) must hope that the retirement will bring to maturity those powers of heart and mind which can, if properly cultivated, turn a great violinist into a consummate artist. Just now Yehudi has reached a period of transition; neither child nor man, he has lost the divine simplicity of the former without having laid the foundations of the individual style that is necessary in the grown man.

The childhood innocence was gone from his playing, and the song from his violin had become listless and lethargic. The music came more from the head than the heart.

There were some traumas ahead for Yehudi. Henry Goldman, who had donated the "Prince Khevenhuller" Stradivarius to Yehudi early in the boy's career, was now hospitalized and blind. No longer able to attend Yehudi's concerts, which had been one of Goldman's great joys, he asked Yehudi to come play for him. Yehudi desparately wanted to but to do so would have violated one of Marutha's principles—that he never play anywhere but in a concert hall, and certainly not for patrons or royalty. Yehudi relented after an argument, and he went to visit Goldman without his violin, but the hurt stayed with him. Enesco, who normally did not interfere with what he called the "Biblical Menuhin family," took the liberty of chastising Marutha over the incident, but Marutha merely said that, well,

Yehudi would soon be getting married, when he found the right girl, and then he could do what he felt was right.

A number of people noted Yehudi's growing restlessness. Even more, there was his growing rebelliousness. Once he slammed the door of the car so hard that the window shattered. Perhaps Marutha was right. Yehudi needed a wife. Yet ordinary dating was forbidden to Yehudi. It was a daring step for him to take a girl out.

Some normal activities were acceptable: Yehudi was allowed to learn the tango. Hephzibah tried to teach him, but she said at last that he danced "like a duck." He took some ballroom dancing lessons, but there was a strange detachment in his dancing. He had a low opinion of swing, the popular musical idiom of the day. "I don't know whether I like it or not," he said at the time. "I think it's a state of mind. Anyway, I know it makes me drowsy."

Yehudi admitted a terrible desire to return to the concert stage. He told his parents, "I am restless. I feel I am losing touch with my public. You must get me some concerts." But Moshe and Marutha said no. Yehudi admitted that concertizing was an artificial life, with no seeming purpose other than to go on to the next concert. Still, violin playing is what he did, and all that he could imagine doing.

For the press, Yehudi emphasized the beneficial aspects of "Mother's Year." To the *New York Times* he explained, "Even if I were losing two years, it's better than spending the time in compulsory military training as they do abroad." That was before there was a draft in this country.

The San Francisco newspapers reported on the gay, almost frivolous life of the Menuhins. One of the young people around was Daniel Fleg, whose brother Maurice nearly became Hephzibah's husband. The boys were the sons of Edmund Fleg, the writer who had written, among other things, a libretto with Enesco. Daniel spent several weeks in Los Gatos. He was a rather sickly boy and got lots of nursing from Marutha. Fleg truly loved Yehudi, as do most people who spend much time around him.

In his diary Daniel wrote about moonlit walks, dancing and hours of chamber music, but he complained that he found Yehudi's respect and admiration for Moshe and Marutha excessive. This reference is found in an early biography of Yehudi, and Moshe had scrawled in the margin of one copy I have seen: "Poor, pathological, suicidal Daniel." Daniel did commit suicide, but obviously his comment in his diary about the relationship of Yehudi to his parents was a spark of treason in Moshe's eyes.

Yehudi knew that before he could make his instrument sing again, he would have to find out who he was. The fact that as a child he could play simply by instinct testifies to some clarity of vision and sharpness of emotion, but later in life, as Yehudi has admitted himself, the influences of adolescence and approaching manhood obscured the childhood clarity. It was not that his intuition was failing him, but just as a scientist first perceives a truth by intuition, then verifies it by deduction, so Yehudi now needed to analyze his intuition in order to save it.

Yehudi was at the time suffering no more than the pains that accompany the transition from boy to man. There is a lot about Yehudi today that suggests that the man never completely won. Enesco recalls that when Yehudi was sixteen he had warned the teenager that he must now become a man, and a look of utter terror spread across Yehudi's features. Enesco decided years later that Yehudi was a man who never stopped being a child, and it was not until later in life that Yehudi began tackling these problems, as we shall see.

The regimen of his first sabbatical was good for Yehudi and "Mother's Year" ended with a stronger violinist returning to the concert stage. He had accomplished this in part by indulging in the rare luxury of not even touching his instruments for weeks on end, even while his musical education was continuing.

One of Yehudi's major intellectual efforts during this first sabbatical involved research with original musical manuscripts. This fascination was partly inspired by his old teacher, Busch, who had emphasized the composers' original intentions. Yehudi loved to pore over manuscripts, point with glee to a stroke of the pen and speculate on the mood it might reflect. Thus when a German publisher, Wilhelm Strecker, sent Yehudi the score to Schumann's "Lost Concerto," the moment was right. Yehudi and Hephzibah played it through, and instantly Yehudi was convinced that it was the "historically missing link of violin literature," the work that came between the great violin concertos of Beethoven and Brahms.

Furthermore, as Yehudi delved into the work, which was written by Schumann in a few short months in 1853, just before the composer entered into a great and losing battle with insanity, he became convinced of its importance and virtues. "Schumann's last prayer was that his violin concerto, in a way the creation that laid bare his soul, be widely known," Yehudi wrote.

But the great violinist Joachim, for whom it had been written, felt quite the opposite and said in his will that the work should not be played for a hundred years, which would have ended in 1956. Joachim had known and worked closely with Schumann, and the strain of watching the composer's mind crumble into insanity made it difficult for him to consider this last major composition with any kind of objectivity. He thought it second-rate and wanted it buried in the archives of the Prussian State Library in Berlin lest it damage the composer's reputation.

But the more Yehudi studied the score, the more excited he became about the work. After a San Francisco recital in October of 1937, Yehudi ended his first sabbatical by playing the Schumann work in December, 1937 at Carnegie Hall.

The *New York Times'* Olin Downes, who had written so extravagantly of Yehudi's first Carnegie Hall Beethoven performance in 1927, now wrote of this latest performance:

> It was to be seen that in the intervals since Yehudi's previous appearances here things had happened. He first played like a child and a seraph. Then came the years of change, experiment, growth in various and perhaps at times conflicting directions at the hands of different teachers and in the working out of various ideas. No doubt the complete ripening is yet to come, but the performer of last night was neither child nor boy. He was a young man, and the change in his appearance was reflected in all the interpretations. He played with a power that never became mere muscularity, a fire that was not a matter of pyrotechnics, a sensitiveness and dawning poetry which show the forming of an artistic individuality which promises to fulfill all the expectations aroused by the earliest appearances.

However, Downes was not favorably disposed towards the work itself. He said it was the product of a tired man, that it had lost its spark, and chided Yehudi for insisting that it was an historical link in violin literature.

Yehudi rather enjoyed the conflicting views of the gentlemen of the press. Yehudi's reappearance was in itself big news, but the tale of the "Lost Concerto" added fuel to the fire. Everyone agreed that

Yehudi's performance of Schumann was masterful. About the work, however, some critics claimed to perceive signs of the coming incoherence and insanity that would plague poor Schumann's last days, while others concurred with Yehudi, saying that the work represented the real, noble Schumann.

Yehudi, now taller and slimmer, for the first time wore a full coat and tails. Hollywood rushed to cash in, and sent emissaries to Los Gatos with offers of thousands of dollars. Moshe issued a long public reply:

> Between Yehudi Menuhin's musical art and Hollywood, as it is constituted today, there is an abyss that cannot be bridged. The pure, simple, integral and complete art of Mozart, Bach and Beethoven, Schumann, Brahms and Hollywood's motion picture synthetic, commercial, made to order art, are two different irreconcilable worlds, which no fakir, no money and whitewashing can get together. The message of the masters of music is completely delivered through the medium of the talent of genius, plus a fiddle, strings and a bow, and no acting, dancing or dressing by male or female partners is called for to illustrate, elucidate or convey the immortal sonatas, concertos or symphonies of Beethoven, Brahms, Bach or Mozart.
>
> Other musicians can do what they please about films, but Menuhin will remain alone, an independent, freelance, pure concert artist, who will travel the length and width of our little world, with his Strad, from city to city and from continent to continent, bringing in person his music and message to the music lovers of humanity. Hollywood's scientific and financial process and triumphs seem to spoil the vision and sometimes even the decency of its promoters. No pot of gold will buy Yehudi's art to be prostituted for acting and dancing or any other sentimental dramatic concoction. When Hollywood will wisely awaken some day to recognize a new field of pure music, and will apply its technical, scientific and organizational talents and equipment to the field of recording in sound films honest-to-goodness, good and pure concert music, they will find an open mind on the part of the Menuhins.

Not too many years later, Yehudi would come to resent the stridency, if not the sentiment, of the statement his father made in his name, and would even toy with the idea of becoming a matinee idol. He did appear in one film, "Hollywood Canteen," and did the soundtrack for a film on Paganini called "The Magic Bow."

Moshe's statement may have been harsh, but at least one of his offspring still concurs with it. As I have already described, Yaltah, who spent many years living in Hollywood, believes that although many good musicians come to work in the studios, and despite Los Angeles' pretentions to being a music center, anyone who stayed there for very long was almost inevitably corrupted. "They all came and sold their souls to Hollywood," she says. Recently, however, Yaltah has modified these sentiments, since she now understands that having to make a living does not necessarily make one a corrupt human being.

TWENTY-THREE

Marriages

Yehudi used to say that the kind of woman he would marry would have to be like his sisters or mother. But the inevitable would happen. Just before the beginning of his sabbatical, Nola Ruby Nicholas and her brother Lindsay had gone to Yehudi's concert in Melbourne in 1935. Nola urged her brother to study Yehudi's handsome face. She wanted to go backstage but she was too afraid.

Nola eventually became Yehudi's first wife and Lindsay became Hephzibah's first husband. Despite the Nicholas' wealth, they did not measure up to Marutha's high standards. She called them "those peasants."

At a matinee at the Royal Albert Hall, on March 20, 1937, Nola and Lindsay again came to hear Yehudi perform. If Nola had been impressed before, she had more reason to be impressed this time. The pianist lost his score, and the concert was forty minutes late in starting. But Yehudi brought the house down by playing unaccompanied Bach, and the well-wishers and camp followers came backstage in even greater numbers than usual. The reviews were ecstatic.

After the concert, Yehudi was introduced to Nola and Lindsay backstage by Sir Bernard Heinze, conductor of the Melbourne Symphony. Nola was a robust, unpretentious young woman, and Yehudi liked her at once. He invited her and her brother to tea with himself and his family back at their hotel. This was easy to arrange since both families were staying at the Grosvenor.

It was only a slightly more complex task for Lindsay, Nola, Hephzibah and Yehudi to arrange themselves into two young married couples. After the tea the four went for a ride in Nola's new Jaguar, and over the next few afternoons and evenings they were together every chance an excuse could be found. Plainly, Yehudi was taken with Nola.

Yehudi was married to Nola Nicholas in Caxton Hall, Westminster, on May 26, 1938. More than two hundred needle-women had worked day and night for a couple of weeks to complete the bride's trousseau, the Associated Press gleefully dispatched.

Nola was a carefree young socialite with plenty of time and money to take shopping trips to Europe. Yehudi was a strange, intense young genius; he lived in deep waters and could see that existence with Nola might be pleasantly lived on the surface.

The year 1938 was an ominous one for the world, and probably the Menuhin who understood this the most was Hephzibah. Unlike her brother and sister, there was something tough about Hephzibah, as a young woman and as a pianist. Hephzibah's cold, appraising intelligence made her a match for her mother, but she is also a woman with a need to be dominated by her men. Her musical partnership with Yehudi suggests this, and her present marriage to her second husband, Richard Hauser, suggests it even more.

Hephzibah makes no bones about comparing Richard, a social organizer, to Yehudi. She believes that both are men of the same caliber, both deeply committed humanists, but Richard's work is social and political, while Yehudi's is primarily musical. Today, Hephzibah waits hand and foot on Richard, although Richard says things such as "My wife is too good for me," and "Frankly, all the Menuhins made lousy marriages." Hephzibah is an intelligent, capable, opinionated woman, but she defers to Richard's every viewpoint and enforces his word as law.

During my visit with Hephzibah in London in 1973, she told me of a conversation she and Richard had had while walking in Hyde Park. Hephzibah remembered another walk in 1938 with Maurice Fleg. Fleg had come to propose to Hephzibah, and Hephzibah had once loved him. But she told Fleg that she thought she was falling in love with her Australian suitor, Lindsay. So Fleg went back to Paris, and Hephzibah and Lindsay continued their courtship. Later Fleg was killed in a concentration camp.

As Hephzibah and Richard walked through Hyde Park, she thought of Maurice Fleg and speculated that if she had married him instead of Lindsay, she would most likely have been killed in the concentration camp, too. It is interesting that Richard, the man for whom she left Lindsay, bears a striking resemblance to Fleg.

During her courtship with Lindsay Nicholas, Hephzibah was anxious to get out of her parents' home; Australia and Lindsay were beckoning to her. She had not yet begun to think and care about the world, as she obviously does now. She was still, quite frankly, a spoiled young woman whose depth had not yet been plumbed.

The poor Nicholases, especially Nola, did not know what they had let themselves in for. Nola was, as has been said, an extravagant but unpretentious, vigorous Australian woman, whose father had invented an aspirin substitute that netted him a fortune during the First World War. But Nola was not as innocent as Yehudi. Not too many nights before their marriage, one story goes, Yehudi had made a witty remark in passing, and she had impulsively hugged him. He allowed her to do so for a few moments, but then he shyly disengaged himself. Hugging and kissing would be all right only after they were married, he said.

The marriage was arranged, of course, by the elder Menuhins. Moshe even undertook to tell his son about the birds and the bees, but he was too bashful about the matter, and so he asked Aunt Edie to obtain a sex manual which he could present to his son.

After the wedding, Yehudi brought his wife home to mother, who began organizing her daughter-in-law's life as well as her son's. Yehudi did not object. Hephzibah, however, had been trying to get away from home for a long time, and Lindsay was her big opportunity. Her sole interest in life would be playing music for Lindsay, perhaps teaching him Italian, and otherwise being a dutiful wife. This was her vision of her "Biblical marriage."

Although Lindsay owned a 23,000 acre sheep ranch, and would on occasion fly to London just for a special soccer match, life in Australia was simple. When Hephzibah had a miscarriage, Lindsay cared for her without the aid of expert medical advice. Life was very basic in the great outback.

Yehudi stands with his bride, Nola, outside Caxton Hall, Westminster in 1938

Nola probably began sensing her potential problems with Yehudi as she returned to the States with the Menuhins aboard the *Ile de France*—it was June of 1938. She was approached by the chief steward, who asked if she wanted her trunks in her cabin. Marutha answered for her: "No, they will all remain in the hold."

"But my evening clothes are in those trunks," Nola responded.

"You will have no occasion to wear them on this trip," Marutha replied.

That kind of thing would become a familiar refrain from Marutha, who would often inform Nola on the eve of Yehudi's concerts that she was overdressed. "This is Yehudi's performance," she would say. Once when Nola was pregnant and taking a bath, Marutha marched in with a neighbor. "That's my grandson," she announced proudly, pointing to Nola's stomach.

Nola was expected to assimilate into the rather severe Menuhin household schedule. Not only was she unaccustomed to such a life, but she must have found her treatment rather demeaning. Her husband was unable to do anything about the matter, because he did not know how else it should be. When Marutha reproached Nola for giving Yehudi a cold, Yehudi did not stand up to Marutha. Nola begged Yehudi to consider the idea of the two of them living somewhere else, even if just for a short time.

She finally convinced Yehudi that they must move away, at least as far as Villa Cherkess at Alma which was, by this time, finished and uninhabited. Only Yaltah was left at home with her parents.

Marutha had tried to arrange a marriage for Yaltah to the son of Keith Pulvermacher, then the editor of the London *Daily Telegraph*, on condition that Pulvermacher's son change his Jewish name. "Marutha," said the senior Pulvermacher, "that Jewish name has been good enough to get us into Buckingham Palace." The match never came to be.

Yaltah thought she had found her love, however. She was busy writing romantic letters to William Stix, son of a prominent St. Louis Jewish family. A young attorney for a Senate committee, Stix was in love with Communism at the time, as were so many others. Yaltah's marriage (she was sixteen) to Stix lasted six months. She says that she was a naive adolescent girl who had no idea that there was anything more to love than writing poetry. The shock of learning that this was not the case quite unnerved her.

Despite newspaper stories to the contrary, Yaltah was not happy to return to her parents' home after her short marriage. The two elder Menuhins and their daughter would sometimes drive over the hill to Santa Cruz, and there would walk on the beach. Yaltah went on hikes and wrote poetry. She also made some recordings in London with Yehudi, but she had no real career of her own. Nonetheless, music was the most important thing in her life. It is how she has always kept her sanity, she says.

To this day when Yaltah gives a concert, Moshe sends her the clippings, reminding her that the only reason people come to hear her is her name. When Martin Bernheimer, now the music critic of the *Los Angeles Times* but formerly of New York, reviewed a concert of hers and said that Yehudi and Hephzibah "had better watch out," that Yaltah was playing better and better all the time, Moshe did not send her a copy of that review.

Yehudi and Nola both took the unhappy sister under their wing, and arranged for Yaltah to live in Australia with her sister and Lindsay. But Yaltah decided on another course of action. She took the name of Kate Davis, the daughter of the publisher of the San Jose *Mercury*, whose parents were friends of the family, and ran away to New York, where she enrolled at the Juilliard School of Music. Her teacher there commented that for one with the name Kate Davis, the blue-eyed, blonde-haired young woman certainly looked Russian. He started calling her Katania. Soon he had her teaching other Juilliard students. For Yaltah, the "Kate Davis" episode was a personal triumph.

Yehudi, too was going through the process of making at least some breaks from his father. The task of informing Moshe that he was prepared to travel alone or with his wife was not easy for him. Yehudi knew how much his comradeship meant to his father on those tours. Nevertheless, Yehudi began taking care of many of the details of concert life that up to then he had not even been aware of. He discovered real joy in performing various tasks, even carrying his own violin case, something he had never done as a young prodigy. He also became a father. His daughter Zamira, named from the Russian word for peace and Hebrew for songbird, was born on September 29, 1939.

Certainly, it was not easy for the elder Menuhins to have all their brood run off. Hephzibah was by this time the mother of two sons, and Marutha would take great joy in the letters from Lindsay telling "What a grand little mother Hephzibah is." Yaltah did come back home again, after New York, and was again alone with her parents, without the companionship of brother or sister. She bided her time.

Although it was the eve of World War II, Yehudi and Nola seemed quite happy. In 1940 Yehudi took Yaltah, his wife and his daughter, and sailed for Australia to visit Hephzibah. They stayed at Lindsay's ranch and spent long hours making music. Nola gave birth to a baby boy named Krov, a word meaning blood in Russian and battle in Hebrew. The name was inspired by the Battle of Britain.

Yaltah returned to Los Gatos during the war, but she did not stay with her parents long. She went to a dance, met a young soldier named Benjamin Lionel Rolfe, and married him in Reno on October 18, 1941. I was born a year later.

TWENTY-FOUR

The Holocaust

IN 1937 MOSHE PUBLICLY denounced Zionism. He wrote a piece for the *American Hebrew* in which he called his former friends in Palestine "Fuhrers of Israel" because, he said, they were teaching Jews to be "intolerant of Gentiles." Since he was Yehudi's father, the press naturally took instant notice. It was the first of many articles in which he sounded what would become a familiar theme of his. "The greatest enemy of humanity is the professional nationalist and organizer, who exploits the innocent memories of a people, throwing salt and pepper into the tender wounds of torn humanity. God only knows how many parasites of this kind, professional Jews, thrive in our midst today," he said.

One gets the feeling that Moshe never did grasp what happened to his people through that holocaust. To him the one constant villain throughout was the "professional Jew." Moshe's obsession with the very term shows how powerfully personal the concept was to him. The "professional Jews" were somehow his tormentors. His uncle, or "grandfather," the rabbi, whom Moshe felt was the cause of his childhood sufferings because the rabbi had arranged his mother's second marriage, was the worst of them all. "Phooey on the Rebbe!" one can almost hear Moshe exclaim, then with that quick, darting mind of his go on to something else.

It may not have been a righteous position, or even an admirable one, but it was a principled one. Years later, when Moshe wrote *The Decadence of Judaism in Our Time,* his vanity press book, his old friend and patron Sidney Ehrman, then nearing a hundred years of age, wrote a preface to the book in which he spoke of Moshe's principles.

Of course Moshe could afford to be principled. His son's success brought him the opportunity to retire rather early in life. He had worked hard as a young man, so hard that in his thirties, Moshe had suffered a minor heart attack in Australia; yet he never stopped working. But now he could afford to write, think and garden in the comfort of Rancho Yaltah, his Los Gatos home.

How much was he changing? In 1938, Moshe was defending himself against people who said the Menuhins were anxiously trying to shed their Jewish identity while climbing up the social ladder. He pointed out that half of the friends who visited the Menuhins' home were members of orthodox synagogues. No, Moshe emphasized, what he was saying was a matter of principle, even if he was not above being affectionate with the people who counted, and nasty to those who didn't.

If Moshe operated from inner beliefs which had developed out of his own needs, so did his son. One of the most powerful and damning books about the holocaust was released by the United Nations just after the war. It was called the "Black Book," and was a massive study of the Nazi crimes against the Jewish people. It is a book that is impossible to read without feeling the monstrous horror of the crimes. A handful of influential Jews were responsible for the study, two of the most prominent were Albert Einstein and Yehudi Menuhin. One wonders how Moshe could ignore such documents and turn so ruthlessly against Israel.

One of the things that Moshe did years later and which Yehudi found especially hard to swallow was to write for a neo-Nazi newspaper in West Germany. Yehudi did not sleep at night for a time because of it.

By the time Yehudi, Nola and Yaltah had returned home from Australia, the war was in full swing. Much of the Europe which Yehudi had known and loved was either under the Nazis or fighting desperately not to be. A Lurline liner brought Yehudi, his wife and children and twenty-nine pieces of luggage home from Australia. He responded to the reporters' inevitable questions by saying his favorite hobby was being with his wife, and yes, he admitted to them, he had fallen from a horse which he had tried to ride in Australia.

He also permitted himself some philosophizing about the relationship between war and music, but only after emphasizing that "the message of music can only be delivered through music." He said that the influence of Africa, with its agitated rhythms, had been reflective of the world. He predicted that after the war the influence of jazz would lessen and some new form of music would evolve with melody that "would be the expression of a people's aspirations" and with a purer rhythm.

The war would be the beginning of Yehudi's real awakening, his maturity, for it brought home to him what he would later feel was the unreality of the world his parents had created for him and his two sisters.

Yehudi's draft board was split three to two in favor of giving him an exemption from the Army. Normally a father of two would have been given an exemption for financial reasons, but Yehudi did not have these. One board member said Yehudi was "just another American," but the majority voted with realtor John Whitsenant, who said that Yehudi was "overweight anyway, and besides, he could injure his hands by washing them or throwing hand grenades."

Perhaps it was the decision of the draft board that spurred Yehudi on to take the most dangerous and difficult touring assignments of any artist. Yehudi visited soldiers on the battlefield, young men his age, and saw, even if from a distance, the horror and ugliness of their lives. It was during the war that he first began to drive himself compulsively, as he still does.

The reality of the holocaust was also brought home to him by his close relationship with pianist Adolph Baller, who now teaches at Stanford University. Baller was a Pole, and when the Nazis took over his country, he was thrown into a concentration camp for the crime of being Jewish.

"What do you do?" the Nazis asked him. He replied that he was a pianist, so they took a hammer and methodically beat his fingers bloody.

Baller made a dramatic escape from the camp and came to New

York, where he was reunited with his wife. She had also escaped, but from a different concentration camp. Baller then came to California to meet Yehudi, and the two became close friends.

Baller had been a child prodigy pianist, making his first appearance with the Vienna Philharmonic at eight years of age, and he was an exceptionally good accompanist for Yehudi. The two of them spent the war years touring, although Baller disliked it. The slightest noise in a hotel at night would awaken him. He was not completely loved by the elder Menuhins, but then they were always uncertain of anyone their son befriended and whom they did not know themselves. Marutha used to complain that Baller played too loudly for Yehudi, but this was not true.

Yehudi's rapid maturation during the war was also an attempt to put behind him a variety of things his father had done, sometimes in his name, which he had found distasteful. None of the Menuhin children agree with their father's adamant anti-Zionism. They believe that it is the result of his bitterness over his childhood. It is apparent that Moshe is a bitter frustrated man; he is certainly often inconsistent to say the least. To me Moshe preached that the coming age would belong to the working man, not the intellectual. When it came to his son and the Musicians' Union, however, he carried on like the staunchest anti-unionist. Moshe wrote in a mimeographed tract:

> It is just as if you had demanded that husbands and wives hold Union cards and regulations to govern their privileges and duties together; or as if the Poets and Prophets of old, or Christ and the Apostles had been forced to get Union cards, and be submitted to blind Union discipline.

As far as most of the world could tell from stories in the press, the specific incident that sparked the whole controversy between Yehudi and the Musicians' Union was a concert at the Shrine Auditorium in Los Angeles which Yehudi was to play with the Los Angeles Philharmonic. The orchestra had recently been organized, and part of its contract stated that all soloists must be union members. Yehudi objected, saying that he was not against trade unionism, but simply that, as a solo artist whose only work was on the concert stage, his interests were best represented by himself and not by a union. As if to underline that he was not anti-union in principle, he pointed out that a good many of the family's friends in San Francisco thought of the Menuhins as "reds" and "Communists."

Actually the whole story was more complex. There were two competing organizations representing musicians. One was the Musicians' Guild, which Jascha Heifetz had helped organize. Yehudi says it was Heifetz who personally approached him in a New York hotel. They had a long meeting during which Heifetz argued that Yehudi should join the guild. Yehudi was somewhat shocked when Heifetz openly worried about the influx of European musicians after the war. Yehudi diplomatically stated that he would not join the guild at that time.

This endeared Yehudi to James Caesar Petrillo, head of the newly-formed Musicians' Union. Petrillo told Yehudi that he ought to quickly join the union and suggested that if he did, the biggest, best-paying concert that had ever been organized for a musician would be organized for him in Chicago. In addition, Petrillo promised Yehudi that he would get to meet "all the important people." He passed on Petrillo's offer, too.

The Musicians' Union under Petrillo had a constitution former President Nixon would have loved, Yehudi explains. Its first rule was that it is the president's duty to enforce all the regulations of the union's constitution unless he does not want to.

On June 8, 1942, Yehudi did join the union. That event was explained by Petrillo:

> There was Menuhin. He used to talk about his art and his God and his fiddle. Then one day, when he was supposed to play in Philly, we told the musicians that he didn't hold a union card, and they walked out. So now him and his God and his fiddle, they're in the San Francisco local.

During the war years Yehudi was showered with medals and honors by heads of state and even by the Pope. He played in factories and troop camps around the globe. When he met General DeGaulle in London, the French leader extracted a pledge from the violinist to give the first concert in Paris when that great city was liberated. He was the first foreign violinist to play in the Soviet Union—without State Department approval. He was received there like visiting royalty. People waited in line twelve hours to get tickets, and all of

Yehudi during his first "jam session" plays the St. Louis Blues in 1943. After the session, one of the players told his buddies "This guy Yehudi did all right"

the greatest musical luminaries came to greet him. Yehudi even had the somewhat strange distinction of surpassing Frank Sinatra's attendance record at the Hollywood Bowl during this period.

But the place that seemed to affect him the most was London. On one of his many returns from abroad, he talked of the "mystic and moving impression" he had watching the half moon over that blacked-out city. He was even optimistic about the buildings that the German bombs had levelled. "The damage has been so cleared up that one has the feeling that the space is being cleared to build finer future cities," he reported, naively. "How wrong I was," he adds now.

In 1945, in San Francisco, Yehudi played the Beethoven Violin Concerto to open the United Nations conference, and a few months later he played a charity concert in Berlin with conductor Wilhelm Furtwängler.

Soon after that, when he showed up to play a concert for 2,000 Jewish displaced persons, only fifteen were actually in the audience. The reason for this was that the D.P. camp newspaper had carried a signed attack by its editor, a man called Jonas of Lemberg, who objected in the strongest terms to Yehudi's appearance with Furtwängler.

> When I read of your "human" deeds towards "distressed German youth" and how your new worshippers applaud you, I knew that in your audience there must have sat those two passionate lovers of music Eppel and Kempke, SS men from the Kurewitz camp near Lemberg, who used to have us sing while they shot our brothers down... Wherever you travel, our newspaper will follow you like a curse until your conscience awakens.

The next day Yehudi insisted on turning up at Dueoppel Center, where he faced the two thousand inmates without his violin.

> I have played for the hard-pressed wherever and whenever I could ... You are truly victims of Nazism, but the tragedy is that you have become like the Nazis... You make your judgements on a racial basis; you demand that art and music be pressed into the cause of hate. Love and not hate will heal the world."

The inmates received this lecture in stunned silence, and Jonas relented enough to declare,

We know he does not mean to be a traitor. If Menuhin offered us a concert today, we would all go. Perhaps it is too much to expect that those who have not experienced persecution and camps should understand our feelings.

Yehudi argued for Wilhelm Furtwängler vigorously, pointing out that Furtwängler had been exonerated by a U.S. military court as well as by three different de-Nazification courts in Berlin and Vienna. You may remember that in 1934 Yehudi had turned down Furtwängler's plea to come to Germany. Now, after the war, Yehudi was defending him.

Yehudi says that he came to Furtwängler's defense in Paris quite accidentally. One of the orchestra members had told him that the only German musician the French would welcome would be Furtwängler. Furtwängler had very pointedly refused to play in occupied Paris. Yehudi mentioned this incident to a reporter. The next day, New York papers headlined his comments, making it look as if he had invited Furtwängler to come to America.

Yehudi also pointed out that Furtwängler saved the lives of numerous Jewish musicians and that the great conductor had never gone on Nazi propaganda tours, as did some other well-known German conductors who were politic enough not to get tarred with the brush of Allied doubt after the war.

This episode was the beginning of a difficult time for Yehudi. His self-image was evolving towards that of a citizen of the world, part of which involved an awakening to his own Jewishness, something the Nazis had forced on him. Almost inevitably, as have most Jews who became prominent secular figures, he was considered by other Jews as not Jewish enough. Naturally his father's strident anti-Zionism did not help matters.

After the Furtwängler affair, there was a full-fledged boycott of Menuhin concerts by many Jews. Furtwängler had been hired for a concert with the Chicago Symphony, and immediately a number of prominent artists announced that they would not play with that orchestra if Furtwängler made the appearance. Among them were Horowitz, Rubinstein, Heifetz, Milstein, Stern, Piatigorsky and Eugene Ormandy. Their position was well-expressed by Rubinstein, who declared, "I will not collaborate musically or otherwise with anyone who collaborated with Hitler, Goering and Goebbels."

Furtwängler's only supporter was Yehudi Menuhin. Yehudi said he would refuse to play in Chicago if Furtwängler was not invited. Furtwängler's invitation was withdrawn, and Yehudi did not play with the Chicago Symphony for years.

There is no doubt that the whole Furtwängler episode raises questions no one can easily answer. In Jewish law, only a victim can forgive, and this seems to make sense. Yehudi was not directly a victim of the holocaust, and his taking it upon himself to forgive Furtwängler, nay, to suggest that Furtwängler did not need forgiveness, is not an action I feel completely comfortable with. While I recognize that Yehudi's stand on Furtwängler was certainly a testimony to his Cherkess stubbornness and his "refusal to go along with the crowd," that does not convince me that Yehudi was right. Furtwängler was a great musician and an honorable man who thought he was fighting the Nazism engulfing his country. Yet the fact that he could even consider interpreting the noble stirrings and yearnings for freedom inherent in the music of Beethoven, for instance, in front of a monster such as Hitler, I cannot understand. But there are points in Yehudi's arguments that I cannot dismiss lightly, either. Certainly it must have been difficult for Yehudi to make political decisions given his father's extreme and contradictory positions on issues concerning Jews and the holocaust.

TWENTY-FIVE

Politics and Palestine

I N 1948 MOSHE MENUHIN received a letter from some old friends; Moshe Sharett, who would become a Prime Minister of the new state of Israel, and David HaCohen, who would become an ambassador and an important Knesset member. The two Zionists from Palestine were in San Francisco lobbying at the United Nations for the creation of the state of Israel.

HaCohen had known Moshe as a youngster in Palestine, but they had not been close. He said there might have been some family relationship between himself and Moshe; in any event, Moshe often used to visit his parents' home, HaCohen remembered. Moshe had been among the twenty-one members of the first graduating class of the Herzlia Gymnasium in 1913, and HaCohen had been in the third class. Moshe Sharett, however, was one of Moshe Menuhin's closest friends in that first graduating class. The two of them had roamed Palestine together, and were the most militant of the young Zionists.

In 1948 the taste of victory was on the two Zionists' lips. "Everyone was for us by then," HaCohen reminisced to me when I visited with him in 1973.

Even those rich Jews, like the Lessings and the Rosenwalds and the Guggenheims, who had been against us in the thirties. But after the holocaust they began realizing how important it was that Jews have their own homeland. We were very popular and sought-after fellows.

"But then we hear that Moshe Menuhin is against us," HaCohen said, his voice becoming shrill.

Who is Moshe? He is not a rich man. He is merely the father of a famous violinist. He was one of us. Nobody understood. I asked Moshe Sharett in San Francisco, so what happened to your old buddy? Sharett said he couldn't understand. Here the whole world was for us. They were going to give us our own state. And what do we hear? Moshe Menuhin is against us. So Moshe Sharett sent Moshe Menuhin a letter, inviting him to come up and see us. He never even answered the letter. Nobody understood.

HaCohen's voice grew lower again.

Listen, we wouldn't have held it against Moshe that he forgot us during the thirties. We know how busy he was. He had the responsibility of raising three exceptional children. He was traveling. We wouldn't have considered him a traitor for not being with us through those perilous years. The rich Jews you can understand. They were hardly Jewish anymore. They were assimilated. But after Germany they woke up.

But Moshe. He was, after all, of the first graduating class of the Herzlia Gymnasium. Do you know how important a thing that is in Israel? We would have at least made him an ambassador. With all that experience traveling around the world meeting all those heads of state, and being the father of Yehudi Menuhin, he could have picked his ambassadorship to anywhere.

These days HaCohen lives atop Mount Carmel, where the winds blow up the hill out of the twinkling port town of Haifa. At night, even in the middle of summer, the wind is cold and howls as it reaches the top of Mount Carmel. It was on this very hill that the prophet Elijah dwelt in a cave. Tradition says that when the Messiah comes, Elijah will race across the sky there.

A few years ago Yehudi scaled Mount Carmel to talk with David HaCohen. HaCohen is proud of the fact that Yehudi sat in his Mount Carmel home in the chair across from his sofa, while he, HaCohen, told him point blank his true feelings about Moshe.

HaCohen is proud of many things. He is proud of how important he has been. He believes that his reports to Henry Kissinger on his impressions of China as Israel's former ambassador to Burma caused the detente between America and China. He always takes time out to show off his collection of rare archaeological artifacts. The many-hued objects cover a large wall in the living room, and each is polished to an exquisite sheen. Some are figurines, some are tools. HaCohen hardly needs to tell you they are worth a great deal, but he does.

And again and again he returns to the subject of Moshe. "Why did he turn?" he asked me. "I told Yehudi it must have been mental. He was a nice boy, very bookish, but just another fellow."

Yehudi and Hephzibah have faced the Wailing Wall to come to terms with their Jewishness. They had to do so, particularly because their father had angered the Jewish community. Also, Moshe's anger towards Jewishness forced them to work it out for themselves, as well as with their spouses. If the first marriages of the three Menuhins failed, perhaps it was because only later in life did they find their own identities and the mates that more truly fit those identities.

Hephzibah's political ties are to the left wing of Israel's labor party, for she knows there is truth in some of what her father has said. I once accused her of denying that Israelis had any sense of the poetry that Jews have always had. "No," she explained, "it's just that their energies have gone into hating Arabs. It's very much like the kind of hate my father had for Jews." She believes that it may be true that Jews, as the victims of persecution, subsequently turn around and act as persecutors themselves. But, in fact, she does not believe that Jews are yet finished being the victims of persecution.

Yehudi expressed a similar attitude to me in 1975.

> One of the difficulties is that it is impossible to solve the Middle East situation on any one level. If it were only a religious level, it would be bad enough, but it is political, economic, deeply emotional, subjective and, of course, national. What vitiates the situation almost beyond redemption is the hypocrisy of at least one great power and many smaller ones. These seem totally committed to a total liquidation of Israel.

In Richard Hauser, Hephzibah certainly found a mate who could share her politics. Several years ago the Israeli ambassador to Australia was looking around Sydney for the famous pianist Hephzibah Menuhin (in those days, Hephzibah Nicholas). To his horror, he found her in a garage in one of the worst slums, living there with her new love, a penniless Viennese Jew who had barely escaped the concentration camps. For Richard Hauser she had abandoned her marriage to Lindsay Nicholas, the wealthy Australian. Nicholas' was a way of life which she had not been able to identify with, since her first suitor, Maurice Fleg, had died in a concentration camp.

When Hephzibah moved to London, she lived in the East End, where she and Richard ran a settlement house for reformed alcoholics, drug addicts and recently-released mental patients. If you fall into one of these categories, Hephzibah and Richard will find time to speak with you, give you some money or feed you. But if there is anything about you that smacks of being well-off or pampered, well, that's another thing.

Yaltah's youngest son, my brother Robert, remembers a time when he visited Hephzibah in her hotel room in New York. A physicist who wholeheartedly disagrees with his aunt and uncle about almost everything, Robert best remembers the taxi driver with whom he found Hephzibah engaged in animated conversation. They had begun talking because they shared a common belief in the evils of white sugar and the virtues of health food. Yehudi was there also, so aunt, uncle and nephew began to talk.

"You're not building bombs, are you?" Yehudi asked Robert, who was at that time employed at the federal government's top-secret laboratories in Los Alamos, New Mexico.

The conversation convinced my brother that while his aunt and uncle may be great musicians, they "know nothing about science."

A Menuhin habit which Robert makes much fun of—that of collecting odd characters—is a trait developed as compensation for their childhood, when people had to be carefully screened, so carefully that the children never got a real sense of what humanity was like. Robert was aghast that Hephzibah purchased the cabbie a ticket to London so he could come and work with them at their Center for Human Rights and Responsibilities. He suspects that she gave the cabbie the money for his ticket, but that the fellow never showed up.

It is curious that Richard, to whom Hephzibah has remained magnificently and happily married, states, as I've said, that all three Menuhins—including his own wife—made terribly mismatched marriages. "I'm luckier than I deserve," he says, and he thinks the same could be said of Yaltah's Joel and Yehudi's Diana. All three of

The Pope greets Yehudi and wife Diana at the Vatican in 1965

the Menuhins think their own marriages were made in heaven, and that the marriages of their siblings are disasters.

Yehudi's second wife is a very strong and intelligent woman. The personality resemblance between Diana and Marutha has been noted many times. If Yehudi feels she can do any wrong, he doesn't often indicate it. Diana certainly pulled him out of his tendency to despair at that point in his life. Until the Second World War, Yehudi had had a Biblical concept of marriage; the reality that ended his first marriage shattered the illusion.

The Menuhin children all acquired their present spouses on the way home after the Second World War. Hephzibah changed from a grand haughty lady into one who believes that only the working class is real. My aunt has no sympathy with my mother's concern over the sufferings of people who lead pampered lives. Once, my mother became very concerned about a particularly over-mothered, rich Zurich advertising man whose major problem in life was a disappointing affair with a conniving, alcoholic actress. Hephzibah figured that what the man did for a living was so pernicious that no sympathy should be wasted on the problems of his lovelife.

There is an air of repentance in the energetic way Hephzibah bustles around, washing and cooking for whomever may show up in her house that day. In deference to the many members of her household who hardly know classical music at all, since as often as not they are prisoners or revolutionaries, she likes to say "Back" when she is about to sit down and play Bach on the cheap little spinet in her front room.

Her daughter Clara's boyfriend plays an eighteen-stringed lute, but quite often raucous rock music drifts upstairs from the den, where Michael, an American-born black and an adopted member of the Hauser household, lives.

Today, Hephzibah refuses to hold anything in reverence anymore, and this certainly includes music. The Second World War did something to end that sense of reverence with which her education imbued her.

Even my mother was somewhat radicalized. During the period of McCarthyism in America, she cornered Donald Jackson, who had been the Grand Inquisitor of the House Un-American Activities Committee. Two of her best friends, musicians, had been destroyed by the committee because they had once been Communists. Jackson had been a patron of the arts as well as a politician, and before the hearings, Yaltah had known him in his former capacity.

"Why are you doing this?" she asked him angrily.

"It's how I get my name in the papers," he said proudly.

"At the expense of human lives? Isn't there another way to get publicity?"

Among Hephzibah's eclectic collection of books, there are volumes on Jewish mysticism and on different aspects of the subject of Jewishness. The discovery of her Jewishness was a turning point in her life, for the roots of her identity had been denied her as a child.

After Arab terrorists had killed the Israeli athletes at the Munich Olympics, she played at the memorial concert. But when speaker after speaker droned on about Jewish suffering, Hephzibah found her mind wandering. Yes, yes, she was thinking, but what about *all* human suffering?

The Israelis are fine and lovely people, and Hephzibah is now deeply conscious of her ancestors, but with a sly grin she will suggest that perhaps their "great religious delusions" have continued on for a bit too long. Her husband also comes from a long line of rabbinical wonder-workers. Richard is quite impatient with the whole lot of them. Hephzibah finds enchantment in the poetry of the traditions, but Richard, who tried after the war to settle in Israel and found it not at all to his liking, thinks the tradition is dead and should be forgotten.

When Hephzibah married Richard, she found solace in this warm, comfortable Jewish man, who was such a contrast to the reserved, trim Australian family of her first marriage. She still adores Australia and, after all, some strapping sons of Australia are also her own sons. "They are tough and mean," she says, but that is what Australian men are supposed to be like.

Certainly it could not have been just coincidence that in the Hauser marriage, two old rabbinical lines were merged and that their marriage today is concerned with making a paradise on earth.

In the late 1940's and 1950's, Yehudi's interest turned to the Holy Land. Part of the reason was somewhat self-motivated. He had to do something to show the Jewish community that he was not altogether in agreement with his father's opinions. Also, his own actions with

Furtwängler had not earned him many credits with the Jewish community at large.

But there was a larger reason too. If I was raised with the phantoms of my past, it was worse for the immediate Menuhin offspring who did not even know they had relatives. The first time Yehudi learned differently was in Moscow during the war. A couple of "nice but normal" people came backstage and introduced themselves, saying that they were relatives of Marutha's. Moshe was not present this time to deny the relationship as he had been when Yehudi met his aunt Batja.

But by far the most memorable meeting was in Israel, in 1951. Then, Yehudi and Hephzibah, and later Yaltah, in her own concert tour of Israel, met all the immediate family. Again, Moshe had vehemently denied their existence and called them impostors. But his nephew Hochy vividly remembers the details of Moshe's childhood in what was then Palestine. Hochy had always loved his uncle. Moshe's half-sister, Vera Greenspun, is still living in Tel Aviv, a stoic old woman. She was one of those who met Yehudi and Hephzibah at Lod airport. Moshe's full sister Mussia, who is now dead, was also there.

Yehudi, Hochy and Vera have all described this meeting to me. Yehudi said it was a major experience in his life. "It was the first time we realized that we weren't Adam and Eve. We had relatives just like other people. It was a tremendous relief."

A decade later, Yaltah and her third husband Joel Ryce went to Israel to perform duo piano. When Yaltah saw her cousin Hochy Zuriel, she was moved to tears because Hochy has Moshe's face. If there was any relief for Yaltah from the Cinderella story that was her childhood, it came during moments of love shown by her father, and she knew there was no denying that this was Moshe's kin.

While Moshe's reaction to his early life of pain was to run from his family and his roots, the Menuhin children had to dig for theirs. Mussia was so bitter towards Moshe and his children that at first she did not want to meet them at the airport. The night the plane landed at Lod airport, the Menuhins were greeted not only by their relatives but by a crowd of angry demonstrators and plenty of journalists. There had been fiery debates about Yehudi in the Knesset, but he proved himself equal to the challenge and clarified his position. Later he and Hephzibah played concerts all over Israel.

That first night, though, Yehudi and Hephzibah met their relatives at a reception at Vera's house. Vera is very close to Hochy, and is the eldest in the family since Mussia's death. Vera told Yehudi and Hephzibah the whole story of the original breakup after the Russian Revolution, in a voice heavy with suffering and sadness. Yehudi and Hephzibah believed that Moshe would let bygones be bygones and join in the reunion, and they kept sending telegrams to Los Gatos, hoping to heal the split of years.

Both Yehudi and Hephzibah were sure that Moshe would wire back. But Mussia said bitterly, "You don't know my brother. He won't respond." She was right. There was no answer from Los Gatos.

One of the tales that Yehudi and Hephzibah heard explained for the first time was the matter of Nachum Sher, Marutha's father. No, he wasn't some mysterious prince, as she had built him up to her children. No one knew much about him even though they had housed him in his old age in Jerusalem. But they agreed that he was "a plain, simple man." Although he had left his wife, Nachum Sher was a very religious man. He went to the Holy Land first and there he was associated with a small synagogue in Jaffa. The synagogue had stood until three or four years ago with his picture on its wall. The neighborhood had always been poor, for it was primarily a settlement for Egyptian Jews, and most of its synagogues today are Sephardic. It is still the poor part of Tel Aviv, the place where the "black" Jews live.

The relatives explained that old Nachum Sher, living in Mussia's household, became very bitter because he knew that his very own grandson was becoming world-famous, and he could not even hear him play. As the old man's health deteriorated, Mussia asked him not to be so bitter. After all, she would remind him, the great Levi-Yitzhak of Berditchev never spoke ill of anyone, not even those who sinned on the Sabbath.

Moshe's mother did not have a much better fate. Sara Liba lived until 1939 and spent most of her declining years in Palestine, moaning about Moshe. The relatives begged him to write to her. He never did—so they say.

One must remember that most of these tales came from Mussia. Although in her youth Mussia had been a bit revolutionary and had even been considered little better than a prostitute for walking through the old part of Jerusalem in high heels with a feather in her hat, she was a loyal Hassid. More than that, she was an attendant secretary to the Lubavitcher hierarchy. Thus she could be expected to have little sympathy for Moshe's rebellion. The doubts that plagued him about religion did not plague her.

How much hatred there was between Moshe and Mussia can be judged by the fact that when Moshe and Marutha finally did send old clothes and a little money to Nachum Sher, they insisted that none of it go to Mussia's family, even though it was they who were taking care of him.

To complicate matters further, Mussia was no weak sister. Known as "Mussia with the lamp," she was a social worker in the old quarters. At any time, day or night, she might be playing the role of midwife and doctor. Not surprisingly, she and Hephzibah became close very quickly, for if ever there was a woman with a born instinct for social work, it is Hephzibah. Hephzibah probably found her true ancestor in her aunt.

Nonetheless, one can certainly see why brother Moshe would not share Mussia's enthusiasm. The Lubavitcher rabbi's order to their mother to remarry was obviously given to keep the Hassidic aristocracy pure, at the cost, in Moshe's mind, of making him an orphan. No doubt Mussia would not see it that way. She was already married when these events occurred. Her own arranged marriage was to a man Mussia did not love but who had more than a quarter of a million dollars in gold bullion. It was later expropriated by the Turks during World War I. The Turks also took her husband prisoner of war in Damascus and killed him.

Later in their Israel stay, Yehudi and Hephzibah went to Kibbutz Maagan Michael on the coast road to Haifa, several miles outside of Tel Aviv. There, they met their aunt, Batja, Louis Menuhin's widow. She had helped to found this showcase kibbutz when she had returned to Palestine from California in 1933, after Louis had died and Moshe had turned against her. Between talks with Batja, the Menuhins relaxed on the kibbutz patio beneath the incredible night sky. I too have been to Maagan Michael, in 1973, and there can be no sky so black, so velvety as that one. The sky felt alive, and the stars seemed to be keeping some very important secret.

TWENTY-SIX

East Meets West

THE FIRST PART OF YEHUDI'S life was spent nurturing his musical gift in a world cut off from everyday reality. Then, he devoted his life to sharing that gift with the world. Now, one senses a struggle to unite the inner and outer worlds he mastered so early and so easily. Like his ancestors, Yehudi might be expected to play his ancestral role of great wise man, even while enjoying the material comforts of fame and fortune. To combine these two worlds would be no easy task even for the greatest of wise men. Certainly Yehudi must be given great credit for having looked to the East, both in his music and his yoga, for the balance necessary for uniting materialism and spirituality.

One who believes that Yehudi is a true wise man is Princess Irene, formerly of the Greek monarchy, who now lives in London. She is related to the British royalty, and she spends considerable time with Yehudi and his wife Diana in London. I felt some resentment towards her because, unlike my uncle, I have no patience with the basic assumptions behind royalty. Yehudi thinks royalty can add something to a society. I could just as well live without it.

On one occasion, I listened to Yehudi and Princess Irene discussing the "servant problem," and I thought, "Damn the servant problem." When Yehudi offered me a ride in his Mercedes Benz limousine, I declined the honor. I really didn't want to ride through the streets of London that way, even though, I must admit, I had done so with my mother.

Yet, I did like Princess Irene. When I talked with her, I quickly felt that there was something sad and discarded about her, that there wasn't an iota of bad intention in her, despite the fact that one couldn't say the same thing about her mother, the former Queen Fredericka.

While Yehudi was out of the room, Irene asked me what my book was about and then told me she had learned of the Hassidic tradition through the writing of Martin Buber. That immediately commended her to me, for back in my room was a Buber work I was reading with great fascination.

We naturally began talking of Yehudi, and his relationship to that tradition, and she confirmed my thoughts when she said, "Yehudi's whole personality became clear to me and I understood who he was when I read Buber." She had been struck by the uncanny similarity between the Hassidic wise men and the gurus of India. When she discovered that Yehudi was descended from generations of wise men, it was a revelation to her.

Although Yehudi may sometimes dismiss his Hassidic lineage, he has confided to me on other occasions that when he recognized his long line of ancestors he began to understand himself, even though he has said he is not a person concerned with family trees. It is obvious even to Yehudi that much of his identity has come from his ancestors, despite the ambivalence with which he relates to that identity.

Yehudi's immediate attraction to yoga occurred during his difficulties in the postwar period. Israel and India both became important to him, even though he discovered yoga in a place no more exotic than a New Zealand doctor's office. Yehudi found a book on yoga while waiting to see the doctor, and by the time he arrived in California, yoga had become his passion. My mother went to Piatigorsky's house where she, the great cellist and her brother were going to play trios. When she walked in, her brother was standing on his head. She said something, no doubt with some humor intended, about the difficulty of playing while upside down.

Yehudi didn't see the humor. He snapped, "Can't you see that I am upside down?" When Yehudi insisted on showing Yaltah and

Yehudi's yoga caught the media's fancy. This 1967 photo showed him sitting in "an Indian (cross-legged) position" at the Drake Hotel in New York

"Grisha" (Piatigorsky's nickname) the yogic practice of sticking a piece of string through one's nose, she was disgusted.

It is clear that my uncle is not particularly religious in the traditional sense. Since World War II, he has had much to do with creating a Western interest in both Indian yoga and music, yet he only practices Hatha, or physical, yoga, not the spiritual kind. "I concentrate by playing the violin," he told me, but he has not experienced those great transcendental states of mind usually connected with yoga.

Yehudi's seeking was certainly reflected not only in his private life, but in his professional life as well. The *Saturday Review* (April 26, 1966), using some hindsight, described the fifties as a time "when Menuhin was at war with his instrument." John Warrack wrote in *Gramaphone* (November, 1958):

> About Yehudi Menuhin's playing, there has long been prolonged controversy. Only his most blinkered admirers maintain that nothing has happened to ruffle his development—or indeed that there has been development—since he first appeared as an infant prodigy. Those who genuinely admire him have preserved their faith in his innate artistry while being troubled at the technical faults that have beset him—faults like unsteady bowing and downright bad intonation that in an artist of Menuhin's calibre and achievement are so elementary that they must spring from obscurer physical causes.

Yehudi curtly replies to such criticism that he believes, like the Chinese, that intellectuals would often be better off engaging in manual labor. He finds critics "too concerned with comparative values, not ultimate ones."

In any event, Yehudi was finding his redemption in the East, and that fact was no doubt connected with his own sense of ancestry, which he said developed as he went around the world meeting its peoples. In February of 1953, *Life* helped launch the West's fascination with yoga on a large scale by running a spread about Yehudi's discovery of it.

The magazine quoted Yehudi as saying that yoga gave him a sense of "general well-being." It showed Yehudi on various pages in assorted yoga contortions and went on to say that his music had been revitalized by it. "Whatever private difficulties he has had with his art, he seems to have conquered them," the article said.

Despite my mother's initial doubts, she did start delving into yoga, but she was as unable to get me to stand on my head as she had been to teach me Russian. One exciting thing did happen, however: one day Marlon Brando called and talked to my mother about yoga. That was exciting for me because we had just seen him in "Teahouse of the August Moon," one of the few Hollywood movies my mother ever allowed me to see.

It seems that Yehudi is of the opinion that if only violinists, nurses, teachers, prisoners and presidents would bind themselves in knots, breathe deeply until lightheaded, clean their nasal passages with string, twist their spines and walk erect, with their sights to the stars, then everything would be much better.

Yehudi's passions for natural food, yoga and ecology grow out of his belief that a good musician has to oppose all that is inhuman. He also believes that "music is by nature civilizing." Music, according to him, is formed by "deliberate application and precise thought;" thus its standards of "thought, insight and effort" are good ones by which to compare everything else.

Of course Yehudi is a purist about music. "The great people in the world of jazz and classical music have lasted a long time," he explains. Yet he was an admirer of the early Beatles. "They were a spontaneous group that came off the streets of Liverpool, and that's the way a certain kind of folk music should happen." On the other hand, he recently walked out of a Rolling Stones concert because he was stunned by the fans' need to "shout, cheer, stamp their feet and climb on the seats."

> In my world more is expected of the artist than of the audience. Here it is in fact the audience's performance—the musicians are merely the trigger. If you took an electric drill or a pile driver, tuned it so it sounded a tune and amplified it a hundred times, it would sound to the people nearby much as this concert sounded to me.

On one occasion during my stay in London in 1973 Yehudi was genuinely pleased when I joined him in a long discussion that turned away from politics and into metaphysics. Yehudi himself is convinced that a new religion will emerge, something neither Jewish nor Christian but relevant to these times. He believes that all the existing institutionalized religions have retreated from the concepts that their particular prophets preached. His new faith would change the traditional morality wherein God created man as dominant in the universe. His new morality is based on "spirit and mind infusing all creation," of which man is but one form.

Yehudi's art is a genuine search for unity. The belief in truth and beauty is obvious, and everything he does on the violin reaches for truth and beauty. He tries ever more to distill the essence, to find the purest tone wherein are contained all the most harmonious things that are this universe, things far away, yet of which we are a part. His art is really not so different from that practiced by his saintly ancestors in their prayer. What they and Yehudi have tried to attain is a mystical union.

Certainly Yehudi's metaphysics do not quite include the kind of heaven that so moved his Hassidic forefathers. But that is not to say he is a materialist rather than an idealist. If you ask him what reality is, you come away with a slightly paradoxical duality. It is not materialist or idealist, he says. "They converge." He says that there is a reality behind the external reality. No doubt he explains this concept better with his violin than with his words, but nonetheless the words must give some illumination of the man.

He takes a pencil and draws concentric circles on a piece of paper. "Reality," he says, "grows in concentric circles. When you are a baby and when you die are the two times in your life that you see through all the levels of reality." He draws an arrow outside the circles, an arrow pointing to the greater universe *out there*.

> You see, in this first circle reality is what you touch and smell. Later on it is school, where all to often one is subjected to a regimen that kills everything within although some sense of discipline, inner discipline, must be acquired. In the larger circle of reality you worry about your job or your food or the opposite sex. All these are fine and necessary things. But most people never go outside these realities. Only a few do: real gurus, artists, mystics, a few of the really great scientists. These people have a sense of the universe constantly, that same sense that all human beings have at birth and near death.

"You know," he pauses, "in India, when a great teacher dies, he knows that he is going to die. He sees no difference between life and death. So he summons his disciples, and his death is not an unhappy occasion."

One should not presume from such remarks that Yehudi is overly mystical. He does concede as I have said to having strong feelings, at times, of links with the long line of mystics from which he comes. He admits to having felt that eerie sense of connection with past generations which, he says, causes you to see your own life in proportion. But Yehudi probably would not offhandedly describe himself as a Hassid, but rather as a violinist or a conductor or a father.

Certainly Yehudi is not proposing a return to the old Hassidic framework. He believes in its reality, the reality that Hassidism became and was to the generations of Russian Jews who lived by it. He believes in it in its indigenous setting, in its own time. But, he says, he can well understand why the younger generation rejects such religious frameworks, which are now failures because they so often were based on superstition. Yet, he argues, "men need a framework, and the current generation is without one. Hence they have this terrible sense of living in an accidental, haphazard universe, which it is not. Science also has not been able to replace the superstitions of religion. I doubt that it can by itself."

It might strike one who is not a mystic able to cross the line between life and death that Yehudi is a pessimist. He believes that harmony is a fact of the universe, but he also believes man's future quite likely will be beset with a wave of catastrophes simply because man has been playing God too long. "Man will discover he cannot play God," he says.

There are, as I've suggested, similarities between Yehudi's heaven on earth and the heaven that is constantly uppermost in the minds of the Hassids. The Hassidic attachment to nature was no small matter. Again and again the sun and the stars and the rivers and the trees and the green hills make up the universe of Hassidic lore. Again and again the mystics of Russia went out into nature where, if they weren't quite peering into the face of God, they were surrounded by an emanation of Him. The threads between man and nature are seen in Hassidic spirituality as they are by today's more political environmentalists, among whose ranks Yehudi has been for years.

God, to a Hassid, is not someone who came and created. He is constantly creating, and what better place is there than the country-side to see and feel that? Just as Schneur Zalman took his grandson for a ride in the countryside to listen to the birds talk to each other, Yehudi's father, Moshe, took him for rides in their old Chevrolet convertible while the soft, warm California spring breeze blew through their hair.

In Yehudi's Utopia, there are no soft drinks or food additives, and technology is more discretely and unobtrusively harnessed, not so much to conquer nature as to harmonize with it. Yehudi's heaven on earth rather reminds one of that world profoundly visualized by R. Buckminster Fuller, who comes from a long line of New England preachers. In Yehudi's heaven, people become more contemplative and profound. The cheapness of the commercial culture is replaced, the ugliness of the profit motive abolished, the Machine Age, with its digital dialing systems and computerized controls, replaced.

Ours might look like a glorious age of cybernetics, but when it is freed from itself by the wrench of history, according to Yehudi, Utopia will have turned out to be somewhere else.

All this living in the celestial upper regions is too ethereal and flimsy for me. For one thing, it requires a Diana, the wife who says "no" for Yehudi. He supports some twenty artists at any one time, and plays as many benefits as paid concerts, yet he is besieged by constant requests. Diana says no.

Not that Yehudi can't be pretty direct, but it is a directness for the sake of the ethereal. When the New York Philharmonic asked him not to play encores because they wouldn't fit into a radio broadcast, he instead made a speech to protest the control over music by "extra-musical forces." "I am not sure you are allowed to applaud either," he told the audience. "I am sure that if Bach could realize what damage two or three minutes of his music would do to the traditions and budget of this great orchestra, he would be very sorry."

No doubt the management of the famed orchestra did not appreciate Mr. Menuhin's "etherealness" just then. Even though economics contradict the spirit of a concert, these days the economics must win out. The ethereal person would opt for the spirit, of course, and a *live* performance is still a special occasion that Yehudi wants to preserve.

In the early sixties, Yehudi stormed out of St. Andrews Hall in

Yehudi, Ravi Shankar and David Oistrakh are shown together at a
United Nations Day concert in 1958

Glasgow after finding a boxing ring set up where he was to rehearse. "I won't play here," he said. "I have seen concerts taking place in all kinds of concrete monstrosities, but I have never seen a boxing ring in a concert hall. That remains Glasgow's achievement."

Yehudi met Ravi Shankar, famed Indian sitar player, in 1952, and became an early apostle. In 1955 he played with a group of Indian musicians in New York. Since it was such an unusual concert for that time, he was asked to explain it in the *New York Times* in April, 1955.

> The only parallel in our music is that found in the twelve-tone system of Schoenberg, which builds intricate compositions on the unalterable sequence of an established succession of notes. There is no ego in this music; the Indians have no Beethoven whose genius is honored age by age, for, instead of confining creation to rare, immortal individuals, it is extended to every artist who plays. Gradually, across the ages, our music has evolved from this mysterious form, now so strange to us.

Shankar played with Yehudi at the Bath Festival in the early 1960's. For two days, Yehudi was coached by Shankar. He wore a silk tunic and sat cross-legged on the stage for the performance. In 1962, Shankar and Yehudi recorded their first album together, "East Meets West."

Shankar, of course, was admired by such giants of the popular music world as Dave Brubeck and the Beatles' George Harrison, and in one joint television interview, Yehudi and another Beatle, John Lennon, had a difference of interpretation about Shankar. Lennon said that the climax of Eastern music would be a golden age when there would be no war. Yehudi replied that he was "despairing of the golden age, but would accept this music as a golden moment." Only a member of the generation coming of age in the sixties could display a greater naiveté than Yehudi.

When the Asian Music Circle was formed in London in 1953, Yehudi became its first president. But by 1962 the invasion of the West by the East was so complete that he was stating his concerns in the London *Times* about whether the Indian musicians were becoming too Westernized; they were forming *orchestras*!

Yehudi also initiated the first musical exchange between Russia and the West during those terrible Cold War years. He was not really an outsider to either side of the Iron Curtain, and he pointed out that his parents were Russian Jews who both retain a deep attachment. He had played in Russia during the war, and again just before the Iron Curtain went down. In 1956 and 1957 he played throughout Eastern Europe, thereby starting the first cultural exchange programs in years. The Soviets sent David Oistrakh to England. In 1963 Yehudi conducted the Moscow Philharmonic in London, and David and Igor Oistrakh joined him in the Vivaldi Triple Concerto. In 1964, he played with another Russian, the great cellist Rostropovitch.

For the last two terms he has been president of the UNESCO music council, and in 1971 at the Moscow Music Congress, he spoke about Aleksandr Solzhenitsyn as "an indication of the vision and greatness of men and women evolving in this vastest of lands." It was a powerful speech, but not a word appeared in the Soviet news-papers, although everything else at the conference was duly recorded by the Russian news agency, *Tass*.

To Yehudi, the battle of East and West, at least as it is expressed in the difference between Russia and the capitalist world, is "a pox on both houses." He condemns the "brutalizing of mind and spirit for the immediate" on the one hand, but he also condemns "the will to dominate which would proclaim a superiority of one group, system or symbol over another," an obvious criticism of the Soviet Union.

Yehudi's criticisms of the Socialist bloc were once about to cost him his third term as music council president. The Russian delegate protested Yehudi's remarks about Rostropovitch, who has since gone into exile from the Soviet Union. But when it came down to voting, the vote was unanimous for Yehudi, except that Poland and Bulgaria abstained. Yehudi had refused to take back his comments, saying that he was a violinist first and then a president and could only speak from his heart as a violinist.

Yehudi is not pleased by the suppression of artists and intellectu-als in Russia. He asked Oistrakh why he didn't say anything about it. Although Oistrakh was a good Communist, he agreed that for Jews and writers in his country, it was not good. But he said that he didn't speak out because "I am an old man with a heart condition."

It may have been a natural step for Yehudi to move from interest in Eastern musical forms to a desire to mold Western music directly, as a conductor. Although it has only been since the sixties that Yehudi has been known as a conductor, his first experience came right at the end of World War II. Antal Dorati told Yehudi, "You have the makings of a conductor." He subsequently talked Yehudi into conducting a concert in Dallas. At the first rehearsal, Yehudi reports, his first piece was the Meistersinger Overture. "I lifted my baton shyly, apologetically. The orchestra responded with Wagner's stupendous C major opening chord. It nearly blasted me off the podium. Obviously it had nothing to do with any gesture of mine. Gradually you come to know how little as well as how much a conductor has to do." Later in the same rehearsal he found himself making suggestions about dynamics, phrasing, balance and so on. "On the night of the performance, I was so nervous that I nearly fell on my face while mounting the podium, and had to be helped on by the concertmaster. Everything seemed to go reasonably well. At any rate, I wasn't stoned."

1959 was the first year Yehudi began conducting with much public notice at the Bath Festival, where he did, among many other things, Bach's Brandenburg Concerti. In 1961 Ernest Fleischmann, manager of the London Symphony, came to Yehudi with a crisis. There was an upcoming concert with no conductor of note able to take the engagement. It was then, Yehudi remembers, that he really discovered conducting was in his blood, that the orchestra could be as much an instrument as the violin in recreating music the way he imagined it should be. But as a conductor, Yehudi did not get his results by autocratic means; rather, he established a rapport with the musicians, at least musically.

Yehudi's conducting of old friends, such as the musicians that make up the Menuhin Players, is very successful. When there is discord, his presence will bring people together. In Los Angeles, however, I saw him fail miserably with the Los Angeles Philharmonic. He is not the kind of commanding figure who molds people he doesn't know.

Modesty and humor are his hallmarks. He will tell a double bass player that the only reason he, Yehudi, dared become a conductor was that all the musicians knew how many mistakes he made, so he would not be bashful in mentioning theirs. Yehudi is not a typical conductor. He creates an ambience simply because, in the words of one musician, "We know what he wants."

When he conducts, the words "tenderness" and "sweetness" are frequently on his lips. "That was a bit fierce, but I liked it," he said to the musicians at a recording session I witnessed. That seemed to be his gentle way of telling them to soften the sound.

According to Yaltah, the sense of rapport that he can create among musicians is almost magical. He asks a double bass player to play tighter, adding, with a grin, "Oh, what I meant was you needed another drink." Then he tells the story of a cabbie who said to him, "Oh, you professional musicians, that means you must play every note right." There was appreciative laughter.

Yehudi's charm and wit do put people at ease. During one of the recording sessions I witnessed, harpsichordist George Malcolm was setting up to record. Since harpsichords are very quiet, they tend to be drowned out by other instruments. The recording engineers suggested pulling out a violin or two. "Does that mean that with each reduction in the string section, the recording will improve?" Yehudi asked with a grin.

Yehudi has said to me that he does not see any great conductors in the world presently, not on the level of Furtwängler or Toscanini. However, he thinks that some of the younger ones show promise. He praised, for instance, Seiji Ozawa, although he added, "He's great on everything but Beethoven, to whom he leaves no breathing room."

During the last ten years or so Yehudi has been both despairing and hopeful about the world. About music in general, he says,

> The problem is that there is almost too much variety. No time has been so rich in choices, and perhaps the choices are too great. That is why everyone has to find such an individual and subjective style. In these times music has to be more personal and difficult to categorize. In the past, when a rapid change was much less the norm, traditions incubated, and a composer grew out of them. Now this is far less true.

He believes the quantity and quality of new violinists in the world is astounding, and they will no doubt equal those of his generation. He believes that the Beatles did a better job of communicating with the postwar generation than classical musicians. Yet he can be acerbic when he talks about pop musicians who go into studios and lay down track after track, doing their—as Yehudi spits it out— "phu-bop."

He is proud of the fact that London is the center of the world's greatest classical music today. He believes that American orchestras have priced themselves out of the market. Part of that varied musical scene in London is a strong electronic music movement, members of which do not look warmly upon Yehudi. Indeed, one evening in a small French town, Yehudi, Hephzibah and Yaltah found themselves stranded in a concert hall with no audience. The audience was to have been a local music group, torn by dissention over whether to allow these acoustic dinosaurs the right to play. Yehudi is willing to grant that some genius will probably come along in the next twenty years, who can truly use electronics musically, and not just haphazardly as he now believes to be the case.

"During my lifetime I have seen an incredible growth in musical interests and audiences," he told reporters in San Francisco. "I know there has been a growth in everything, in the popularity of liquor, cigarettes, divorce. I don't know whether the musical growth is greater than those, but it is marvelous."

It may be significant that Yehudi believes strongly in the apprenticeship system. That was the essential method by which his ancestors maintained themselves as a dynastic line of wise men. He has his own apprentices, but he also teaches large classes. His advice often includes the suggestion that for instance the student wear only underclothes while practicing, since violin playing is mostly a solitary thing and "one should be completely at ease" while doing so.

One might ask, why underwear? Why not nothing at all? Maybe being naked would backfire. In the back of his head, the student would always be expecting someone to burst through the door while he is deep in the throes of the Beethoven Violin Concerto. The whole idea is to keep relaxed. "It is a mistake ever to pick up a violin without being completely relaxed," Yehudi says. "To achieve unity from fingertips to toes, a player must have a feeling of floating in oil." Perhaps a true wise man floats in oil...

Has the Schneersohn/Hassid line been resurrected in Yehudi Menuhin? Is Yehudi a true wise man? If the phenomenon of Yehudi

Menuhin has been explained better by a study of his great ancestors, certainly this understanding has served to put some distance between Yehudi's wisdom and that of, say, the Baal-Shem. I don't think Yehudi would disagree, and it is to his credit—it may even be his greatest claim to wise man status—that he does not pretend to such status even while others push it upon him. Yehudi's mastery of his own instrument, his developing skills as a conductor, his innovations in music education, and his dedication to international world peace are, if not signs of a great prophet, at least the mark of a great man— no small achievement. I think you would have to credit Yehudi's parents with having provided for their genius son an environment that on the one hand fostered his musical genius, but on the other, limited his human experience. One wonders what Yehudi might have been had he, like the Baal-Shem, broken away from the established, priestly fold within which he has always lived.

TWENTY-SEVEN

Synthesis—
The Menuhin Struggle

THE ELDER MENUHINS, Moshe and Marutha, are now very old. They live a quiet life in Los Gatos, and Moshe seems more involved with the next life than he does with this one. His funeral is completely planned and includes a recording of Yehudi playing the Bach E major concerto. Another piece featured will have Yehudi and Yaltah playing; as befits the parents' conception of her, the piece is not an important work. Yet another selection will be Dvorak's "Songs My Mother Taught Me." There will be no mention during the service of Moshe's feelings towards his wife, only his children. Nor will the issue of his relationship to Jewishness be mentioned.

Yehudi will also play Ravel's "Kaddish." Moshe has said of this work: "I loved this melody, this truly old Jewish melody, although I have no use for the contents of the prayer, the Kaddish, which are archaic and tribalistic." (The Kaddish is said at or after the death of a Jew, and is considered by even the least religious to be a most sacred prayer).

Perhaps music really does speak better than words. The Bach concerto in E major has a haunting sadness to it, a sense of the sadness that comes from contemplating death. How did the young Yehudi play that prayerful music with such dark moodiness? How does a boy know of such things? It was as if the son spoke of the horrors the father had experienced but could never truly resolve. There is an

My father took this photograph of Yaltah
with Moshe and Marutha during one of
many summers spent in Los Gatos in the
early fifties

assumption in this culture that children cannot understand the vast, flowing tides of ideas and history, and yet at what time in life do the stars shine the brightest?

Moshe was of that generation of Jews uprooted from one land and forced to make their way to another. It is the archetypal Jewish story, the Jew always ready to go into yet another exile, another land. It is Yehudi who will speak for him, through his music, just as it was Yehudi, the child, who seemed to incarnate all that Moshe had to give up in his early years of struggle.

Although the Menuhin children love and respect their parents, they are now deeply involved in this life with all its disturbing contradictions. Certainly, as I've said, Yehudi, Hephzibah and Yaltah all felt the need to discover the past that their parents had separated them from, and this meant coming to terms with their Jewishness. Yet the influence of their internationalist parents would never allow any of the Menuhins to take the easy way out—they are, indeed, citizens of the world, while at the same time they live the lives of aristocrats, the intimates of royalty, intellectuals and great artists.

One day, while visiting the Menuhin clan in England, I went from the political atmosphere of Hephzibah's home to a concert in St. George's Cathedral at Windsor Castle, conducted by Yehudi. As the Missa Solemnis by Beethoven rolled out, I found myself wondering just what was the role, the purpose of this unique Jewish family of mine. Were they, even Hephzibah, mere court musicians? Is all their social activism, political committedness, socialist idealism merely the icing on a classical, aristocratic cake?

Yehudi would argue that his music is for all the peoples of the world—kings and prison inmates, Palestinian refugees and Israeli kibbutzniks. He tells the story of his performance at a prison. When the announcer said that the first piece would be by Mozart, the audience groaned. By the time Yehudi was through, however, the audience had seemingly changed its mind and decided that classical music had something to offer them.

But I keep thinking that there's something of a museum piece about my family. The ethereal passion, the liquid unpredictability of Yehudi's playing sometimes seem out of touch with these soulless times. But then maybe it is right not to be a part of these times. As the divinity of the Beethoven Mass revealed itself that day at Windsor Castle, I was very moved. And it seemed right that a Jew, in fact Yehudi, "the Jew," was conducting the Mass. Somehow that gave the performance symmetry and synthesis, and I could not ignore my pleasure in this spectacle. At times like these, one can almost forget that so often poetry and music are created at great human cost.

What of the children of Yehudi? How have they come to terms with their membership in the Menuhin tradition? Yehudi's daughter Zamira has been pampered and has not had to work, although she is now an airline stewardess. So sheltered has been her life that when I brought a woman to her house who was describing the experience of working in a sausage factory, Zamira did not understand why this woman had not quit. Having to work from necessity is a concept Zamira never seemed to have considered before. This naiveté or otherworldliness, as I like to call it, is my uncle's strongest suit. Societies demand it in their geniuses, and even the genius' family is ethereal. Zamira could only see that to have a job in a sausage factory would be a convincing argument in favor of vegetarianism.

Certainly both Zamira and her brother Jeremy inherited the Menuhin taste for searching—Jeremy thinks the Menuhin moodiness is due to "our Russian blood." Zamira has gone through several stages, including a flirtation with the Catholic church. Jeremy went back to Los Gatos, hoping to find his identity at his grandparents'. He was sorely disappointed. He, too, sometimes wishes his father were different. He claims his father is so much a public man that he is distant even with his own son.

"He's a good and kind person, hidebound and puritanical, perhaps, but good." Once Jeremy wanted to bring his girlfriend home to stay at the Menuhins' house in Highgate, London, for a week. His father strongly objected. It was his mother Diana who prevailed.

Jeremy is most adamant about defending his father artistically. He is the only musician of Yehudi's offspring, and like the two Oistrakhs, father and son often play together. Jeremy is a pianist. When asked why his father's playing is sometimes less than his best, Jeremy replied, "I am distrustful of any artist who always plays well." He subscribes to the theory that an artist should always be trying to do more than he can do, and thus he is often condemned to failure.

Perhaps the contradictions in the world are so mirrored within the Menuhin family that synthesis is the only way the Menuhins survive. In some senses, the Jewish experience can be described as a search for synthesis by a tradition-bound subculture surviving constant exile within foreign cultures. If Moshe was the Menuhin least willing to come to terms with the contradictions within him, perhaps Yaltah is the Menuhin within whom synthesis and sensitivity are the most apparent. She believes that behind life's vale of tears is a cosmic mechanism that the annointed can manipulate. Among the annointed ones, only Marutha toils in the *dark* side of God's kingdom, according to Yaltah. My mother's world, especially emotionally, runs very deep, and it shows in her music. Her experiences and the influence of Jung's ideas, have made her open to the mysteries of the psyche.

Once Yaltah went to a seance. The medium was an uneducated woman, and it was unlikely that she would have known anything of the Hassidim or of Yaltah's connections with their high command. But she told Yaltah that she saw a man in a black coat and a beard standing behind her. The beard and the black coat were certainly the trademarks of Yaltah's ancestors. The medium imagined the ancestor must have been a grandfather or even a great-grandfather, and said that the man was repeating one word over and over again, but she could not tell what the word meant, since it was in a language she did not understand. The word sounded like "shida." "Shida," the man kept repeating over and over again.

Several months later Yaltah was in the Zurich house of a good friend of hers, a man who happens to be a Hassid as well as a noted professor of the Old Testament. She did not tell him why she wanted to know what the word *shida* meant, because seances and the like are taboo for Hassidim. Messing around with spirits or anything akin to black magic can be a very dangerous affair, especially for a woman. (Hassidim begin their days with a prayer thanking God for not having made them women.) So Yaltah could not say what the circumstances of her hearing the word were.

The professor said that *shida* is the Hebrew word for "order" or "oasis." The very fact that this seemingly nonsensical word had a meaning is amazing enough. At that point in her life, however, the words order and oasis had great meaning. Yaltah's has not been an easy life. She was suffering then even more than usual, as the result of some difficult personal affairs. And if ever a kindly grandfather had a word of reassurance for a descendant, it could not have been better than that expressed by the word *shida*.

It may be that *shida* is what the Menuhins' struggle for. Certainly one enters *shida* while listening to the Menuhins play music. Perhaps Moshe will finally find peace within the *shida* conjured up at his elaborately planned funeral. But if *shida* is such a struggle for those blessed with as much as the Menuhins, one can imagine how difficult it is for the have-nots of the world. For them, oasis and order are out of reach. It is as if the Menuhins, knowing of their gift for the entry into the higher realms of order and oasis feel a special responsibility to bring others with them. Moshe taught this to his children, but it may be that his lessons were too restrictive, his contradictions too severe. As the Menuhins grew into citizens of the world, their sense of responsibility grew to encompass all the world, and Moshe's simple black-and-white vision became increasingly transparent. Perhaps total freedom from their parents will be the only way the Menuhins will ever achieve the great syntheses they seek.

TWENTY-EIGHT

Hephzibah Breaks the Mold

O F COURSE THERE IS more than struggle and pain in the Menuhins' lives. There is, I am happy to report, growth and change, and as is the case with everything Menuhin, these are accomplished with great style and spirit. I remember when, some time ago, Hephzibah stopped being my aunt. She did this so that we could choose whether or not we wanted to be related. This happened in London, where we were sitting on the floor of her house half a block from the Thames. She was cutting clippings out of newspapers for the files of her Center for Human Rights and Responsibilities, and chattering on about a number of different things. Suddenly she said, "Repeat after me: I divorce you. I divorce you, I divorce you." I did so. We laughed and went on chattering.

It seemed light-hearted, the right thing to do at that time. But there was also a twinge of anger. I wasn't sure I wanted to divorce my family. I thought of my mother's remark about Hephzibah's daughter Clara: "If Clara thinks she has problems because her parents love the world before their family, she should be glad she did not have our parents who loved only their family."

But Hephzibah is serious about this matter of families. She believes that rather than forming families around common ancestors, families should form themselves "by affinity"—similar to the concept of extended families. An event that illustrates her belief involves

Yaltah who was recovering from an operation at the Florence Night-ingale Hospital in London. Yehudi and Hephzibah had sneaked over to see her several times, at odd hours. But one afternoon Hephzibah came with the whole motley crew of the settlement house she and Richard were running at that time.

The receptionist of the shabbily genteel place asked who the patient's family was.

"Us," Hephzibah laughed. "But oh," said the confused receptionist, "only family can come in." "We are all family," Hephzibah said for the last time, and everyone marched up to see Yaltah —more than a score of them.

My mother thought the episode humorous, but absurd too. Obviously these people were not all her family, yet she really appreciated all the attention. And she thought it rather ironic that Hephzibah, who insists she wants to recreate families by affinity, still leaned close to her as everyone was departing, and said, "It's nice to be able to take care of someone you really love."

Hephzibah is not as much of one mind on the subject as you'd think. When she is being affectionate towards me, she will say that I walk and look like one of our rabbinical ancestors. And if I boast of some accomplishment, she remarks, "The genes will tell."

She is not militaristic about Israel, but at the same time, she is fearful that Jews will once again be persecuted. She likes the toughness, aggressiveness and even the arrogance of the Israelis. Yet intellectually she is convinced that all the old paternalistic structures are going, and she adds, "Good riddance." And yet in the next breath she'll continue, "To be without a family would be like being a drunk, sleeping on the banks of the Thames."

When Hephzibah played for the Dutch royal court at the 1964 presentation of the Erasmus Prize to Martin Buber, she felt the pull of her ancestors. "The old Buber was a real Hassid," she said, although present-day Lubavitchers do not believe so.

> He was a fine figure, with his flowing beard and gentle eyes. The Dutch royal family is a stunning example of enlightenment and human sweetness. Imagine that when the procession walked into the hall, Buber was at the head, even ahead of the Queen, who was

Yaltah and Hephzibah playing together in New Zealand in 1952

standing in respect for him. Prince Bernhardt made a magnificent speech summarizing Buber's work.

Afterwards, Hephzibah happily noted, the Prince gave her the largest bouquet of roses.

With Hephzibah one goes so quickly from the sublime to the earthy. The last time she and Yehudi came through Los Angeles, we spent a day in the swank Polo Lounge of the Beverly Hills Hotel organizing the Los Angeles Center for Human Rights and Responsibilities. I think Hephzibah expected me to take over after she left, but I was unusually reticent. The Los Angeles branch floundered as quickly as it had arisen that afternoon. Once Hephzibah was gone, there was no one to accomplish anything.

The specific reason for organizing was that Hephzibah stumbled onto the fact that the Vietnam veterans in the Veterans' Administration facility near UCLA lived in absolutely horrible conditions. I knew this, of course, but I found it somehow amusing that Hephzibah had found out about it from her chauffeur. She had pressed him into the organization.

My problem was that I felt the very paternalism she said she was fighting against in her attitude towards me. Here she was, barging in on my complex life, wanting to give me new duties in things she thought were important. I was supposed to put my life aside. Hephzibah says she finds no hope in elitists, be they in socialist countries or capitalistic ones. Elitists are always the true enemies of human progress, she says. And yet there, in the Polo Lounge, all I could think of was how absurd it was to be discussing the evils of the elite in this plush bar. I am reminded of my own early Marxist rantings in the comfort of Alma. If we are going to put down the elite, let's go to some sleazy coffee shop in Hollywood where the other half lives.

Yet there is a method and perhaps synthesis in her madness—and madness it does appear to be when you walk into the Center's offices in London, near the Thames. You might see a dozen prisoners crowded into her tiny kitchen, Hephzibah washing dishes for all of them, all the while carrying on a conversation. Instead of prisoners, her guests might be mental patients, South Africans or Irish revolutionaires. And be careful of the phones—the South African secret police have ears everywhere.

Hephzibah is enthralled with the notion that the world is changing. She sees classical music audiences growing smaller each year,
and says she is not sure that is so bad. The piano in Hephzibah's
home is a cheap, tinny-sounding spinet. On rare occasions she
escapes her busy life and visits Yaltah to play on one of the three
beautiful Steinways there.

Yaltah wishes that her sister would come back to "noble" music.
But by her comments one would think Hephzibah is a little sick of
music, although she plays magnificently. Music has merely become
her entré to the rebellious members of the ruling classes who will, she
believes, help effect great social changes.

The Center has isolated sixty-one crises of modern life, and
warns that because of their synergistic effects on each other, the
world will face a great crisis, bigger than the sum of the whole, very
soon, that will either lead to a dark age or a renaissance, depending
whether or not mankind listens to the theories of her husband,
Richard.

You've heard of these crises, no doubt: violence, apathy, alienation, changing man-woman relationships, the generation gap, the
accelerating rate of change, noise pollution, lack of privacy, the
deterioration of cities, the decline of art and beauty in ordinary
people's lives, the increasing ugliness of the urban environment, the
emphasis on rationalism at the expense of intuition, a surfeit of
charlatans with "jerry built" remedies, the decline of the family in
both developed countries and the Third World, the decline of neigh-
borhoods, the growth of strong centralized bureaucracies, the
increasing division between the "haves" and the "have nots," the
increase of scapegoatism and torture around the world, the decline of
democracies and the growth of dictatorships, and finally, the growth
of the consumer society, which Hephzibah believes has replaced
Marx' "opiate of the masses"—religion.

The Center has plans for community organizing to deal with all
of these problems and more. Hephzibah's more than modest contribution to all of this is financed by her piano playing. If Hephzibah
does know that she and her husband have little chance of saving the
world, nevertheless, as a true Menuhin, she is dedicated to that goal
with her last ounce of strength. Hephzibah is fond of saying that the
choice is between a renaissance or a catastrophe, and put that way,
you can see why she refuses to entertain doubts about what she's

doing. Long ago, she discarded the naive notion that music by itself is an answer. Now she uses music mostly as a Robin Hood tool, a way of taking from the rich and giving to the poor, which obviously comes from the tradition of socialism her father came out of in Russia at the turn of the century. On the other hand, one would be hard-pressed to describe Moshe as a socialist in a political sense today. He, as much as Marutha, saw his offspring as natural aristocrats. Hephzibah has little patience anymore with people given to elitist notions. It is clear that more than any of the three children, she has broken out of the original mold set for her by Moshe and Marutha.

TWENTY-NINE

The New Jerusalem

WHILE HEPHZIBAH SEES THE world poised on a precipice between a renaissance and another dark ages, I anticipate, at best, a more gradual evolution. During my lifetime it seems as if a terrible mediocrity has fallen across the land. People are less alive, less eccentric—or so it seems. Our economic system has evolved to a point where power is so concentrated that even its possessors have become cogs in the machine. Because of the need for a transient labor force, able to pick up and move anywhere without roots in any one place, the corporate state has eliminated the extended family of several generations that used to exist on American farms. The nuclear family has been reduced to apartment-sized units. The welfare system is supposed to make up for the insecurity this elimination of the extended family created, but it doesn't really. Husbands and wives trade each other in on new mates with almost as much regularity as they buy new model cars. People's personalities are molded so they can be plugged into the system whenever and wherever they are needed. Thus, it is not surprising that uniformity is the highest virtue, despite the lip service paid to individuality. The grey, corporate men have taken over even the newspaper business, which not so long ago was still a great holdout of eccentrics. The television world never had to rid itself of eccentrics since its primary concern always has been to sell products by using formulas and cliches.

It is hard to imagine a family like the Menuhins flourishing in such a world. As I uncovered the tradition behind my family and, in the process, grew to feel closer to it, I began to see the impossibility of such a tradition in my own life. The eccentric Hassid in me has grown, while much of the Menuhin idealism has died. No longer when I hear Beethoven do I necessarily feel that great sense of social and historic change his music once made me feel. No doubt, if history were now rumbling and thundering on the verge of some emancipating revolution, Beethoven would be the appropriate accompaniment. During his time feudalism was being replaced by a more democratic and literate industrial order. There seemed room for optimism then. The Utopia Beethoven heralded was, he believed, on the horizon. These days, his Utopia seems to have become our nightmare—at least, some of the time.

One night recently in the tear-stained face of my wife listening to Beethoven's Ninth Symphony, my cynicism vanished, and I realized that there might be such a thing as a musical composition good for all time, which is what I had always assumed Beethoven's works to be. Still, I wonder whether there will come a time when this culture will have nothing left in it to sustain such a piece of music as the Ninth; its hopefulness and prayerfulness, its revolutionary fervor will all have become irrelevant. The consumer society will have triumphed and my only thoughts will be of deodorants and toothpaste. This would please the system, but my god, what is it doing to us, let alone our music and our art?

Perhaps we need not worry whether there will be more prodigies, but rather whether there will be more cities like the San Francisco of the 1920's. San Francisco, via Jerusalem and the Hassids, created Yehudi, and the catalysts seemed to be good fun, sun, clean air, unspoiled water and, of course, powerful parents. But is it that simple? If so, then if we could only bring back this earlier San Francisco, we might see Yehudis and Hephzibahs and Yaltahs growing up by the scores. But going back home is not possible. Though Yehudi is still the naive child, the ethereal dreamer in certain respects, he discovered long ago that he cannot recapture the world that nurtured him, the world which he, as a child genius, seemed to effortlessly command.

But where was his home anyway? This book has been a journey through the many homes in the Menuhin past. Hephzibah talks about yet another, a home yet to come—a New Jerusalem; a place where prodigies would blossom aplenty, prodigies in everything. And now the world needs them more than ever because it has so many more problems.

Yehudi, too, has a New Jerusalem vision of sorts. Thirty years ago he devised a plan for the reformation of New York. In a recent interview, he described the new New York in physical terms:

> New York should have been, by every right, the greatest city in the world. . .the inhumanity of the city itself should have been combatted in many ways. Purely architecturally, I suggested that all the lower floors of the apartment houses be taken out so that the pedestrian would have a free ride all over town—in other words, he would not be squeezed between immobile buildings and mobile traffic.

Thirty years ago, Yehudi might have actually thought it possible to reconstruct New York, but today, the idealism is balanced with a touch of resignation if not pessimism. About his New York plan, Yehudi added: "Naturally it won't happen because—unfortunately— what should happen, rarely does. Except in art and in personal rela- tionships, at times." Yehudi's great plans for saving the world have been tempered over the years by common sense.

I hope, like Hephzibah, that we are heading toward a renais- sance. But often as I drive to work or walk through downtown Los Angeles and see the hordes of bums—not old alcoholics but young men and women—I fear for the worst. It seems that as mediocrity, as blandness has increased, so has a great new class of Untouchables invaded American cities. Teenaged boys and girls offer their bodies for sale on street corners not far from my house. Not only has life become plastic and yes, sleazy, it has become cheap. Sometimes it seems pointless to listen to Yehudi playing the Beethoven Violin Concerto when I am filled not with hope, but with revulsion for what we have wrought.

I've never seen Yehudi angrier than when he's talking about Muzak. Muzak seems to bring out all his anger at his and the world's failed prospects, and unfulfilled dreams. I can easily understand Yehudi not liking Muzak; but his tone of voice shows his feelings to be much deeper than mere irritation. It took me some time to figure out why he gets so upset. Muzak symbolizes much of what the Menuhins have struggled against.

The Menuhin idealism has unresolved contradictions at its base as well as genuine synthesis, expressed as music and humanitarian activism. Moshe, as we have seen, grew up with the terrible feeling of being an outsider. He came from the ghetto and wanted to make sure he never had anything to do with his own past, his family's tradition. Yet, paradoxically, he recreated the feeling of the feudal Lubavitcher court in his own children, and walled them off from the same twentieth century he was so anxious to participate in. It was a highly artificial construct as his children were to feel later in their lives. In short, Moshe always felt out of place in the modern world. Yet how desparately he wanted to be a part of it. The motivation behind most of his projects was always in large part the desire to participate, to be a part of the world he could never really join.

Yehudi, who has always felt that his mother shaped him most, is more his father's son than he cares to admit. Yehudi's career, nurtured and protected by Moshe, was part of Moshe's vicarious participation in the world. I once told Yehudi that I had heard the story of how Moshe would put his baby son down to sleep with the record player going. Yehudi didn't particularly deny the story, but he said it embarassed him. "It makes me seem as if I was programmed to be a violinist right from the beginning like I was only a computer."

Of course Yehudi was not a computer, but nonetheless there may have been a lot of programming by Moshe. So much of Yehudi's concept of the world is based on Moshe's life-long activism; Hephzibah also learned well her father's lessons. After all, in similar circumstances, many families may not have had the driving compulsion to understand the politics of the world outside the pretty estate walls. There was no chance of avoiding politics with Moshe in the house as he first and foremost strove to understand the world politically. What indeed is the message of Hephzibah's work by which she thinks she can save the world? Ultimately, it is nothing more nor less than participation. For both Yehudi and Hephzibah, participation is the antidote to alienation. And for Yehudi, alienation is symbolized by Muzak, a species of music that is meant to be listened to without participation by musicians or audience. How bored the musicians are as they play their Muzak scores!

Yehudi first encountered Muzak in the late thirties, in a Toronto cowshed, where it was used to increase milk production. "Bach and Mozart worked better than the jagged music of a later day," he said, trying to be funny about something for which he had little humor. "Even Struass didn't do as much for milk as Bach did," Yehudi added.

> I find today we are all being reduced to the level of cows. They are milking money out of us as we shop... I try to listen to music, but that music is not meant to be listened to. It's meant to permeate our ear subconsciously like subliminal advertisements; to give us a sense of support, companionship and comfort, even if it's only a reflection of our own vacuum. It reflects musically the vacuums we have in ourselves, but I don't like vacuums compounded. I'd rather not have any music; then when I listen to music, I'd rather it be music of my choice. Yet it seems so overwhelming in its application; it's become such an industry. It's psychologically well supported and written with the definite aim of being unobtrusive. I look on it as a kind of surreptitious, secretive invasion of my privacy. It's meant to invade me, like a germ, like some virus which takes possession, and is supposed to alleviate my soul.

To illustrate his idea of music as a means toward participation, Yehudi contrasts his response to Muzak to that of an audience at an Indian music concert by Ravi Shankar:

> ...following every rhythmic inflection, keeping the time, listening with all their hearts, or even dancing. The association of the player and listener becomes increasingly great in proportion to the participation. But participation is not expected, it is rejected with piped music. That contributes nothing but degradation.

For the Menuhins, participation means to share in the common lot of this world. The better the goals and feelings we share, the better the participation. When Yehudi was young, his participation was limited to his violin. Of everything that had happened to him on his first and only day of formal education, he remembers best looking out the window at a tree. "That seemed to me the most valid element in the whole picture," Yehudi has said. He doesn't remember the teacher or his fellow students.

He now says he didn't like groups as a child because "I was a real violinist, and being a violinist is a solitary profession." As he grew older, however, the need to participate grew stronger. He became an avid chamber musician and conductor.

Chamber music is stressed at the Yehudi Menuhin School at Stoke d'Abernon, on the Surrey side of London. While the school (founded in 1961) is often compared to the Russian music schools, Yehudi thinks a great weakness of the Russian schools is that they are geared to producing soloists, and they have too little chamber music. The Yehudi Menuhin School teaches only three other instruments besides the violin—viola, cello and piano. The school diet as well as its extra-musical academic offerings reflect Yehudi's particular tastes, especially his idea that music is a participatory experience. My mother has taught there, but I know she is a little bothered by the fact that the piano doesn't get the reverence she thinks it deserves. Yehudi argues that there are already enough unemployed pianists in the world—and that's surely true.

Violin playing is a supreme act of participation, as is the playing of any instrument, or the writing of a book, or the making of a building. I have long been intrigued by Marx's notion that all human wealth is created by man's only real resource, his labor. Playing the violin beautifully and poetically, or doing anything well, is the most exalted form of wealth. It is a highly individual act but also a universal one.

Today, the world is torn between socialism and capitalism, a conflict that Yehudi and I have discussed in connection with the whole idea of individualism. So much of assembly line and corporate work does not allow the kind of involvement that Yehudi values so. He told me once that he believed the profit motive had once been a noble impulse in man's history, but for the most part it no longer is.

Then he went off into a long tribute to the glories of individual initiative. While his verbal dance to the virtues of the system did not entirely convince me, what else, I thought, could a Yehudi Menuhin believe? And besides, Yehudi had spent a great deal of his life around people who have every reason to celebrate capitalism over socialism.

Not surprisingly, Yehudi is a master at seeing everyone's point of view. Perhaps as a compensation for his father's extreme views, Yehudi learned to consider all viewpoints. He would not be the great interpreter of music that he is without this technique. In his heart, though, I believe that Yehudi is somewhat of a radical, even a socialist.

While I believe that some kind of human socialism must develop one day out of American capitalism, I could never, as the Chinese attempted, reach down and pull out my roots and abandon them totally. I think a sense of origin helps each person decide where to go, to the extent that he has the power to decide. To my mind, the question still to be answered is where is the hope of the world? Is it Cuba, China, Russia, America? Where will the New Jerusalem be? Both Yehudi and Hephzibah answer, America: "No other country holds such a promise for the future. I see no other country that has as many alternatives as America," says Yehudi. When during the Vietnam War, I was contemplating moving to another country, Hephzibah advised against it. "The fight is in America, for that is the country that will determine things for the world." She was then planning to move to the Chicago ghettoes to organize tenants' unions.

The difference between Yehudi and Hephzibah is considerable. Yehudi is less concerend with workers' and tenants' rights, and more concerned with the spiritual. He says civilization must change.

> It cannot go on indefinitely making more motor cars, and producing more Coca-Cola, not only because of the depletion of our natural resources, but because of spiritual needs people are now discovering. We have discovered certain capacities for love and understanding, things that are independent of the motor car and materialism.
>
> We have also discovered that it is no longer possible for one part of the civilization to live at the expense of another. It is no longer possible for one nation to live at the expense of other nations, so there is a growing realization of basic values that will have to be restated.

In *To Jerusalem and Back,* Saul Bellow reports his sense of the emptiness and purposelessness of American life on his return to Chicago from the Holy Land. (But he does not see socialism as offering any solutions, as I do.) My first glimpse of California after my Israeli visit left me with feelings much the same as Bellow's. While in Jerusalem, though, I did look forward to coming back to California, but wished that there were some place where Jerusalem and California could be combined; perhaps the world that Hephzibah envisions.

Then, one night after I had been back in the States a while, I had a dream about being in a city I seemed to recognize, yet could not name. I saw a long street both elegant and dilapidated, new and old, with many trees, but also bathed in the flat glare of a large yellow sun. The main boulevard was long and wide, with five-story apartment buildings on both sides. When I looked more closely, I realized the buildings were a combination of such places as I've seen in parts of London and San Francisco. There were also Spanish-style wooden balconies such as the one I had in Los Angeles. I kept walking down a boulevard that sloped to a beach. I realized that the ocean in my dream was the Mediterranean, not the Pacific—yet the place was not Haifa or Tel Aviv. It had the sun-drenched quality of both Jerusalem and California, but it was neither of them. For a long time I tried to figure out what or where the city was, for I felt very much at home in it, more at home than I had ever felt anywhere.

The dream had something to do with my discovery of the historic forces that had been shaping my family for hundreds of years. It reminded me of the hopeful orthodox refrain, "Next year in Jerusalem," which Marutha used to think so funny. The Menuhins, and their Schneersohn ancestors, have always yearned for a new home. First it was in Lubavitch, then in Palestine, then in New York and San Francisco. Alma, Moshe's dream for a Menuhin court, never worked out, and now the three Menuhin geniuses have found a home in Europe. Yehudi believes that Switzerland, where he lives a part of each year, is the only place in the world where there is order without tyranny.

For me, a new home would have to resemble the world of my dream. Although I know that the dream was a one-time creation of my mind, it is still the beginning of something new, something not yet fully formed. Yes, history has shaped the Menuhins, but dreams can shape history. Wasn't Moshe shaping history according to his dreams when he "programmed" Yehudi? When I am leaning towards a religious or mystical interpretation of the Menuhins, I see Yehudi as something of an angel put on this earth at a time that is poor for the incubation and survival of great souls. Moshe saw in Yehudi the fulfillment of all his dreams, and whatever resentment I feel towards my grandfather, I am very grateful that the best of his powerful qualities found their way into his son and daughters. That the three Menuhins have survived the transition from their precocity to their adulthood, given all the obstacles that these chaotic times have thrown across their paths, is a miracle in itself—many prodigies never accomplish this feat. That the Menuhins have been playing beautiful music in almost every country in the world for over fifty years makes them a truly monumental family.

The power of the Menuhin music has brought me many pleasures throughout my life, but the intensity of their emotional machinations has often brought me pain; out of the pain came the need to understand the Menuhins not just as a family of great artists, but as my all-too-human family, a family with all the emotions, hatreds and frustrations of any other family. If Yehudi and Hephzibah thought as children that they were Adam and Eve, I came to feel like some lesser being living at the edge of the garden. Just as Yehudi and his sisters were thrilled to meet their relatives in Russia and Israel, to break out of the protected garden of their childhoold, my encounter with my relatives and ancestors helped to give form to my chaotic emotional life. Moshe's rejection of me was balanced by a new identification with the historic Menuhins, and the God of my childhood could no longer control me as he once had.

What of the future of the Menuhins? Coming closer to the Menuhin past has helped me to understand the present-day clan, to see them as participants in an historic transformation. The three Menuhin prodigies were a transition generation: from the world of the classics to the modern world of avant guard music, jazz and rock and roll; from the orthodox Hassidic tradition to the modern world of social activism, revolution and anarchy. The old cultural mechanisms by which young brainy children were brought into the Menuhin clan are now gone—arranged marriages are out of fashion. A new mix of blood, genes, brains, karma—call it what you will—has entered the Menuhin line and the old gene pool out of which came the Schneersohn dynasty is no more. Almost all of us are marrying outside of our family or culture; we have assimilated.

What this means for the future of the Menuhins is, of course, difficult to say. Without the genetic link to the Schneersohns and without the psychological and cultural supports needed for the nurturing of the family tradition, I think it not unfair to assume that Yehudi, Yaltah and Hephzibah are the last hurrah of the Schneersohn dynasty. I am personally not at all saddened by this prospect; yet something in me, perhaps that quantity of the Schneersohn spirit that I was born with, wonders if there might be some way in which the

Menuhin greatness will continue. Perhaps the ultimate meaning of the Menuhin miracle is that no matter how brilliant a tradition may be, it must be open to the world around it—it cannot, in a world that is now "one world," shut itself off entirely. The Lubavitchers in Brooklyn can continue to be the museum pieces that they have become, but the world will and is passing them by. The Menuhins, although they have lost the purity of their Schneersohn heritage, may be the very best that came out of the Lubavitcher tradition. The Menuhins have tried to become as universal as possible, even if ironically they have remained Hassids in many subtle ways. It may sound unreasonable and arrogant to talk of the Menuhin descendants becoming a new breed of aristocratic philosopher-kings; yet I think there is, in the way the Menuhins participate so actively in our perilous times, something that can be transmitted to their children and to their children's children, and to the world. I'm sure that some of the Menuhin commitment to peace, justice and art will find a way to survive down the line. If the Schneersohn tradition was transmitted via blood and genes, the Menuhin tradition will continue, perhaps, as a celebration of values.

My sentiments on the subject of the future of the Menuhins are usually less generous. When it seems doubtful that the world will survive, the fate of one family's tradition is of less concern. Perhaps, like my dream, the Menuhins will have happened only once. Yet I know that the world's children will live one day in a New Jerusalem, and that they will create the Utopia that makes New Jerusalems possible. And as long as people keep searching for Utopias, whether in private moments of music- or love-making, or in world political movements, the Menuhin tradition will live.

A publicity photo of the three Menuhins taken in the fifties

INDEX